We Are What We Think and What We Eat

By Roger Dufau

First published by Dog Ear Publishing
4010 W. 86th Street, Ste H
Indianapolis, IN 46268
www.dogearpublishing.net

ISBN: 978-1-4575-1540-8

This book is printed on acid-free paper.

Printed in the United States of America

To the whole human "family"
and
with special thanks to
my mother and each of my grandmothers,
who introduced me to the bliss of unconditional love

Table of Contents

Part II

Introduction

This book was inspired by a dream that refused to go away.

In 2005 my wife Kathleen and I took a vacation on the Caribbean Island of St. Martin, a place that is a delightful mixture of French culture and Dutch enterprise. After our third night there I woke up in the morning with the vivid memory of a strange dream. A beautiful "being" bathed in wondrous light appeared and spoke to me. His presence filled me with awe, especially as he seemed to know all about my hopes, feelings and desires. We spoke together for some time and it was he who gave me the insight that you see above: "You are the result of what you think and what you eat." He then suggested that I needed to find out more about the significance of those words in my own life, and that I should share my insights with the world.

But this wasn't the first time that I had encountered the idea. I had read of it before in a book about the American psychic, Edgar Cayce, famed as the "sleeping prophet". The words were from one of the thousands of readings that Cayce gave while in trance states, states in which he received information from spirit. "We are what we think and what we eat," emphasizes both the power of the mind to create an individual's reality and the responsibility we all bear to take good care of our bodies. Cayce taught that the body is "the temple of God". He and his followers believed that the source of those particular insights was Jesus Christ.

All of Cayce's readings are still available in a library maintained by the A.R.E. (Association for Research and Enlightenment) located in Virginia Beach, Virginia. This organization has been in existence since 1932 and is still very much active today. I will discuss its work more fully at a later stage in the book when I describe my near-death experience. I'll just say for now that the A.R.E. helped me to make sense of what I had gone through. And perhaps the roots of my St. Martin dream flowed, at least partly, from that life-changing event.

1

In the morning after this dream I had the urge to explain it all to Kathleen, my wife. She didn't laugh or tell me I was crazy, she was just very puzzled - as was I. But after that we both filed the dream away in the backs of our minds and got on with our lives. Everyday routines and the pressing business of making a living took over, as they always do. But the dream was not willing to forget about us. It returned every month, repeating the same message: I needed to reflect on the importance of our food and our thoughts, and to share my insights with the world.

Then I began to rationalize the experience away. I decided that it was a sort of 'wrong number', a perfectly good dream for someone, but clearly not meant for me. After all, literature and writing were never my strong suits, even in my native France. And here in Canada, with English not being my native language, the idea of writing a book seemed even more ridiculous. None of this mattered to the dream. It continued to return every month like clockwork. Finally one night, I decided to stop arguing, and said that I would accept the suggestion and try to write the book. But I insisted that I get help so that I wouldn't make a fool of myself. I was told that as I went along everything would fall into place and that no one is ever alone. All I had to do was honestly observe my life experiences and report truthfully what I learned.

But before I could begin I had to ask myself if I saw any basis for hope, both for myself, and all of humanity. What must we do in order to evolve spiritually? We are told that the present millennium is destined to be a time of spiritual awakening. But this is difficult to believe when all we see around us is human short-sightedness and the endless repetition of harmful acts. I asked to be guided and pleaded to be made worthy of such an undertaking.

Even so, I began by doubting everything, and constantly procrastinating. Many years went by in this way until one day in 2008 I found myself resenting my work as a chef for the first time, work that until then had always been a source of great pleasure and satisfaction. The very next day I woke up with painful shingles on both sides of my body, and also on my chest and back. Yet I still went to work and kept on going. My reasoning was that I had "much to do".

It seems that at your soul level or that of your sacred self, all is possible. In my case my spirit had clearly decided to give me a wake-up call. Since I hadn't been listening to the message from my dream – that I was supposed to be writing a book – something had to be done to get my attention. But of course I still kept on working. So I received another reminder. This time the pain in my body was dramatically increased. Both ankles swelled up and turned a dark red, and being on my feet as my job demands, became agonizing.

I did call a dear friend, who is also a chef, to help me finish the next day's work as I had made a commitment that I felt I should respect. But as soon as the preparation was done, I went to the local hospital. I was barely able to walk. The nice doctor was puzzled by the overall picture and asked for a long list of tests to be done. He finally sent me home late at night, but I was given no pills or treatment of any kind since the results of the tests were not yet available. I was to see my own private family doctor the next day and he would decide what course to take once he had received the test results from the hospital.

But as it turned out, my doctor was not available the next day so I had to wait yet another day. All this time, I knew in my heart or higher self that I had created the whole thing! So I decided to make peace with myself, and in quiet time and prayer, I renewed my commitment to get on with "the book". Once that decision was made, everything started to change and over the next few hours all the pain disappeared, and with it the ugly appearance of my body also started to slowly fade away.

When I finally saw the doctor my condition had become very mild. One of my ankles was still a bit swollen and the skin was still somewhat red. Yet even these reduced symptoms were enough to make him quite concerned. He brought in a colleague for a second opinion and a young doctor in training was there as well. They gave me an impressive-sounding name for my illness and then the two senior doctors went off to confer further. In their absence the young doctor told me that the name of my condition meant that no one had the faintest idea of what it was.

The upshot of all this medical attention was that I was to see a skin specialist in the next few days. Three days later, while I was still waiting to see him, the young doctor called to see how I was doing. I told him that my symptoms were all gone and that in fact I had been intending to drop by and ask them to cancel the appointment with the dermatologist. I asked him if they wanted to see for themselves. He said they would take my word for it.

These events only make sense if you accept that there is great power in acting in harmony with the higher self. Taken by itself, my story is only an interesting anecdote, but it does strongly suggest that there are larger realities than the everyday ones to be discovered and analyzed if you have the courage and audacity to pay attention. This experience and others like it over my lifetime have influenced my beliefs in profound ways. Some have been confirmed, but others had to

Here is my mother holding me with my cousin, Maritchu, center. (1944)

be let go. I have been able to do this objectively because of having the good fortune to have always been surrounded by family and friends who have encouraged me to question anything that makes my intelligence rebel or even just doubt. The great works of politics, philosophy and spirituality touch us all, but I believe that every idea needs to be tested, no matter how great its authority may be. No one has the right to dictate our truth to us.

I hope to convince you in the course of this book that humanity can create the conditions for the world to become a safer and more just place for our children and grandchildren to live. If we as a species can find a way to do that, I am certain that life on this planet can be sustained for countless generations to come. I hope that these ideas will resonate with you and that I will have contributed in some small way to a future in which the human race finally comes to accept love over fear. But now I would like to take you to the beginning of my story.

PART ONE

CHAPTER 1

My Basque Childhood and the Legacy of "Amatchi"

I was born in 1943 in a place called Saint Jean de Luz in German-occupied France. Saint Jean de Luz is in the Basque region on the Bay of Biscay, very close to the Spanish border. My father and mother were both born in Paris and in my mother's case, that's a story in itself. She had been adopted by a Basque family in Sare which is fourteen kilometres east of Saint Jean de Luz, just at the beginning of the Pyrenees. My adoptive Grandmother's sister was the Chef de Cuisine at the home of the fabled Rothschild family on Avenue Foch in the heart of Paris. As an adolescent I once visited my uncle who also worked there. The Rothschild home was just behind L'Etoile where the famous Arc de Triomphe is located.

A tale of love and intrigue involving the Rothschild household surrounded my mother's birth. Her biological mother was the daughter of a wealthy Parisian family. She had fallen in love with a Polish military officer and became pregnant with his child. As the year was 1922, her parents acted quickly to prevent scandal. My grandmother's sister was given a sum of money to take care of the "problem" with the help of the *Assistance Publique Francaise*. The young woman had her child in due course and my grandmother left her Basque country home for the first and only time to travel to Paris. There she took the newborn into her charge and travelled back home to introduce her to her eight brothers and sisters. One more child was born after my mother's arrival, making a family of ten children in all.

When I was growing up I always marvelled at the amazing number of relatives on my mother's side. She was totally accepted by all of my grandmother's family despite her clear blue eyes and light complexion – very different from her Basque family. She was nicknamed the "Parisian white sheep". During the war when she became a leader in the French resistance, her BBC code name was "the mouton blanc" or the white sheep!

We often asked our mother how she felt about not knowing her real parents. She didn't seem to mind as she loved her adoptive mother and family very much and was loved by them in return. Nonetheless there were times when nostalgic curiosity and longing surfaced, but she didn't dwell on them. In the main she didn't seem to suffer too much from the circumstances of her birth.

Some time after my parents had passed away I was attending one of the many family reunions that occur at funerals and a very old aunt of mine (the oldest of the family and the last to die – at 93) was telling me the familiar story of my mother's birth. I thought I already knew all the details, but it turned out that my mother had withheld an important fact. My aunt added one more shocking detail to the tale. Not long after my mother's birth, her biological mother and the Polish officer committed suicide. I was left stunned and completely speechless by this revelation. It made me wonder if the nature of her parents' deaths had caused my mother pain. Did she feel that she was somehow the cause of the tragedy? I'll have to wait until I see her again to find out the answer.

Yet as interesting as my mother's history is, it would be very unfair of me to leave out my father's side of the story. My paternal grandfather originally worked in the Boulognes-Billancourt area of Paris at the first Renault automobile factory. He was also very politically active and was involved in founding Le Party Socialist which was created to address social concerns and to bring a much-needed sense of fairness to the issues of the time, especially those affecting working people.

Despite his interest in politics, he and my grandmother eventually tired of the hectic pace of Paris and moved to Ciboure, which is separated only by a river from Saint Jean de Luz. There, my grandmother, who like my maternal great aunt was a *cuisiniere*, found employment cooking for the renowned artist Pierre Labrouche. In the course of her work there she often served meals to M. Labrouche's great friend, the composer Maurice Ravel, who had his family home in Ciboure.

I have much-loved memories of days spent with my grandparents there, helping my grandfather with his garden, feeding his many rabbits, or looking for hidden eggs. I had to watch the chickens as they often laid their eggs outside the coop in other parts of the property. In those days chicken meat was more valuable then beef or fish! My grandfather's chickens were truly free-range - unlike the so-called free-range chickens of today. (In subsequent chapters I will address the conditions in agro farming.)

Sadly, those happy days came to an end when my grandmother passed away quite young from a blood clot in her leg. That in turn led to a fatal heart attack. Even harder to bear was the fact that her death could have easily been prevented. At the time of her death she was staying with her daughter and didn't want to bother anyone by complaining of not feeling well. So no doctor was ever called.

With her death my brother Michel and I had to become much more self-sufficient. What we missed most was something that we had taken for granted when she was alive – unconditional love. It was her nature to give, and then give some more. As children, we never thought about it. For us, things felt great or lousy. No psychology there, just pure experience. But we certainly noticed when that all-enveloping embrace was suddenly taken away. Fortunately I still had my other grandmother (the Basque one) in the country. And in her case, I realized how much I loved her well before she passed away.

One of the reasons my grandmothers were so important to me was that my parents were almost always busy trying to make a living. Not that this was unusual at the time. There were few luxuries available to most of the people we knew. After the Second World War the atmosphere was very restrictive. People were divided by politics, and religion was rigid and controlling with endless do's and don'ts. We weren't allowed to eat meat on Fridays and we had to go to mass on an empty stomach for purity's sake! We also had to confess our sins at least once a week. Even at home, my family life involved many chores. As I have said, life in those days was completely absorbed with trying to survive, and we all had to help. As I was the first born, a great deal was asked of me but I didn't see that as unusual in any way. School was no picnic either - with physical abuse generously distributed. I didn't enjoy it at all and consequently I didn't perform well, often sneaking away from classes and going fishing instead.

And fishing provided a welcome respite. Whenever my brother and I needed pocket money this is what we would do, and since Saint Jean de Luz was a fishing port, we had access to all the equipment needed to catch shrimp, eels, crabs or sea bass. When the tide was very low we would find shrimp and crabs and when it was rising, the sea bass would show up in abundance. (While it may be true that the Bay of Fundy's tides are more extreme, ours were pretty impressive as well - about six metres during the equinox. The difference was enough to play in, but our tides weren't dangerous like the Bay of Fundy's.) So fishing was not only great fun but profitable as well since my grand-mother would always buy whatever we caught.

But of course I always had to return to my real world sooner or later. And in this world I wasn't thought to be particularly good at any-thing judged important. I was looked down on pretty much every-where: at school, at church, even at home. My father was away at sea most of the time and my mother had a lot to cope with on her own. She wasn't exactly patient or gentle with us. Loving kindness was not a big factor in the scene. So what little free time we had, we spent on the street, the beach, or at the fishing port.

As you might expect, in these economic circumstances having a meal out or seeing a movie were both very rare treats. And vacations - except for going to visit relatives - were unheard of. These are not complaints, just descriptions of the way things were. When you don't have a basis of comparison with other ways of living you just get on with your life. I can't say that my life was particularly happy however.

But lest you think that I bore no responsibility for my misfor-tunes, if the truth be told I was a "difficult" child. I had a hard time accepting authority. When ordered to carry out some task I would often do the opposite - or even worse completely ignore the request. And it wasn't that there weren't consequences. Force was very much in use in those days. There was general acceptance of spanking as a cure for almost any transgression. You were not only subject to such discipline from your parents, but you were almost as likely to receive it from teachers, neighbours, or even the local priest. My mother often lost patience with me but it was my father (when he was home) who was assigned to "correct" me – often with very little sense of what had actu-ally happened.

But our relationship changed because of events that I still remem-ber vividly. I should first mention that my brother Michel, through the brilliant tactic of screaming and crying - even before being punished - managed to avoid most spankings. On this memorable day I was sus-pected of being guilty of a crime that had actually been committed by my brother. While my father was making up his mind, my brother went into his usual performance. So naturally it was decided that I must be to blame. Now my father was a very strong man, as he was the chief mechanic on a tuna fishing boat and he could easily lift heavy equipment or even large tuna fish. But in my outrage at being falsely accused, I had decided in my little mind not to cry no matter what. So when my punishment began, far from sobbing and repenting as my father expected, I screamed in rage using words that were far from contrite. After a few minutes of this, my father suddenly stopped, looked at me and began to laugh. I told him that I would never cry as I was innocent. Then I began to laugh as well. I was eleven at the time and he never laid a hand on me again. He went to my mother and told her that she would have to do her own dirty work from then on. A new respect for my father was born in me that day. Much later, my mother and I solved the problem of our dysfunctional relationship, but it took the death of my beloved Basque grandmother to make it happen.

What I didn't realize at the age of eleven was the fact that I was rebellious because most of the discipline I received from my parents was coercive and not loving. As I grew older I was better able to distinguish between demands that were arbitrary and those that were simply necessary. But I still wanted to be asked to do something rather than told. This is still one of my struggles in life. You can request almost anything of me and I will most likely be happy to agree, but I have to be the one to decide. I have since come to realize that the core issue was, and still is, trust.

When I was between the ages of seven and twelve, my mother preferred to have me out of the way during the tourist season. This was because she was extremely busy with her large fruit and vegetable store in a good part of Saint Jean de Luz. It was for this reason that I had the great good fortune to spend the three-month summer holiday with my Basque grandmother in the small village of Sare which, as I have mentioned, was a few kilometres to the east of my home town. Those summers are the source of many of my most treasured memories. They were particularly important after the loss of my grandmother from Ciboure.

Life in Sare was great. We lived in a farm house right in the mountains. There was no electricity at the time, or running water but we always had lots of water available in the tank at the side of the house. It was filled with collected rainwater as well as fresh water from a local source. Not having the modern conveniences that were available to me in my parents' house didn't bother me in the slightest. I was with my beloved grandmother and that was all that mattered. (I never knew my Basque grandfather as he had passed away before I was born.)

My grandmother was not very well off, but in that area, everyone's financial situation was similar to hers. In fact agriculture was still done in the old manner – manually, or with horses or oxen. But they were good people, genuine in their dealings with one another, true to their word, and always willing to help.

My grandmother's house. This photo shows the renovated home. (undated)

But the greatest difference in Sare, was in the nature of my relationship with my grandmother. When my grandmother wanted me to do something, unlike my parents, she would ask, not tell me. She would gently inquire if I wished to help her, or perhaps go somewhere, or participate in some activity. Maybe I would like to share something with the group? Without even consciously realizing the great difference in how I was being treated, I found myself saying yes almost all of the time. I felt like a respected member of her family. And to top it all off, she trusted me completely and gave me total freedom to do whatever I wanted on many afternoons.

What a difference from my life at home with its endless restrictions! Over time, I learned to speak Basque. My mother spoke Basque, French, and Spanish, but my father spoke only French. So at home it was all French and at school as well. My father was never able to communicate with my grandmother as she spoke only Basque. I often translated for him.

I remember only one negative incident in a perfect and totally loving relationship with my dearest *Amatchi*, the Basque name for grandmother. I was far from perfect of course, but I was never scorned or spanked for mistakes or poor behaviour, just gently reminded that they weren't appropriate. It was made clear that it would be appreciated if I learned from my errors and tried to avoid repeating them. But the exception to this generally positive interaction came out of my desire to play smart. I had just learned a new sentence from Basque neighbours who were close to my own age. At the time my knowledge of Basque was mixed at best, a fact that probably played a role in the incident. In any case, you can imagine my grandmother's reaction when one day, for no reason whatsoever, I said to her, "You are a sorceress."

My Amatchi wasn't amused and for the first time in many years, I saw her sad and almost speechless. In my cockiness and embarrassment I didn't apologize, but I went to bed that night with a heavy heart. I hardly slept, and in the morning I rushed to her in tears and asked her to forgive me. I promised that I would never again call anyone a bad name – especially not her. She hugged me and accepted the apology. All was well again!

Before she passed away, incredible good fortune made her life (and by extension, ours) very exiting. A famous singer, Luis Mariano, who was of Basque origin and quite wealthy, bought my Amatchi's house. He completely renovated it and turned the old and humble home into a very luxurious one. But more than this, he was a kind and generous man and invited my grandmother to continue living in the house as his concierge. He paid her very well just for being there, never really asking her to do anything to earn her salary. I remember her marvelling at the good fortune that allowed her to continue living in her now very beautiful home, and to even receive money for doing so. Luis was kind to my family as well. We received many beautiful gifts and he often made us welcome when he entertained his many friends. Some of the ladies were so beautiful that even in my little boy's heart, it was like falling in love over and over! I swore that one day I would marry someone just as beautiful, and many years later, I did.

Luis had his own chauffeur, who drove either a white Cadillac, or for fun in the country, a red Jeep. I wanted a jeep like that from then on. And when the time came that I could actually afford one, the decision to buy one was very easy and the enjoyment in fulfilling a lifelong desire was very great. Later on in life that experience, among others, led me to realize that dreams are not far from the conscious desire to create their reality.

As an adult I enjoyed many beautiful performances by Luis Mariano, in Paris at the Chatelet Music Hall where he was the lead artist. Those performances and others by his colleagues opened up my eyes to the fascinating world of entertainment. I also had the good fortune to meet many of these artists in person at Luis' Paris home where one of my uncles was the caretaker. He made it easy for me to be invited there.

But now back to my childhood days. In the summer of 1955, when I was in my twelfth year, I returned once again to the mountains, but this time I stayed with my aunt. As it turned out, this was to be the last summer in my beloved Sare. My dear Amatchi passed away in July and when I learned of her death I was heartbroken. "Who is left to love me now?" my heart seemed to cry. My parents loved me of course, but they didn't give me the affection and understanding that my Amatchi had. School was more like penance and the church made me suspicious: I had no belief in or love for the strange, often nasty, and very demanding God portrayed in the Catholic teachings of those days. So the great hole left by my grandmother's departure not only made me an even worse student but also more difficult to deal with at home as well. Even friends couldn't begin to fill the gap in my life.

One day, when I was twelve, watching the railway track not far from the station, I began to consider a fast way to end all of my misery. All I had to do was throw myself in front of the train just before it passed, leaving no time for the engineer to stop. As I waited for the train, still not quite sure whether or not to commit this extreme act, I was completely numb with no feelings of any kind. My mind seemed to be entirely focused on watching the tracks. I didn't believe in angels at the time but there was at least one on call that day. A very sweet girl named Maïté came by and asked me what I was doing there? I had long had a crush on her and but had never dared approach her. How on earth did she happen to be there and what made her suddenly decide to talk to me? Of course those were only my thoughts in hindsight; at the time, I just reacted as would any young man in the presence of the girl of his dreams. Maïté asked me to go some place with her and my mind was now filled only with thoughts of love. Since there was clearly more cause for hope than I had imagined, I decided to get on with my life.

One day, not very long after the railway incident, during an argument with my mother, she complained bitterly that my late Amatchi had been able to get anything out of me, but as for her and almost anyone else, virtually nothing. At that I found myself asking, "Do you really want to know why? She took me at my word and asked why.

I explained that my Amatchi had never told me what to do but instead always asked me if I wished or could do something for her. I told my mother that she and the others just ordered me around. None of them ever asked me politely. In addition, they often called me insulting names such as, good-for-nothing, lazy, or even worse. My Amatchi had never called me such things.

After this clearing of the air, a few days went by and I didn't even notice that my mother wasn't bossing me in her usual manner. One day she asked me if I could do a particular chore. The idea was to help her to get things ready for supper. She explained that if she had to do it alone everything would take too long and supper would be late. Without even thinking I said yes and did what was required. My mother seemed very pleased and thanked me. What followed, without my even noticing at first, was a complete change in my mother's attitude toward me and my brother, and in her way of dealing with us. My sister was too young at the time to notice what was going on, but she certainly benefited as well. As the eldest, I was gradually trusted with more and more responsibilities, and my efficiency in carrying them out was much appreciated

After that time, as long as my parents were still alive Michel, my sister Denise, (changed as an adult to Valerie) and I had a loving and trusting relationship with them. There were no lies and no games. Now it's true that my brother and I were still responsible for various misdeeds now and again, but nothing too dramatic or dumb. We were reprimanded when appropriate, but the tension was soon over and trust was quickly re-established. Even our friends enjoyed spending time in our house as they too were treated as equals by my mother and father. They loved spending time with us so much that their own parents began to wonder what was going on.

But it is not just the nuclear family that is central, the extended family is also very important in Basque culture and on days off from school (Thursday and Sunday, later changed to Saturday and Sunday), our parents usually set us free to do what we wished and that often included visiting relatives in Sare. The Basques are traditionally a hospitable and generous people, especially if you are introduced by one of them. I could take my friends to any of my mother's family there and always count on being welcomed - even if we were unexpected. On our bicycles the trip would take about an hour and-a-half. Even apart from family, Sare alone was well worth the effort as it occupies a picturesque location beside La Rhune, a mountain which marks the beginning of the Pyrenees.

Now of course no family exists in a vacuum; there is always a social and cultural context. And as my formative years were so influenced by Basque culture, I'd like to provide a brief overview of Basque history and traditions. My home town of Saint Jean de Luz has a very old port with stories of navigators going far back in time. Some of these early Basque mariners reached the shores of North America long before Christopher Columbus. Frequent destinations on those long-ago voyages were Newfoundland and other areas of what are now Canada's Maritime Provinces. The Basques travelled there in the course of following the whales as they migrated to the northwest from the Bay of Biscay.

The same can be said of the Spanish Basques whose seafaring skills helped the Spanish to reach South America. The riches of Spain and the history of their powerful fleets owe a lot to the shipbuilding abilities of the Basques as well as their astonishing navigational abilities. It was in no small part due to the Basques that the Spanish were able to travel around the world, establishing trade routes to places as far away as the Philippines, and ultimately throughout South America. The tragic loss of Spanish power has a lot to do with false beliefs and ideals. As a way of comparing Basque values and Spanish ones, the example of the Spanish armada that was sent to attack England in 1588 is very revealing.

The Basques have always had a collaborative and cooperative culture that is suspicious of hierarchy. In contrast, sixteenth century Spain was a monarchy in every sense of the word. The reigning Monarch, Phillip II, firmly believed that members of the nobility possessed great gifts simply by virtue of their blood. The planned invasion of England was initially well-planned, but the untimely death of the experienced Admiral Santa Cruz left Phillip with some big shoes to fill. However instead of choosing an experienced leader, he appointed the very reluctant and utterly unqualified Duke of Medina Sedonia to the post of commanding a tremendous fleet of some one hundred and thirty vessels. The result of the king's poor decision, combined with a storm that further aided the brilliant English seafarers was for the Spanish, a catastrophe. The disastrous defeat and the loss of a huge number of ships marked the end of Spanish naval supremacy.

So the Basque belief that intelligence, talent and values are far more important than blood, turns out to have a highly practical value. The Basques are not large in number, the whole region comprising only seven provinces spanning the French and Spanish border, but they have always fiercely defended their own against invaders. They have managed to survive since the beginning of recorded history, over thousands of years. No one knows exactly how long. This tiny culture has always managed to survive, sometimes against incredible odds. Nothing has ever been able to force them to abandon their language, traditions or their unwritten laws.

One of the most interesting of these traditions is a society organized around "houses" which trace their lineage back through many generations. The identity of every Basque is drawn from membership in one of these houses. Within these houses, men and women have different responsibilities but their roles are equal. The leadership of the house may be inherited by either a man or a woman, the decision being based on ability rather than gender. Such equity has ensured the continuation of the houses even through times of historical turmoil.

Despite any impressions that may have been created by the media, the Basques are not naturally separatists, but they insist that their culture and identity be respected. They are a very open people, happy to mix with and learn from other nations. And historically this is what they have done, as their destiny has always taken them out into the wider world. The total assault on their culture that they experienced in Franco's Spain led to the creation of a movement for Basque independence called the E.T.A. (Euskadi Ta Askatasuna). The E.T.A. and its sister organizations is both a political and military organization. It began to seek Basque independence in the latter years of Franco's rule and continued to do so even after Franco's death in 1975, but the liberalization that came with democracy in Spain has gradually reduced it to increasing irrelevance, especially since the late nineties. It would be nice to say that the Basque experience under Franco was an isolated example, but sadly, destruction of vibrant cultures by powerful political and economic forces is as common today as it has ever been.

The American writer Mark Kurlansky has written an insightful book called *The Basque History of the World*. In this work he describes the Basques as Europe's oldest nation and ironically, one that has never been a country. He also notes that the Basques are a fascinating people whose origins are not only unknown, but who also speak a language unconnected to any other on earth. Kurlansky paints a fascinating picture, but the truth is that the old Basque ways, even their value system, are gradually falling prey to modern life. The reality of a highly competitive world of business has tempered traditional values like being true to one's word, sharing of possessions, living peacefully and respecting others. Even once-powerful family ties are being weakened. What has survived almost intact is the language, the traditions of the feast, Basque songs and dances, and sport in all its forms, old and new. The Basques are a people who above all value joy in life. They are a people of celebration.

It is interesting to note that Basque ideals are echoed in the work of the American writer Neale Donald Walsch, in which the key elements of

life are described as Joy, Truth and Love. He states that these three elements are essential in order to glorify life. Neale's *Conversations with
God* series is a modern-day publishing phenomenon having sold over
eight million copies and been translated into thirty-four languages.
Each book in the series was on the New York Times Bestseller List -
the first, *Conversations with God, Book I, An Uncommon Dialogue*, for two
and-a-half years. All the books come from an extended, ongoing mystical communion with God. I have had a long association with this
remarkable writer which I will outline, along with an examination of his
worldwide spiritual work, in a later chapter.

CHAPTER 2

The Learning Curve

My communion in the Catholic tradition at 12 years old. (1955)

Despite its many failings, organized religion at least attempts to provide people with richer lives than they might have otherwise. And as you might expect, since I grew up in France, my first exposure to spirituality was the rituals of the Catholic Church. I still remember the preparations for my First Communion at age ten or eleven, and for my Solemn Communion at age twelve. Much of what we were told was rooted in the fear of God, but that was not true of the teachings concerning Jesus Christ. Here we were taught about pure love and it is for those kinds of moments that I am grateful to Catholic teaching.

But even then, I was not one to accept things blindly. In one of our bible classes, I gathered the courage to tell my priest, Father Jean, a friend of the family, of my reluctance to love such a "nasty" God who always seemed keen to punish and torture us with the prospect of eternal damnation and Hell. I went even further, and whether I truly believed it or not, I told poor Father Jean that I didn't want or need such a God. The dear man was sincerely surprised and shocked by my stance. He could see that I wasn't acting, pretending or making a grand statement to impress my friends. It even surprised me that I had gone so far to provoke him. The good Father went to great lengths to make me see what a loving God we were blessed to have. Still, I wasn't convinced and it took me many years to come back to searching for a spiritual connection. My wise mother forced me and my brother and sister to go to church up to the age of 12, the time of Solemn Communion. Thereafter we were free to practise our faith or not. My father was never part of the decision process. He was a staunch atheist like his own father and didn't interfere one way or the other. So when I was twelve, the Church and I went our separate ways. After that my brother and I only went to church for funerals. My younger sister was to later follow the same pattern.

As I have mentioned, Father Jean was a long-time family friend, but the relationship was based on much more than his role in the Church. During the war, he had been a member of the resistance, as was my mother. Our family doctor, Dr. Sperader, was also a former member of the *maquis* and in fact he had been leader of the *Reseau Comete*, a resistance network that operated in the south of France. The still-living wartime comrades were treated to my mother's generous hospitality at least once a month. No longer united by a common enemy, their deeply opposed religious and political views were on full display. As a child I listened with fascination to the fierce debates that took place at our kitchen table. Despite the fact that I was still a child, some of these concepts resonated with my impressionable young mind. Of course I wasn't allowed to be part of the conversation, but I was keen to linger about as long as possible before being sent to bed.

So even though I no longer went to church, those religious debates (among many others) that I had taken in so eagerly at the kitchen table were still present in my mind. Without being consciously aware of it, I was waiting for another chance to discover more about the nature of spirituality. That opportunity was to come in a completely unexpected way through a mystical experience.

But that revelation was still a long way off and for the time being my growing up continued to be very ordinary indeed. School remained a place that was more characterized by misery than joyful learning. At the age of twelve I was put into a class for students with learning problems. In those days you had to be fourteen to quit school and my new classmates were simply putting in time until that special birthday came around. No one seemed to care that for most of them the time spent in school was totally useless and unproductive. The majority learned absolutely nothing! But at least they weren't being smacked around for their lack of ability or motivation. These boys were bigger and stronger than the teacher so they could at least remain ignorant in peace. In this new environment I suddenly became the "smart one" and I was always happy to share my know-how with my new comrades. Consequently I was the friend of all and never had to put up with bullying - or even harsh words. My good relationship with my fellow students led to a surprising incident many years later, but I will save this story for a later chapter.

As things turned out I didn't have to wait until I was fourteen to leave this interesting class. A teacher who was a friend of my parents recommended that I be placed in a more challenging environment and I was miraculously given a second chance. This time I resolved to try very hard and to get as involved as possible - with some of my subjects at least. I quickly realized that I was far behind in some areas and I made my own decision to catch up in Mathematics by taking correspondence courses. In this way I hoped to make up for years of laziness and sleepiness. I took courses that involved everything from basic arithmetic to algebra and geometry. This last was especially useful when later I successfully passed an examination to qualify for entrance to a private aeronautical school. The test required that you demonstrate an aptitude for "space geometry", the ability to visualize objects and design them three dimensionally using industrial techniques. I mention all this to show that once the mind focuses completely on a goal, success is far more likely. I'm not suggesting that any of this is necessarily easy, but with ability, intense vision, and hard work, most obstacles can be overcome.

My sudden transformation was a puzzle to my teachers and I found it amusing that they didn't trust my rapid progress. As though I were "milk on fire", they slyly watched my every move to discover how I was managing to cheat. But mathematics is a precise discipline and they finally had to accept that my high marks were indeed deserved. (I didn't feel any need to reveal the fact that I was also taking correspondence courses.)

My newfound success at school made life there much easier to cope with and things at home were mostly very congenial as well. So now that these major parts of my life were coming along nicely I began to feel the need to discover new things. I enrolled in a jujitsu course to learn how to defend myself. Alas bullies were plentiful and it took very little to end up in stupid and senseless fights. But once I began to master this martial art I discovered that people stopped bothering me. It was never my desire to provoke anyone before I took jujitsu, and now they had stopped antagonizing me in return. The big difference seemed to be that I wasn't worried or afraid anymore. Somehow I came to sense that you communicate your mood to others. With understanding that came only many years later I learned that there are indeed very subtle waves of feeling that we project to the outside world. Some of us are very sensitive to these vibrating energies. Women are particularly gifted at detecting them.

But jujitsu was not the end of my explorations. The next step in my search was to find, for the first time in my life, a direct connection between diet and health. The motivation for this discovery was a classic teenage one – pimples. I was lucky enough to be spared from having them on my face, but I had huge ugly ones on my chest and back. It being summer in an ocean-side city, hanging out with friends on the beach was an everyday pleasure – at least for some. I was so self-conscious about those blemishes that swimming and sunning, especially with girls, was torture. And this was how I decided to become a vegetarian.

The few remedies for acne that existed in those days didn't work and I was growing increasingly desperate until the day that I was waiting to meet my friend Jean in his father's shop. Jean's father was a vegetarian and had two small outlets selling natural products and remedies. As I waited I heard him discuss a health issue with a customer. He seemed very knowledgeable and ended the consultation by suggesting a naturopath for the man to see. Thus encouraged, I knew Jean's father well enough to trust him so I confided in him about my health problem. He was kind and humourous in his response. He asked me if I was willing to be mocked and despised - perhaps even by my own family - should I decide to become a vegetarian. (In those days, (1958) vegetarians were a very rare breed.) Then he gave me a lot of good advice and when he had finished I had made up my mind. My mother had a fruit and vegetable shop with plenty of what was required, and I wasn't concerned about being scorned. It seemed that I had nothing to lose.

Jean's father had said that I would need to have my family's agreement if he were to advise me and so I had to tell them. They were shocked. They couldn't see how such a change in diet would affect someone's health. And in any case, my pimples would go away after puberty. Nevertheless they agreed and I became a vegetarian. Of course I was indeed mocked and despised at school, but despite all the problems of living in a sea of omnivores I persisted. For a time I was even a pure vegan, not just refusing meat and fish, but anything that was not of vegetable origin. Some of my relatives and friends thought that I had gone crazy. But after only two weeks noticeable improvements could be seen. My energy level was much more "sparkly" and not only that, but I was thinking more clearly. Overall, I felt more alive. Clearly what I was eating was having a huge effect on my wellbeing – as it would on anyone's.

To be a vegetarian or vegan requires not only avoiding dead animals, but also not eating anything that may have an animal product as an ingredient. For example most cheeses, allowable for so-called lacto vegans, contain rennet, a substance taken from the lining of a calf's stomach, and from those of certain other young animals as well. Another challenge for vegetarians is finding the right foods to provide the body with adequate protein and amino acids, both found readily in meat. The chosen foods must also contain all the elements needed for any healthy diet, vegetarian or not. Finally, it is essential that dishes be found that suit the individual's personality and temperament. But of course in this day and age there are many prepared vegetarian dishes available, meals that require only the knowledge of how to operate an oven. Sadly even though it is much easier to be a vegetarian in the twenty-first century than in the 1950's there are new dangers that accompany this situation.

These widely-available processed vegetarian foods often mix too many starches and can contain high levels of sugar and/or salt. In addition, by buying these prepared foods would-be vegetarians not only fail to learn enough about proper cooking techniques but also never discover their own bodies' specific needs. In other words there is a lot to learn in order to adopt a healthy vegetarian lifestyle. So if someone gives up meat out of revulsion or because of a current fad, the result may well be serious health problems despite possibly noble intentions. Later in this book we will look at what has been tried over and over with great success.

When I became a vegetarian my day began with a variety of fruits for breakfast - without any cereals. It had been suggested to me that the two did not mix well. One or the other was fine, but not both together. For lunch I would have a light meal consisting of various salads accompanied by whole meal bread and followed by a few nuts. For dinner, the basic ingredients were a variety of vegetables, a starch or two, such as polenta, couscous or whole meal rice, and legumes such as beans, chick peas and lentils. I would make a ragout of the legumes and vegetables, spicing them to lift up the flavours then cooking them in their own juices in patapar (parchment) paper. I can tell you that there was no suffering on this diet. These meals were feasts. The other family members enjoyed the food as much as I did but would add fish or meat as they wished. Sometimes there would also be dessert, but not every day – about two or three times a week on average. This was as much as I ever wanted in any case, but my brother and father would have preferred more. (My mother once came home with boxes of sweets and invited my brother to have as much as he wanted. He gorged himself to the point where he actually threw up. Point made.) My health improved dramatically on this regime. My previous skin problems disappeared and I was able to go to the beach without being embarrassed. Playing sports was equally comfortable for me. I was thoroughly delighted with my body's new look. I was to stay a vegetarian until I was eighteen years old.

At this stage in my life I was eager for new challenges and experiences and it so happened that I had reached the age when I was able to look for a good technical school. An excellent one was only fifteen kilometres away, and it offered an exam for sorting out your abilities. The twenty-two who scored highest were deemed suitable for specialized training in aeronautical manufacturing. My friend Jean and I had an older friend who was already enrolled in such a program and he encouraged us to give it a try. But there was another hurdle first; that was to qualify for admission to the actual training program which would take place at a company called Avions Breguet, later called Dassault. It was a good thing we didn't know that there were two hundred and thirty people competing for very few places; we would probably have given up without trying. When the entrance exam was over I felt that I had done okay, but probably no better than many others. I really didn't expect to be accepted. However, about a month later Jean and I learned to our great joy that we had both been offered positions. When we went to tell our now former school not to expect us for the next year, to our great surprise those teachers who had given us such a hard time, seemed genuinely happy for us and offered their congratulations. Their good wishes made us realize that these teachers had a human side and that their strict treatment of us was the result of good intentions. It may well be debated whether such methods are the right way to motivate young people, but their hearts seemed to have been in the right place.

Our four years at Avions Breguet were good ones. We had a lot of hands-on work with interesting machinery or involving manual expertise, mixed with classroom-style technical schooling. The latter included a lot of mathematics – mostly spatial geometry, a discipline necessary for much industrial design and the skills involved in accurately reading plans (drawings). We learned a tremendous amount and we were further motivated by the fact that we were learning something that would give us the means to earn a living, a fact which made us feel proud and useful. Such an atmosphere made us work much harder at solving problems than we would have wanted to do during our earlier school experiences. And as a further bonus, all our work was done by the end of the day at five o'clock. There were also breaks for sports some days, and we had lots of time off: each year we had four weeks of paid vacation - two in summer and two in winter. We were also free on all public holidays.

By 1961, I had successfully finished my diploma after three years of study. As a result I was offered either an additional two years of study to get a higher technical qualification or the opportunity to begin work at the factory immediately after the summer vacation. I went on to a further year of training and was prepared to begin another when the proverbial bottom fell out of my plans. I was almost eighteen years old by this time and at that age military service was obligatory in those days. I applied for but was refused a temporary dispensation to finish my technical training. I could begin work at the factory, but I would be allowed to stay there only for a few months before being sent to fight in the Algerian war. Even though a national aircraft manufacturing capacity was key to France's future, the politicians of the day couldn't see the importance of something so new and untried. The beginning of the computer age in the 1970's produced similar incomprehension among elected leaders. The long and short of it is that if I had been at a public university I would have been able to continue my studies, but my school was a private one so I was looking at the prospect of fighting in a brutal war for a cause I did not believe in. Thus in 1962 my journey to Canada began.

But first some background. The thought of refusing to serve in the Algerian war did not happen overnight. I had always been interested in the history of French involvement in Indochina (Vietnam), as many know, a futile war that ended with France's humiliation by the Viet Minh at the battle of Dien Bien Phu in 1954. This defeat led to France's surrender and withdrawal. I could see a similar pattern starting to take shape in Algeria and I wanted nothing to do with it. A number of my friends had already been conscripted and none felt that the war was an honourable one. Many did not return. The circumstances, France's attempt to suppress a desire for independence in one of its colonies, had nothing to do with the circumstances that had led my parents to fight Hitler. It was not a matter of cowardice or fear, but simply that I was not prepared to risk death in the name of oppression.

But long before these events took place, I had grown up with the knowledge that my mother and family doctor had been active in the resistance during the war. The horrors of that conflict were part of my family's history. Not surprisingly I developed a strong anti-war mentality. What I did not mention before was that my Basque grandmother's house in Sare was a key part of the underground network. Because of her proximity to the Spanish border she was asked many times to host and hide all kinds of people who were in grave danger. Some were members of the maquis who had become fugitives, some were Jews, and others were even Canadian and American pilots who had been rescued by the maquis after being shot down. So my decision to refuse military service was hardly a surprising one. And when I shared my decision with my family, they made no attempt to talk me out of it. On the contrary, they immediately went to work to secure me permission to go to Canada.

My mother had powerful connections as a result of her wartime work and I also had the support of my uncle Camille who worked for Interpol in Paris and had close contact with the Canadian Embassy. With all this influence working on my behalf I was able to get a Canadian visa very quickly.

CHAPTER 3:

A Fresh Start, Adapting to a New Country

When I left France and arrived as a landed immigrant in Montreal it was the middle of winter, February 4th, 1962. The plane I flew over on was a Lockheed commercial Jet that covered all that distance in a little over eight hours. And apart from the speed of the flight, it was also a marvel to me that the landing had even been possible with all that snow around. Arriving in a strange country might have been a little overwhelming had my friend Jean not been waiting for me at the airport. He had come to Canada with his father the year before.

That kind and sweet man, who taught me how to be a vegetarian, had not had an easy time of it. He had once been a chef, but after nearly dying from food poisoning from eating tainted game meat, he became a passionate advocate of vegetarianism. Sadly, in the 1960's he was too far ahead of his time and after three years of trying to interest the good people of Saint Jean de Luz in meatless living (and two failed shops) he was forced to declare bankruptcy. His brother had gone to Canada as a pastry chef in a place called Club Esterel in the Laurentians north of Montreal. They needed a good French chef there and with his brother's help Jean's father secured his visa and work.

Jean and I had kept in contact. He hadn't had any problems with emigration as at the time he was a minor travelling with his father. I myself had to wait to be eighteen in order to be classified as an adult and legally able to go by myself. Jean and I both intended to continue our careers in the aircraft industry with the only major Canadian manufacturer, Canadair.

When we went for our interview there, we were told to first study English for at least three years then come back. I asked why, since Quebec was supposedly bilingual. It turned out that technical drawings and even instructions on the floor were exclusively in English. I asked if the company subsidized English courses and if we could be given some low level job in the meantime as we needed to support ourselves. The interviewer bluntly replied that this was our problem, not his. We left disappointed, knowing now that without English our chances of decent work in plane manufacturing were pretty much non-existent. Not surprisingly, in later years Jean and I were very sympathetic to the attempts of Quebecers to preserve their language and culture in the middle of an English-speaking continent.

Fortunately we had a back-up plan and that was going to work at the Club Esterel with Jean's father and uncle. However, unlike them, we would be going there as labourers, hired for snow clearing. But, after we had spent a month clearing snow, Jean's father (by now executive chef) convinced his boss, Mr. Simard, to offer us work in the kitchen. We both accepted even though we would be working twice as much for less money.

Our duties began very early each morning when we had the responsibility of feeding eighty construction workers who were there to work on a hotel expansion. We sometimes had them for lunch as well. We also had to assist in preparing meals for the regular guests – a much classier affair. I quickly realized that I had natural abilities as a cook; all my helping in the kitchen at home was serving me well. Of course I had much to learn, but as many of the local workers were somewhat indifferent to their duties, I was able to shine by comparison. Jean's father quoted the old adage to me about the one-eyed man being king in the country of the blind. He appreciated both my willingness to work efficiently and my ability to quickly master his many requirements. In turn I greatly admired his mastery of his craft. As a boss, he was kind and patient and I was grateful for all that he was teaching me.

But the money was still almost non-existent. We were paid twenty-seven cents an hour on the basis of a fifty-five hour week. However as the locals didn't take their work seriously and sometimes went missing, we often had to cover for them on our days off. Those lost days of rest were never replaced – especially not mine as my abilities were getting increasingly sophisticated and specialized and I was needed in the kitchen most of the time. In fairness however, our food and lodging were both included.

Another sacrifice I had to make concerned my vegetarian diet. In 1960's Quebec the supplies available weren't anywhere close to those on offer in France and either you kept to a meagre diet with little choice or you compromised and adapted to survive. I chose to adapt, as did Jean. We tried a bit of everything and it made life much easier. My flexibility also worked well for Jean's father (still a vegetarian) as he was able to have me try a lot of food that he didn't eat himself.

But that change certainly didn't mean that I was willing to gobble up doubtful food. I was still very particular about what I ate, and I remain so today. I am more of a vegetarian than an omnivore and I continue to begin my day with fruit. Later on I like to have some real coffee with whole meal rye bread and with almond puree. Sometimes I also enjoy a fruit spread or jam. My diet also includes free range eggs and chicken when available, and the chicken must have been properly raised on natural foods. I mostly avoid pork but I will sometimes have beef or local lamb. In season, I buy fresh organic produce from local farms and occasionally dairy products if they have been produced without harmful additives. And of course, as the son of a fisherman I like to have all the beautiful fresh fish that I can find. Desserts I have rarely. The result of this diet is that I am seldom sick and my energy level is very high. And if the need arose I would have no problem in becoming a vegan again. So all that youthful experimentation, in France and at Club Esterel continues to shape what I eat today.

But to return to my tale of life in the Laurentian Mountains, after many months of little but work, Jean and I began to feel deprived. Our days consisted of work, sleep and eating on the run. They were rewarding in many ways, but we were young and wanted to meet girls. We also craved the chance to experience some culture beyond a bit of television now and again.

So one day we took a taxi to the closest tavern for some entertainment. We had no idea, until we saw a sign, that we were underage in Quebec. At the hotel where we worked we were given wine and beer as we had been in France. It had never occurred to us that we were being given alcohol illegally. At home it was considered grossly inappropriate to abuse alcohol – or to overindulge in anything for that matter. So you can imagine our surprise when we were faced with an RCMP constable at the entrance to the bar. That the police would concern themselves with drinking was a total shock to us. We tried to follow some couples inside but the officer blocked our way and directed us to the Men's Section. At least he hadn't asked our age.

With serious misgivings, we entered a dark, smoke-filled room with men sitting around tables crammed full with glasses of beer. Why so much beer? Was it a drinking contest? Even more astonishing was the fact that every table had a large salt shaker in the centre. I asked Jean if he thought they put salt in their beer. At that moment a big waiter with a full tray of beer asked us how many we wanted. When we said two he made no effort to conceal his contempt. And then we made things even worse when I made clear that I meant two in total, a paltry one each. Now he was really upset with us. Our French accents stuck out among these rural Quebecois, and they seemed to enrage him even more. He swore mightily at us. Flustered I gave him twice the money he had asked for, making matters even worse. Jean and I each had a sip of beer and then began to notice the dark looks that surrounded us. I whispered to him that we'd better get out of there before someone found an excuse to beat us up. A good call it turned out, as nasty comments were shouted after us.

But our visit to the black hole was not to be the end of our day's troubles. Hoping to impress girls we had dressed for style not practicality. And as it was October, a very unpredictable month in that part of the world, the decision came back to haunt us. The light was dimming fast and the temperature was dropping. With no taxi to be seen, we began the long walk home as a blizzard struck. Our attractive but thin jackets and our fancy shoes were no defence against the elements. We walked hugging each other like lovers in an attempt to keep warm, barely able see the road ahead of us. And just as we thought that things couldn't be worse, we heard the sound of a pack of dogs howling and growling deep in their throats. Then as we got closer to a small hill we could see what the woods and snow had hidden from us: these were no dogs; they were wolves. Jean held me even more firmly and asked if I thought we should run for our lives. I said no; I thought our best chance lay in ignoring them. And somehow it worked. The whole way back we couldn't tell whether they were following us or not but they didn't attack. The rest of the walk, until we finally saw the lights of the hotel through the snow, and then a passing car, seemed to take forever. But now we knew we were safe. And who knows? If it hadn't been for those wolves we might have at least suffered frostbite or even frozen to death. As it was, we suffered nothing more than damaged pride. And in a strange way I felt grateful to those wolves. It almost seemed as though they had been sent to save us. To thank God would not have fit my beliefs at the time, but now I wonder. Naturally Jean and I have retold the story many times - with a bit of exaggeration for dramatic effect, and lots of laughter.

As time went on, life in the Laurentians became less and less appealing to us and in November of 1962, Jean and I finally made the big move to Montreal. We arrived at the Dorchester Bus Station without the slightest idea of where to go, so we arbitrarily chose to walk to the right and see where we ended up. Eventually we found ourselves on

Rue St. Denis in Old Montreal where we decided that we liked the look of the interesting old houses and apartment buildings. One had a room available so we took it, paying two weeks in advance. We were not the only tenants and soon began to notice that the other residents seemed mostly very angry and extremely impolite. Our impressions turned out to be correct as we often heard screaming, swearing and banging doors in the middle of the night. Then one night we actually heard gun shots followed by the arrival of the police. They questioned us along with the other tenants. That was enough for us and in the morning we decided to move on. The landlord refused to refund us anything so we lost a week's rent, but that didn't seem very important under the circumstances.

For our second attempt at finding suitable lodgings we chose the very middle of the city. As we explored the area we marvelled at the sight of the vast construction project that would become Place Ville Marie. Coming from a small town we had never seen or even imagined such a gigantic structure. Finally our wanderings led us to Rue Bishop, the site of another rooming house. This time our prospective landlady, Hannah, was German and we wondered if our two cultures, with their long history of tragic conflict, could live together amicably. My instincts told me that everything would be fine, but Jean was considerably more hesitant. What decided the issue for me was the fact that her sweet and calm face reminded me of my grandmother. I chose to trust her and that decision turned out to be a blessing as she knew exactly what to do to help us. It was like coming back home.

Hannah had lost her husband not long before and while she had a daughter the latter did not live in Montreal. As a result, she more or less adopted us and I have to say that we loved it. She was kind to us in countless ways and in return we asked her to tell us what we could do to help with the maintenance of the house.

Finding work turned out to be much more difficult and our money was slowly but surely melting away. We ranged far from Rue Bishop in our job search, still hoping to find something where we could use our technical knowledge. Sadly, not knowing English was all too often a barrier, a barrier made higher still by the fact that all our training had been in metric measurement, when at this time all Quebec manufacturers were still using the imperial system. Jean ultimately found work in a foundry - a far cry from precise and interesting work - but a job was a job, and he took it. As for myself I decided to look for hotel restaurant work instead.

As it turned out there was a very nice looking place that was only two blocks from Rue Bishop so I went in after lunch to talk to the chef.

Working in Montreal as a bus boy. (1962)

He told me that nothing was available in the kitchen but that they were short a bus boy in the "Pavillion," their fancy dining room. As it was urgent that I find work, I much appreciated the suggestion. I was told to wait for the Maitre D'. After some time an elegant gentleman dressed in a beautiful tuxedo came in. It turned out that he was Mr. Fascio, the Maitre D' in charge of a staff of twelve waiters, two captains, and two bus boys. He asked me about my experience. Not much to tell there: I had worked for one summer in the dining room of the Hotel de la Poste in my home town of Saint Jean de Luz. I was fourteen that year and I was to begin my course at Avions Breguet in the fall. But regardless of the brevity of my resume, to my surprise and delight, Mr. Fascio asked me to start work the following morning.

Despite the state of Jean's and my finances, I had to go out immediately and buy some white shirts, a bow tie, black trousers and black shoes. The shopping trip left me almost penniless by the end of the afternoon. That evening we had almost nothing to eat as Jean wouldn't receive his first cheque for another week, and I had forgotten to ask Mr. Fascio anything about my salary or share of the tips.

My first day at work went by somehow. I did my best, realizing very quickly how much I had to learn. But the other bus boy was a kind man from New Zealand and he was very helpful to me though he spoke only English, and I only French, Spanish and Basque (the last seeming particularly useless in Canada). I must admit that I was feeling a bit of the odd man out in my new country, until to my great and happy surprise I discovered that none of the many Italian or Greek waiters was of Canadian origin. One of those waiters, a man named Ricardo spoke kindly to me in French. I immediately recognized his Spanish accent and when I realized that he spoke little French, I began speaking to him in Spanish. We exchanged the usual information, where we were from, how long we had been in Canada and so on. It was then, to my joyful surprise, that he began to speak to me in Basque. We ended up being very good friends and he quickly warned me that some of the waiters would try to sabotage me as Mr. Fascio had chosen me over the friends that they had suggested. First he had hired a New Zealander rather than another Greek or Italian, and then to add insult to injury he had now hired some frog from nowhere, not at all part of the hotel restaurant life.

The sabotage manifested itself on the second busy weekend. I was continually pressured to work faster and faster and I did my best to keep up, quickly carrying out all the dirty dishes and bringing fresh ones in turn. The Greek waiters especially tried to make things as difficult for me as they could. They dumped their soiled plates and silverware on the tray in all directions, expecting me to carry out the big, round tray as it was. However I took the time to rearrange things so that the load would be stable. Then at the busiest time of the evening, one of those same waiters assured me that he had arranged the tray so that it would be safe to carry and asked me to take it out immediately as he needed the space for another tray. I lifted it up and rounded the corner near a table with five diners just in time for the tray to dump half its contents onto the table and its occupants. The noise and splashing attracted the attention of the whole room. I kept on going to deliver what was left on the tray to the washing section of the enormous kitchen, and then I went directly to the change room. I was heartbroken, certain that I had lost my job and that there was no sense in going back to the dining room. I had been there not even two weeks and was only barely surviving on the small bits of tip money as it was, but with all the mess that I had created I still intended to pay for the damages or at least work them off in some way.

As I slowly changed, lamenting my situation, Mr. Fascio came into the change room and asked what I was doing there. I explained that I expected to be let go for dumping the tray, but I intended to pay for the damage. He told me to go back to work, that he was the one to decide whether I was fired or not. Now I had to face the whole dining room. First I went to apologize to the people at the unfortunate table. I expected the worst but they were very gracious about it. Luckily no one had been injured, the only real damage being a bit of a leftover sauce that had splashed onto one of the women. She took it all in good spirit

and didn't make a big thing of it at all. It helped that the house paid for
their meal and dry cleaning. As they spoke French, I was able to thank
them profusely when they left. I was reasonably sure that their kindness had helped me keep my job.

What happened afterwards was even stranger. Of course Mr. Fascio was aware of all the dirty tricks that I had been quietly enduring,
and the next day both bus boys were asked to go to his office. He asked
us what we were earning in tips, both weekly and nightly. When we
told him, we learned that the waiters had been cheating us. They were
supposed to turn over ten per cent of their tips to be shared between the
two bus boys. In fact the actual number was more like five per cent -
and that only on busy nights. I felt sad to learn this, but not truly upset
as I had long observed in my life that people find it easy to be dishonest with you when they believe that you don't belong or are in some way
different from them. Those waiters clearly believed that they were
more deserving of the money than the two outsiders.

Like a dog with a good sense of smell, all my life I have had the
ability to sense when people are dishonest. No matter how wonderful
they may appear, or how hard they may try to impress me, I refuse to
have anything to do with them. If there is no alternative to dealing with
them I watch them like a hawk and cut our association short as soon as
I can. I don't call them names or judge them; I just don't give them my
trust. Life offers many choices as to who we choose to be and what we
decide to experience. Later on in the book we will look more closely at
the Law of Attraction, a principle that describes how we bring the experiences that we need into our lives. Neale Donald Walsch, whose work
I mentioned above adds that our lives have the meaning that we give to
them. My own life has been shaped by a desire to learn to love. That,
for me, is first and foremost. I believe that anyone who uses love as a
touchstone for meaning can never go far wrong. When life's direction
is guided by love, a higher level of consciousness is almost inevitable.

As a young boy (ten at the time) I had not yet fully realized the
central importance of love and it led me to make a terrible mistake. On
a street in my home town two friends, along with my brother and me,
stole some money that belonged to a newspaper vendor. In those days
newspapers were sold on the honour system. The papers were simply
placed on a bench and anchored with a stone. The customer took the
newspaper and put money in a box. So it was a simple matter for a thief
to make away with a few coins. And while I didn't actually steal the
money I certainly enjoyed my share of the candy that was bought with
it. But the problem with crime in a small town, especially one in which

your mother is well known, is that someone is bound to see you do it and report the matter to the parents. And so it was with me and the others. I didn't try to avoid responsibility, taking my fair share of the blame. Surprisingly however, the sky didn't fall. My mother was far too clever for that.

Instead, she took all the young conspirators to visit the newspaper vendor. Our first shock was discovering that he couldn't afford a proper house, instead living with his family inside what had once been a block-house - part of the German coastal fortifications left over from the war. It was all concrete without windows and completely lacking comforts of any kind. The man came out to say hello to us and we boys all looked at each other in fear, wondering what was going to happen. He invited us into a home so poor that the inhabitants couldn't even afford electricity: the one dim light was powered by acetylene. A woman and two children could barely be seen in the gloom. My shame at having been part of robbing such a man was overwhelming. I rushed outside and threw up in some bushes. My mother pointed out how poor they were – as though we couldn't see for ourselves. She had brought bags of fruits and vegetables for them, telling the newspaper vendor that they would otherwise spoil and go to waste if he didn't take them. After that event I swore to myself that if I ever stole anything again it would only be in a case of dire necessity.

And I have tried my best to stick to that resolution. I have never stolen anything since. Some people don't believe me, but I have never even cheated on my income tax. And in fact when I have been audited from time to time, any adjustments have been extremely minor – a few dollars here and there, the result of error or different interpretations of the law, but never dishonesty. Moreover back when I was still a waiter, I would try to get my colleagues to agree on a fair percentage of our income from tips to declare on our income tax. They always wanted to declare nothing at all, but I still paid tax on my tips, even when they mocked me. Three years later Revenue Canada began to audit hair-dressers and waiters, a decision that resulted in a lot of pain and anger. I had my own business by then so I wasn't audited personally, but my ex-colleagues' lies ended up costing them dearly. One refused to pay and left the country; another barely survived as he spent two years working to pay off the debt and clear his name.

This is not to say that tax law is always fair. The middle class, whose income is mostly recorded on paper, clearly carries a dispropor-tionate share of the burden. Workers who manage to be paid in cash, and those among the wealthy who are unscrupulous enough to move their money offshore, seem happy to avoid paying their fair share. Still and all, most of us seem to realize that services must be paid for, and the disadvantaged looked after, so we willingly carry our proportion of the burden despite the inequities in the system. Most of us seem to feel that it is more important to do the right thing than try to cheat the government out of the money that is needed to support a healthy society. In other words, we choose, probably with more than a few reservations, to give the government our trust. In the coming chapters of this book, I will return again and again to the theme of trust.

But trust is essentially a passive emotion. As I look back on my life I have actively tried to build bridges between groups. As I have said, much evil comes from close identification with one's own, and damn the rest. In my lifelong work as a restaurateur I have always been blind to status and station. I have never cared whether you are the ex King of Greece or a mechanic in a service station. I have always treated everyone in exactly the same way. What's more I believe, deeply and sincerely that every human being *deserves* to be treated as the equal of every other.

That view has never been more sorely tested than it was in my early years in Quebec. It was a time of great ferment and fierce debates often raged around me. To my puzzlement, I was sometimes accused (being French) of somehow being complicit in my ancestors' failure to defend New France. I had no idea what they were talking about so I made it a point to learn about Quebec's history. Then I was better able to follow what was going on. My Francophone friends felt themselves to be victims because of events that took place over two centuries ago. And of course the Anglophones had an entirely different way of seeing the same things. There really were "Two Solitudes" in those days. But even when I had gained a much better grasp of what was being talked about, I still couldn't persuade my friends to leave the past behind. My youthful optimism led me to think that I could bring the two sides together. Suffice to say that my efforts were not appreciated. I quickly learned that mindsets held since childhood were not going to be changed by anything I said or did. So I made friends with the moderates and let the ragers rage. I learned to listen and remain silent. But I have never given up on the idea of being a peacemaker. I will return to this theme later on.

As things turned out, my time in Quebec was not to last long. Things were going very well in terms of work, and I was getting increasingly better positions and greater pay, however, my unresolved military situation had not disappeared. I had not been granted a dismissal by the French Government and as far as the French consulate in

Montreal was concerned, I was still a draft dodger. As long as I remained in Canada, the label didn't affect me at all, but if I were ever to go back to France I would be forced to complete my military service and added to that would be an additional length of time to be decided by a military tribunal. The threat would continue to loom over me until I turned sixty. As far as Paris was concerned, I would always be considered French, even were I to become a Canadian citizen. These were matters that I hadn't seriously considered when I came to Canada at age eighteen. I had failed to give any serious thought to what I would do if something happened to a member of my family. And that is exactly the situation that I was to find myself in.

CHAPTER 4

Back to the French Life

In September of 1963 I received news that my brother Michel and some friends had been involved in a car crash that had killed one and seriously injured two others. My brother was one of the injured and he was now fighting for his life. One leg had been crushed and there were other wounds which while less serious were dangerously weakening his body. I made the decision to return home on the spot. When I got there it took a few days to take in the whole situation. By the time I arrived he was out of danger but facing the amputation of the damaged leg. Luckily for him, a young surgeon, fresh out of school, persuaded our family doctor to take a chance on putting the leg together. (This was the same family doctor who had known us since we were children.) Before the operation could take place, the head surgeon had to be convinced as well. After much deliberation the decision was made to try and save the leg. The surgery went on for a long time but it went well, and we had a discrete celebration that night. (He was only eighteen at the time, and was told that sports were now out of the question, but he has managed to have a normal life ever since.) But I still felt that I had to go back and support my brother and other family members.

Facing the now-inevitable I asked the French government to pay my way back to France, so that I could meet my military obligations, but despite being legally required to do so they refused my request. I tried to book a flight but none was immediately available so I tried to find out if I could go by sea. Luckily the Italian cruise ship Homeric was departing from Quebec City two days later, and the fare was very reasonable so I booked passage. The journey was a very pleasant one as I was no longer having to provide food for others and had nothing to do but enjoy my leisure. One of the pleasures of the voyage was a very beautiful girl whom I would try to glance at discretely whenever I saw her. Eventually I worked up the courage to engage her in conversation and we seemed to click. We had a great time together until our arrival in our destination port of Southampton and the sad end of our little romance. But I had mentioned that I would be in the clutches of the military for the foreseeable future and to my surprise she promised to come and visit wherever I ended up in France. She had come to the U.K. to see her family in Epson, Surrey, and as things turned out the English connection would prove to be a very lucky one.

Once back at home in St. Jean de Luz I tried to be as invisible to the authorities as possible, but in a small town no one can hide for very long, and I was fully aware that the local gendarmes would know that Roger Dufau, draft dodger, was back home. No one had asked me anything when I crossed the border from Spain, but I didn't expect that situation to continue much longer. Once I knew that my brother Michel was going to be alright, I decided that the best thing was to go to the police station. My father came with me, and as he knew them all, we had quite a courteous meeting. They pointed out that if they were to go by the book they would have to immediately handcuff me and escort me to a military post. But since I had come to them voluntarily they gave me a week to spend with my family and trusted me to turn myself in on a certain date. I thanked them and gave them my word of honour that I would comply. And I did. I could have sneaked back to Canada by going through Spain, but I felt bound by my promise and also by the fact that my family's reputation was at stake. Yes the war in Algeria was over, and yes I still believed that time spent in the military was a waste, but I wanted to deal with the issue and get it out of my life once and for all.

So at the end of the week, accompanied by a gendarme, I boarded a train at the local station. Our destination was the city of Montluçon about ten hours and three changes of train away. The officer felt no need to handcuff me and we had many lively and interesting conversations in the course of the trip. Here again trust triumphed over the rules and regulations. When we arrived he took me to a military office where we said our farewells. I thanked him for his kindness to me.

I dealt with several different people, none of whom seemed to have any idea how to deal with me. Finally I was sent to a large barracks, still wearing the civilian clothes I had arrived in. Someone took me to a room where I was left by myself. While I was wondering what they planned to do with me next, an officer suddenly appeared and announced that the whole building had just been put under quarantine as two cases of meningitis had been reported. The three hundred men who were in the building at the time would not be allowed out for three weeks. Being the only one in civilian clothes I stood out of course, not only in appearance but because without a uniform I was not subject to military protocols and discipline. Despite all of this I made nice connections with some of the other men.

Then there was the food. The quality of the food was poor and gross, and as a result I ate almost nothing for the first three days. But as bad as the meals were, the manner of serving them was even worse. It was done in such a way that a few people, junior officers, got the lion's share of what was available, while the enlisted men had to make do on very little. The meals were served in a large refectory, with tables seating twenty people. The food was brought to the tables in carts and then large serving dishes were left at the end of each table. Each man took his portion and passed the rest down the table. With reasonable people this system would have worked well, but of course all the junior officers were at the end where the containers of food were first placed. They felt that it was their privilege to heap their plates as high as they wished. By the time the containers reached the last of the privates there would be almost nothing left, the only exceptions being when no one liked the food.

After a few days of this nonsense, I suggested to some of the other men, that the food be served beginning at the enlisted men's end of the table. I asked who would be willing to help me get this idea put into practice. No one else was willing to get involved as they were afraid of reprisals. But I found a way around this on the fifth day, by stationing myself at the officers' end of the table waiting for the food to arrive. When it did, I picked one dish up and asked two of the men to help me carry it. That way I would be the only one responsible. I counted on my civilian clothes to sow some confusion among the officers about how to respond. Despite my civilian clothes, threats were offered generously. But my sheer size and determination prevented anyone from trying to stop me. Attracted by the commotion and my lack of a uniform, a captain rushed over to find out what was going on. I pretended that I knew nothing of military ranks and addressed him as "officer". I briefly explained my personal circumstances and the saga of the food supply. I asked if he thought it reasonable that most of us be starved indefinitely. As a result of this conversation the non-commissioned officers were reprimanded and the food service changed. After that the containers of food were left at both ends of each table.

In the following days, many of the men came up to thank me and ask my name. But of course they were ordinary soldiers, not non-coms. The latter, by contrast, promised to give me all the shit they could think of, and assured me that they would greatly enjoy doing so. I was left with a lot to think about. The prospect of a bunch of angry army officers looking for revenge was hardly appealing. So I was forced to come up with a plan. I decided to act, and in doing so I had to deny my commitments and higher feelings in favour of sheer survival. But of course it's completely natural to respond to threat by acting in self-defence and that's what I decided to do. My education and training made me a better fit for the air force than the army - where I would simply be more cannon fodder. From my time at Avions Breguet I was certified in aeronautical engineering and I was also licensed to fly a glider. Someone at the French Consulate in Montreal had doctored my resume so that I would not qualify for anything but the infantry. I know this for a fact as I still have my military record book. Under "education" it states "*neant*" or in English, none. I had made the mistake of asking them not to send me to military service, so this was their way of punishing me.

But while I had a plan to eventually save myself, in the short term I was still in the army and I needed to find a way to protect myself. So like others before me, I decided to fake an injury – in this case, to my back. This "ailment" would keep me in hospital rather than in training where I would be at the mercy of my persecutors. I pulled this off for some time, until one day my conscience woke out of its sleep and my real self returned. I had been fooling a few of the doctors by mimicking the symptoms of sciatica which I knew well since some of my friends and family suffered from this condition. But one day I faced a new, young doctor who, reading from my file, asked me if I had sciatica, chronic lumbago. Without even thinking, and not knowing why to this day, I found myself answering, "No, I've never had back ache or sciatica in my life, but everything in the army is so pathetically stupid that I had to do something to minimize it all, or maybe even get myself discharged." He looked me straight in the eye and said, "You've said enough. I could send you to jail for six months of solitary confinement and after that an additional year in the military." I was shocked by what I had just said, but I answered that I understood his responsibilities and knew that there were many cheaters.

But instead of turning me over to the military police, as I deserved, he asked what I had done in civilian life. I explained that I had been in Canada working in kitchens and dining rooms. I added that I knew how to make all the American cocktails. To my surprise and delight he offered me two weeks in hospital "for observation" and that during that time I would have a chance to display my abilities in the Doctors' Mess. If they liked me they would manage to find me something to do there while I "convalesced" for twenty-eight days. That meant that I would be out of the hospital and free as a bird. As it happened, things worked out far better than I could have dreamed. The doctors became dear friends and I was able to serve my eighteen months in the military (with no added penalty) working for them. They arranged for me to be accepted by the Medical team at Legouest Military Hospital in Metz, located in France's northeast where I worked in food preparation or catered for small functions. But better yet, as I was still technically a patient I had one day off to "convalesce" for every day that I worked. During this time, Judith, my companion on the sea voyage, and I had been corresponding regularly and she made the decision to come and live with her family in Britain. Metz's location made it easy to get to London or Paris and I was often able to get leave to meet with her. I was also able to visit my family from time to time. All these trips were made possible by the long hours that I had put in working in Montreal - especially at night when the pay is better. Night work has the additional advantage that by the time you leave work, everything is closed and there is nowhere to spend your money.

Buoyed by my success in turning my military service to such good use, and with plenty of free time on my hands, I decided to request reimbursement for my travel costs from Canada, and eventually for returning there. I knew that the French Government was obliged by law to give me the money. But it turned out to be a long, hard fight. The local administrative officers ignored my repeated requests, so I decided to write directly to the Defence Ministry in Paris. That certainly produced results of a kind. The Lieutenant Colonel in charge of the hospital where I worked, ordered me to appear before him. To stress that my presence was not voluntary, he sent two Captains and an Adjutant to escort this nobody without any education into his presence. The interview, if you could call it that, consisted of the commanding officer heaping the invective, which is part of the richness of the French language, on my head, accusing me of an endless litany of petty sins. I didn't take it personally, on the contrary I was in awe of the fact that a military nonentity such as myself could provoke such passion in a senior officer. It came out that this mad rage had been provoked by my letter. The Ministry agreed with the validity of my claim and because it had been wrongly denied, had sent an insulting response to the hospital that was addressed to the Colonel personally. I apologized to him for causing so much trouble, but that I had known that compensation was due to me, even before I left Canada. I told him that I too had felt slighted, in my case because my rightful request had been so cavalierly dismissed.

A month before I was discharged from the service four guys came to deliver a cheque for three hundred and forty dollars. To put this in perspective, a good worker's salary at the time was about eighty to one hundred and twenty dollars a month. My remittance as a second class soldier was two dollars a month. My friends and I had good reason to cheer this rare victory over the notorious military stubbornness.

I was finally nearing the end of my military service and I was at a loss as to what to make of it all. What had I learned? The positive parts were the great friends I had made and the fun we had shared together. The rest would bear more thinking about. One thing at least was clear, that my life was looking a lot more promising now. I was soon to marry my sweet and beautiful girl friend Judith but there was one small complication. She loved her little Anglican church in Toronto and wanted the wedding to be held there. I had no objection at all, but because I was not of her faith her priest wanted me to get a certificate of confirmation from my church in Saint Jean de Luz. I guess he needed to know that I had had some kind of religious upbringing. So before flying back to Canada I went back to my home town and it was wonderful to have a few days of normalcy with my family after my strange time in the military.

Of course eventually I had to tell them that I was going to be married, but in Canada unfortunately. My mother was saddened by my decision but was nevertheless quite helpful about my confirmation certificate problem. She told me that Father Jean was still alive and about to retire. I was happy to reconnect with him after so many years. I told him of my plans to marry, and while he was disappointed that the ceremony was not to take place in his church, he was far more troubled by the fact that Judith was an Anglican. He agreed that differences between the two branches of Christianity were not great, but insisted that I have her convert to Catholicism. By then I was a bit amused and asked him why the issue concerned him so much since I hadn't attended any church services anywhere since the day of my first communion. "Don't all churches worship the same God?" I asked him. "Why is my small request for a certificate of confirmation such a problem?" But he seemed genuinely upset by my indifference to the matter of my future wife's conversion. It troubled him so much that he told me with great sadness that he wouldn't be able to give me the certificate. Further, he went on - and in saying this he seemed to be in anguish - if I insisted on marrying outside of the church despite its laws, he would be forced to have me excommunicated. Without thinking, I blurted out that he shouldn't worry as I wouldn't lose any sleep over it. Tears sprang to his eyes, and I immediately regretted taking his concerns so lightly. To him excommunication meant that I would be damned to eternity in hell. It had never been my intention to cause such pain to an old and dear friend, so to placate him I promised that I would do my utmost to ensure Judith's conversion. I left rather shaken up by the meeting, but in retrospect, perhaps I did manage to assuage his worries somewhat. I never saw Father Jean again as he died two years later, but my family told me that he enquired after me from time to time. His beliefs were utterly real to him and I truly hadn't meant to take them so lightly. But still I had to be loyal to myself as well. I made no attempt to change my fiancée's beliefs, nor have I ever tried to change anyone else's for that matter.

Back in Canada without my certificate, I found that the Anglican priest's position was almost as inflexible as Father Jean's. While in his church I noticed a strange anomaly. In spite of the Anglican Church's proscription of homosexuality, the priest and many members of the choir were clearly gay men, a fact which my fiancée flatly refused to believe. I utterly shocked the priest by pointing out this inconsistency, making clear that it was of no concern to me, but that his rigidity about my certificate seemed to betray a certain selectivity on the subject of church law. Perhaps this was unkind of me but I was getting very tired of church politics. I stated my refusal to believe in such a petty God, and that these endless rules were the product of human minds, not the divine one. Finally he backed down and agreed to marry us as long as I didn't take communion. The wedding took place in January of 1965, with the reception at Casa Loma, a Toronto landmark dating from the years before the First World War.

Now finally married against all odds, it was time to turn my attention back to earning a living. We decided to return to France where my goal was to open a bar and restaurant in my own Basque country. First we found an apartment in Biarritz, then soon after a dilapidated bar and restaurant that looked very promising. Its location was in Socoa, a small town overlooking the beautiful bay of Saint Jean de Luz and Ciboure, with a spectacular view of the Pyrenees. The site was part of the Yacht Club Basque concession, a government property built as a fortress to defend the area against invaders from the sea. It is a massive stone building built by the famous architect Vauban in 1605 and it is still in perfect condition today. I had a bit of money left and combined with wedding gifts we had enough to restore the existing run-down establishment and open an American-style bar and restaurant. We had a wonderful view of the Atlantic on the left and the mountains on the right. It felt good, and knew instinctively that it would be okay.

Le Fort de Socoa - the location of my first restaurant. (1965)

However I was only twenty-two and I knew that I would be competing with long-established businesses with solid reputations. What could I offer that wasn't already available? The novelty of an American bar was a huge plus, but who was I to try and compete with these great established institutions? I truly was the new kid on the block. After much thought and many talks with my family, I decided in favour of simplicity. I would have a menu with five specialties and I would strive to make them of very high quality. Since I overlooked the ocean, making the menu mostly about seafood was a no- brainer. And given that my father worked on a fishing boat as I have said, I had ready access to all sorts of fresh fish. Another resource was a huge Spanish fish market - only four kilometres distant - that by two o'clock in the afternoon was almost giving the fish away.

I decided in favour of fish soup as my first dish, my second would be fresh grilled scampi on a bed of paella rice with huge Spanish mussels. My third item would be hake, a local favourite and caught on a line with only the largest ones kept. The remaining two offerings would be a meat and fish paella, and finally a good sirloin steak for those who disliked fish. There would be no deep-frying as everything would be pan-fried, grilled or baked. Dessert would be a gateau Basque made by my aunt and traditional cheeses of the area. When it came to wines I had much to choose from as some of the Yacht Club members owned wineries in Bordeaux. My cognac came from one of the finest houses, Martell, as M. Martel himself, the current owner and descendant of that very old family, was also a member of the club. I also chose some local Basque wines as they were both cheap and of excellent quality. They turned out to be very popular with my thirsty customers. Starters would be tapas or picadillos served at the bar or table. Once open, we added many assorted pâtés made in the winter, including local salamis, ham (prosciutto style) and salads of all kinds depending on what was available.

To help with the marketing of our new business, I asked key people to pass on a good word for us if they liked what we were serving. Through a neighbourhood connection I found an excellent cuisiniere from a small city called Canal, which is south of Valencia in Spain. Whatever the reason, we got busy pretty fast, and our bar with its large assortment of American cocktails was a huge success. Our bar prices were similar to any high-end bar, but our drink sizes were larger. The drinks were what kept us in business but we never had a complaint about the cost - despite the substantial mark-up typical of bars and restaurants. On the other hand, our food prices were extremely reasonable and the serving sizes generous. Ironically though, it was only the cost of the menu items that people occasionally objected to.

In the main though, everyone seemed happy to spend the evening with us as the atmosphere was very convivial. We served the food family-style with serving dishes in the middle of the table. The customers each had three plates set in front of them so everyone could sample each dish without having everything mixed up on one plate. We took away the plates as they were used leaving the ones underneath for the next course. There was one area of difficulty and that was with the kitchen, which was too small. Further, my cook and her husband were unable to work quickly and efficiently, so the food often took a long time to come. However it was excellent when it finally got there. Luckily most of our customers were on holiday and in no rush. And of course the French love to sit and chat endlessly over their meals. Unfortunately they would insist on bringing their dogs and we would look on in dismay as the pampered dogs sitting in the women's laps would be given the plates to lick off. But that was a relatively small annoyance when you consider that no one abused alcohol or was ever rude. We had a good balance of more affluent patrons, the yacht club members, along with happy locals and tourists. The ambience was very vibrant and conducive to good humour.

This was all despite our punishing work schedule which included no such thing as a day off. We employed four people, not including my wife and myself. In addition to the kitchen staff we had hired two people for the dining room. They were very good, giving friendly service and smiling often. Despite there being six of us, we all had plenty to do – unless the weather was bad. There was only one narrow road to the restaurant and when there was a wind, gigantic waves would wash over it, making it impassable.

So to get supplies, each morning I would go to the market myself, as the road to the old fort was a very narrow single lane which no one would attempt with a truck. I knew my suppliers very well and never argued with prices so my shopping was generally a pleasant experience. From the outset I had told them that I wouldn't argue with their prices as long as they continued to give me their best quality. After all they had to make a decent living too. Trusting them in this way worked out very well. It was only very rarely that someone would try to take advantage of me and I would see this very quickly. If a talk or two didn't correct the behaviour, I would stop dealing with that particular individual. This daily trip was mostly very pleasurable as over time I had formed strong relationships with these merchants. I still observe these principles today and it continues to be highly unusual for someone to take advantage of my trust.

And not only were the days and evenings filled with work to be done, most often I would also be tending bar until the early hours of the morning. Usually my wife and the other staff would go home earlier and I would be working alone. Very late on one such evening I was chatting with a couple of late guests when three rough-looking characters came in. Something didn't feel right and alarm bells were going off in my head. My last two guests sensed it too and decided to go. By now the three toughs were sitting at the end of the bar so trying to act as normally as possible I went over and asked what I could do for them. They were being very noisy and using foul language but I engaged them in conversation hiding my alarm. One of them asked if it was true that I was a Canadian. I replied that I hadn't been there long enough for that. I told them that I was a local and pointed out the lights of my home town across the bay. They looked at each other in surprise. One of them reminded me of an old school friend and he seemed to recognize me as well. Then he asked me, "Say, are you Dufau from Les Cours Superieurs?" Now I knew it was Jeannot, one of the notorious students I had spent almost a year with during my sleepy period in school, when I was twelve. The name of the class was typical of the

French sense of humour since the course was the very opposite of "superior". I quickly got them drinks and we laughed and laughed sharing stories of our memories and transgression during those distant days. Of course I kept refilling their glasses on the house, and as the night wore on, or actually the morning by this time, they admitted that they had come with the intention of smashing up my bar. I never asked why, but I was grateful that they had changed their minds. I invited them to bring their wives or girlfriends for a meal and Jeannot did take up my invitation, but I never saw the other two again.

I didn't tell Judith about that night as she was already having second thoughts about the bar and restaurant business. It had all been too much too fast and that fact coupled with the lack of rest and private time together made for a rather toxic situation. My problems became worse yet when at the peak of the summer season my husband and wife cooking team threatened to quit if I didn't double their wages. I had hired them mostly for the wife who was a great cook, but the husband was a total flop. I only paid him the same as his wife as a salve to his male pride. I asked them for a day to talk it over with my wife. The blackmail was a serious problem for us. They were well paid with bonuses depending on the number of patrons served. They were also fed and lodged. And let's face it, while the restaurant was bringing people in, it was only making a small profit, certainly not enough to justify a large wage increase. And on top of all that, the French social welfare laws of the time added another eighty percent to the amount paid out in salary. Even today, North American worker benefit costs are far lower. So we decided to let them go and I would take over the kitchen myself, while my wife took care of the bar. She was a great hostess and even though she originally spoke only English, her French was getting better by the day.

Our situation was further improved when I hired an older woman to help me in the kitchen. She had been suggested to me by my mother, and between us we were able to work miracles in that small space. With these positive changes, the mood changed in the restaurant. We never wasted time complaining, focusing instead on doing the best we could to prepare good food for the now very large number of people who came regularly. Admittedly we had little time for fine tuning, but we always gave good value both in terms of preparation and ingredients. The latter were always the freshest and best quality that I could get. Some members noticed the difference in atmosphere right away and began to ask me to prepare different dishes for them when things were slower at lunch or dinner. By that time we were into September and the pace was slower,

so it wasn't difficult to try some new things. This was my first opportunity to start creating my own recipes. There were two key elements
present in that situation, ones that continue to inspire me today: a particularly fine food supply and diners who are prepared to give me a free
hand.

As time went on I realized more and more how restaurant life is
about much more than food. Yes there must be magic in the meals but
personal relationships are at least as important. When people sit down
to dine together, at the very least they will share the pleasures of the
palate, but they may also find that they have more in common than they
think. Even if they begin as strangers, they will almost always discover
common ground somewhere. They may even derive enjoyment from
each other's company. In some ways coming together over a meal is
similar to being at a concert; everyone joins together in an experience
that has the power to create a sense of oneness. The things that divide
are put aside for a time and an atmosphere is created that is conducive
to acceptance, tolerance - even peace. Although I was very young, I too
enjoyed this human aspect of the work. I discovered that at its best, service, in small ways or large, constituted a pursuit of happiness – for both
server and served. Over the years as I have observed differences in
class, culture and politics disappearing in the good will created by a
wonderful dining experience, I have often wondered if a restaurant
might somehow serve as guide for the wider world - showing how to
transcend divisions and animosities. Traditional institutions, including
religions, have utterly failed to discover core values that might bring us
together, so why not start by sitting the warring parties down to a
superb meal together and see what happens?

I had plenty of time for such musings as the fall wore on. By mid-
September of that year (1965), we were experiencing some unusual
storms. The sea had become so rough that no one would dare the journey over that narrow road to the Yacht Club Basque. They ran the risk
of being swept into the ocean. To make matter even worse, the equinox
was approaching and that meant even higher tides and with them much
larger waves. So after a week of doing absolutely nothing we decided
to close down until the next season.

Around this time I was approached by a club member who loved
the youthful enthusiasm that we brought to our restaurant. He offered
us the opportunity of opening a restaurant in Pau, a mid-sized city but
the capital of the Pyrenees-Atlantic Department. Pau is not too far
from the famous Lourdes. We were grateful, but we declined his offer
as we wanted to stay on the coast and return to the club the next sum-

mer. We had a great apartment in Biarritz and I had been offered the chance to manage one of the bars at the local casino. It had not been doing well and I assumed that they thought my knowledge of American cocktails would be good for business. I accepted the offer on the condition that we would take a ten-day break before starting work. Since opening our place in Socoa in June, we had not had a single day off. We went to Spain where we travelled all the way down to Seville, stopping wherever our fancy took us. On the way back north we visited the Alhambra. Wherever we went we treated ourselves well, staying only in good hotels. I felt wonderful at this stage of my life. Both Judith and I felt that the fates were shining on us.

After this all-too-brief vacation, I took on my new challenge. Luckily I was able to make the necessary changes without breaking the bank. The Biarritz Casino had just introduced the first American-style bowling in France and our bar opened on one side to the flashy new sixteen-lane alley and on the other to the gaming rooms. The clientele seemed to be a mixture of the young and not-so-young. In addition to drinks I added a small menu - all that was possible as there was no kitchen. I introduced club sandwiches, fancy hot dogs and American-style ice cream. I could offer the last because an American friend of ours had married the daughter of the owners of Glaces Gervais. They were happy to prepare ice cream in the American manner for us - something that nobody else was doing yet. And when we introduced sundaes, unheard of at this time in France, there was practically a stampede.

The other two items required some special ordering as well. For the hot dogs I found a butcher who would make me wiener-style sausages using high quality pork and veal with a light texture to allow for easy steaming. When it came to the hot-dog "bun" I had to deal with equipment that was totally different from the North American type, so some ingenuity was required to make it interesting and good. I needed a baker who would make a longer-than-usual baguette with milk added to the dough. The extra length allowed me to cut each baguette into three pieces. Then to prepare each hot dog I would toast the piece of baguette using a small round heating element that I inserted about a third of the way inside and left it there until the bread was crunchy in the middle. To finish it off I would add butter and mustard and insert the wiener, which was steamed separately, into the "bun". The whole concoction was served rolled up in a fancy napkin. The club sandwiches were also something of a challenge. I had the same butcher who made my hot dogs cook chicken breasts for me as well. But I also needed a square loaf of bread that could be cut into uniform slices. And even though such a thing was unheard of in France, my baker was again up to the demands of my innovations. I served the sandwiches with potato chips that were made freshly to order for us.

The effect of all these changes was a big increase in the bar's popularity, as our younger clientele gave us a lot of free advertising through word of mouth. The ambience was lively and fun, and pretty much free of rudeness and other bad behaviour. To deal with the increased demand I hired some young people to cope with the easy part of the preparation while I managed the rest. As they became more experienced, they were able to learn the more elaborate aspects. Of course many hours were involved. Starting around four in the afternoon I finished up about two in the morning, or sometimes even later. But at least this time I had a day off each week - a welcome change from the club.

Another thing that worked to our advantage was the long wait for bowling. People would pass the time at the bar enjoying our food and drinks so much that they almost forgot why they were there. My boss was very happy with me, not only paying me very well, but sharing a percentage of the profits as well. My income was further augmented by generous tips and my only expense was personal income tax.

However, after a few months I was faced with the choice of remaining where I was or returning to my old job. The premises at the club were leased to me personally so I couldn't just walk away. I decided to carry on at the casino and as luck would have it I was able to find a nice person to take over in Socoa. The board took a bit of convincing but eventually agreed to the change. My original plan in accepting the new job was to recoup the money I had spent renovating the club restaurant, but the casino income was not only vastly superior, it was also year-round. Another plus was the free mornings. The late start of the work day allowed me to spend time with English friends we had made in Biarritz and it also gave me the opportunity to learn how to surf the beautiful beach in front of the casino. In short, it made all the sense in the world to put an end to my first try at being in business for myself.

In those days gambling was a more civilized affair. There was a dress code and the doorman could refuse entrance without explanation if he sensed trouble. This atmosphere appealed not only to the locals but to wealthy Spaniards as well. (Across the border casinos were forbidden and bowling didn't exist). Further, the police were just across the road if they were needed. The games on offer included roulette, baccarat and poker, all ones that involve at least some element of strategy. Slot machines, and the numb stupor that they induce, had mercifully not yet been invented. That said, then as now some were slaves to gambling, but most simply enjoyed it as entertainment. But at least the casinos at that time were all owned by cities and made a useful contribution to civic revenues.

The wedding of my brother Michel and Bernadette.
Pictured left to right: Judith, me, my mother, Michel, Bernadette,
my father and my sister, Valerie. (1966)

But while everything was going well on the work front, I was experiencing stress in my marriage. My wife Judith had a university degree in nursing from Canada and it was a source of frustration to her that her highly specialized training was not recognized in France. Even though her French was good, no one would give her work in her profession, not even in a position with very basic responsibilities. She was experiencing, in reverse, what Jean and I had been subjected to in Canada when we tried to get work in the aircraft industry. These experiences seem emblematic of countries' failure to trust each other.

As a result of this discrimination Judith was pretty much on permanent vacation and after a while she became extremely bored and frustrated - she wasn't the sort of woman to stay at home and live only for her social life. So we decided to return to Canada. My boss at the casino had a hard time accepting our decision but ultimately came to respect it. Another page of my life was in the making.

I had no fear of the unknown as it was all useful experience and I didn't expect my life to stand still. I believed and still believe in adapting to new circumstances and doing my best to make things work. With the experience of many years living this way I think that it's a healthy way to see things, but at that time I was missing a key bit of understanding - namely how to sustain long-term happiness in the face of constant change. I found some of that understanding in the *Conversations with God* books mentioned earlier. Walsch outlines the three principles involved in making life work – whatever form it may take. The first is that life is *functional*, meaning that it works or functions. The second is that life is *adaptable*: in other words it is able to choose the most appropriate and intelligent way to adapt. And finally, life *sustains itself* or finds ways to reproduce itself and evolve in the process. As I gained more life experience I learned the enduring truth of these principles and when something in my life wasn't working, I was able to apply them to see what I was missing. The process helped me to make decisions in the present and allowed me to better foresee what the result of those decisions was likely to be. At the root of the principles is the idea of what Walsch calls the *ME NOW*, a core identity that passes through what we experience as "time". I will further examine our idea of who we are and our common idea of "time" in a later chapter.

CHAPTER 5

Discovering Toronto

In October of 1966, Judith and I arrived in Toronto, our city of choice, but our experience of time did not, unfortunately, include our relationship. It was simply the case that we had each moved on, and we divorced without rancour. We stayed friends, and even today we remain on excellent terms. I found work the second day after we arrived at a fancy restaurant called L'Aiglon. It was situated on Yorkville Avenue, just north of Bloor Street. (At this time the area was well-known as a cultural hub and there was a very active jazz and folk scene. The River Boat, just down the street from L'Aiglon, was a popular venue for a long list of famous performers. The area has since become better known for its luxury stores and condominiums than music.) My interview had been at eleven a.m. and I was to start work later the same day. Before then I had to buy a tuxedo and all the necessary accessories. But a bit of rushing around aside, it was great to reconnect with old-style French service. My colleagues were very helpful and the affluent clientele were pleasant to deal with. My English was a bit rusty but I managed to improve fast enough to keep my position.

In those days life in Toronto was very fragmented: you were defined by your ethnicity, neighbourhood, and of course the status and connections offered by your work and income. But the restaurant industry brings people of varied backgrounds together, sometimes with surprising results. I made a few friends quickly, some from the restaurant scene - but not all. One of our regular customers liked what she called my "continental look" and insisted that I have some photographs done so that I would be available for modelling jobs. I thought the idea was crazy and argued with her, but eventually I went along to please her, certain that she would see the folly of it.

Quite the opposite happened as shortly afterwards I received a call asking me to start my first modelling job. Needless to say my complete lack of experience was a worry, but I decided not to panic and instead decided to do the best I could. After all I still had my restaurant work and if I wasn't suited to modelling it wouldn't be a problem. When it came time for the photo session I surprised myself by feeling free of inhibitions or any nervousness. The shoot went on for a whole day as we had to model a variety of outfits in front of several different backdrops. The models consisted of two beautiful women, a well-known male model and me, the new kid on the block. My sponsor loved the resulting pictures as did the photographer, and I immediately began to receive more and more modelling offers. Despite my unexpected success in my new field I was determined to keep my restaurant work as a backup, but I needed to find a more flexible job to accommodate the increased demands on my time.

Luckily I was able to find such a job at Gaston's in the Markham Street Village, another lively Toronto pocket. Here the atmosphere was much less formal. I dropped my tuxedo for an apron and I could sing or whistle at work as well as being encouraged to talk to and joke with customers with a reasonable degree of freedom. The ambience was one of fun and enjoyment to go with the excellent food. Gaston was more a friend than a boss and we often shared great food, lively conversation and good bottles of wine after the service. I remember this period of my life as light and devoid of any concerns whatsoever. I would get up in the morning almost laughing in advance at the day ahead. I had every reason to stay and enjoy my life as it was, but once again I started to feel that it was time to try something different.

So in 1969 I began to feel attracted to life in California, feeling that this part of the world offered the energy of adventure, even something mystical. I started the process of obtaining a visa at the U.S. consulate, telling only one close friend at first. There was nothing to tie me down as I had no particular girlfriend and my commitment to my work wasn't great – I knew that I could be replaced quickly and easily. But almost a year went by before I was called to the consulate for a final interview. And this time no one was interfering with my application as had been the case with the Canadian embassy a few years before. Instead I had a meeting with a kind and dynamic-looking U.S. immigration officer. He engaged me in conversation, asking me some questions about my reasons for wanting to emigrate. All seemed to be going well until he dropped a bombshell! He asked that if I realized that as a U.S. resident I would be subject to the draft for another three years –

until I turned twenty-eight. He added that I might well be sent to fight in the Vietnam war. I was speechless for a moment. He saw my concern and said that my odds on being called up were about one in fifteen.

That wasn't a chance I was willing to take so I told him something of my history. I explained that I had originally come to Canada because I refused to serve in Algeria. I told him that as much as I loved his country I couldn't possibly serve in yet another unjust war. I talked about the history of Vietnam in the fifties and the fact that decisions made then had led to the present American involvement in Southeast Asia. Back then the Americans refused to help the French with anything more than equipment. That decision, motivated by American dislike of colonialism, led to the French defeat at Dien Bien Phu. The French withdrew to the South of Vietnam effectively dividing the country in two. The communist Viet Minh suspended their attacks on the French because of a promise in the Geneva Accords, the treaty that ended the war, to hold free elections about the future of the country, to be held in 1956. I pointed out to the now-shocked official that his country's fear of a communist electoral victory had caused it to prevent the elections from being held - hence the American involvement in a brutal war against the very soldiers who had defeated the French Foreign Legion.

In the end, the American official turned out to be a very decent man. He said that he respected my views and gave me a tourist visa that would automatically be renewed when it expired in six months. I apologized for all the work that I had caused the consulate and further for not being aware of the draft regulations. We parted on good terms. After all it was not his fault that we live in a spiritually sick world where power is constantly abused. It is my hope that the gradual change in global consciousness beginning to take place will one day lead us all to realize that we are not separate, but one.

My life didn't change much after the California debacle but I did suffer a setback in my restaurant career. I was still working at Gaston's when on a very slow, stormy winter night one of our best customers and his girlfriend braved the dangerous roads to have dinner with us. Unfortunately they arrived at 11:00 pm, just as we were preparing to close. (The only other diners were Gaston, his wife, and Jean Michel another waiter.) Even so, we didn't say a word and made our guests welcome as usual. I had seated them and brought the drinks they had ordered when I realized that they had already had a few. And to make matters worse, there was great deal of tension between them, a tension that made them rather hostile to me as well. Still, I made an effort not to be poisoned by their mood and treated them with my usual kindness and courtesy.

When they finally finished their meal I was greatly relieved as it was now past one in the morning. But my relief was short-lived. They wanted coffee, but kept finding reasons to complain and left their many cups untouched on the table. They insisted that every single cup was either cold or simply not to their liking. I brought a fresh thermos of coffee, clean cups and more cream to their table and asked their permission to leave as I had been working since eleven in the morning. I said that I would prepare the bill and he could sign for the meal whenever he wished. (Gaston allowed only a very few customers to sign for their bills.) I asked Gaston if I could go home and he said it was fine as he would be there for a while longer. I got my coat and was preparing to leave when I noticed that my rude customer had already signed the bill. Jean Michel showed it to me. On it was written, "Fuck tipping." Further, the customer stopped to speak to Gaston privately on his way out. When he had left I spoke to Gaston myself. I told him that it was the guest's right not to tip, but I was not happy at being insulted. I thought about the evening all the way home and decided that if such a thing were to happen again, I would not do anything differently. I went to bed with an untroubled mind and slept soundly.

The next day on my way to work I found myself feeling apprehensive and when I arrived there the atmosphere did indeed seem ominous. Everyone was avoiding me and the usual greetings sounded false. I took Jean Michel aside and asked him what was going on. He didn't want to say much other than to point out the conversation that my insulting customer had had with Gaston. So I went to Gaston and found him far from his usual self. I asked him if he wanted to know what had really happened, but he cut me off, saying that he couldn't accept having any of his waiters insulting customers and that he had made the difficult decision to fire me. I was strangely cool about it, telling him that although I was the one who had been insulted, it was his restaurant and he had the right to fire me if he wished. And with that I said goodbye to him and my colleagues and left

I have often thought about what happened next. Shortly after I left Gaston's I received a long letter from the customer who had gotten me fired asking me to forgive him for his bad behaviour. I called and told him that I was grateful for the apology and admiring of his courage in writing the letter. I also pointed out that I felt no bitterness over the incident and suggested that he too let it go. As it happened there was another connection between us as he was an excellent photographer

The Three Amigos: Me, Mariano, and Jean Michel when we were working at Gaston's restaurant in Toronto. (1967)

and I had modelled for him a few times. I worked for him on a few more occasions afterwards, and each time we met for a shoot we would exchange conspiratorial smiles. Nor was my work confined to modelling; my old boss at L'Aiglon had heard about my dismissal and hired me back to work there on weekends.

One surprising effect of the firing was my decision, after some reflection, to remain in Canada and in Toronto specifically. I also decided to work for myself again. Unfortunately my first crack at the Toronto food scene was a near-disaster, even though I received some unexpected extra help. Around this time my mother and father had separated in France and my mother decided to come and work with me as a partner. Together we opened a place that we named "Le Petit Gourmet". It was located at 858 Millwood Road in the Leaside district of Toronto. There were many apartment buildings in the area, and the Chinese restaurant on one side of us and the Kentucky Fried Chicken (as it was then known) outlet on the other were both doing tremendous business. So we were pretty optimistic at the outset. I personally delivered tens of thousands of menus in the surrounding area and made sure that our prices were as cheap if not cheaper than those of our competition. We also offered free delivery. What we hadn't counted on however was the fact that the word "French" seemed to be extremely unpopular in the area. The locals at best ignored and at worst maybe even actively boycotted us. We quickly realized that we had a disaster in the making. My mother especially, even though she had no awareness of the city, knew right away that we were in serious trouble. I felt badly about having put her in this position but she wasn't at all bothered by my choice of location. That said, we clearly needed another strategy. And fast.

With my mother's support I decided to draw on my modelling and television commercial experience. Whenever I did a shoot there was always food available through specialized catering services. I knew a number of people in the industry and after some adjustments to our menu I went and talked to the people in charge of the various production houses. I was frank about the difficulties we were facing in our business but I offered to compete with the prices offered by their current suppliers. And I even promised that everything would be free if they were ever unsatisfied with our food. The orders took a while to build and that suited us fine. The gradual increase in demand gave us time to get properly organized and learn the ropes of the catering business. And as things turned out no one ever asked not to pay. There was also an amazing and unexpected bonus when most of the production houses chose us to do the Christmas functions and special orders for their film crews.

So again I was faced with the need to change my perspective and adjust to new demands. In addition to the challenges I have described, I also had to learn everything about the rentals necessary to organize and arrange seating for large groups. As luck would have it I called a place named "Gervais". I was completely transparent about my lack of knowledge but the girl on the phone put my fears to rest with her kind and helpful manner. I joked about my situation and said that I wished that I had an angel like her to work with me. To my surprise she offered to come and help me, and in answer to my concerns she assured me that there would be no conflict with her work place. To top it all off, she even promised to find me any extra staff I might need. We had a great working relationship for over a year until she unfortunately (for me) decided to follow her English lover to Britain. By this time my mother and I had not only learned how to make a modest profit, but also, more importantly, we had discovered the neighbourhood where most of our customers came from. And for that reason, in 1971 we moved our business to a location near the Rosedale subway station.

Also around this time a friend introduced me to a beautiful German girl named Katrina and we hit it off right away. We were both unattached and close in age, so before long we were in a relationship. Both of us understood that this would not be a lasting love affair as she was about to return to university in Germany. Nonetheless we had a wonderful time together and my mother seeing me so happy was quick to accept my suggestion that we invite my new girlfriend for dinner. Katrina was very attentive to her and moreover, she spoke perfect French, so one dinner turned into several pleasant occasions.

Now all this time, because of Katrina's fluency it had never occurred to my mother that she was not from France. So when she finally asked her where she was from and Katrina answered that she was from Germany, my mother retreated into a cold silence for the rest of the evening. I was utterly embarrassed even though I knew her reasons all too well. As I have already mentioned, my mother had been in the French resistance and suffered the loss of many who were dear to her - including her favourite brother. All of them dead at German hands. But even though I knew all these things I felt that my mother's were the struggles of another time and a very different generation. I believed that life was renewing itself and that neither Katrina nor I had anything to be ashamed of. But clearly the scars of the war were still fresh and she was unable to accept this beautiful young girl for herself.

When I drove Katrina home that night I asked her to forgive my mother's attitude but she understood completely. She told me that her own father and mother would throw her out of their house if she dared to bring home a Frenchman. Feeling compassion for our parents' pain and expressing the hope that their bitterness would fade with time, we agreed to let go of the incident.

But to my surprise, things turned around very quickly. I had a couple of gentle talks with my mother, not really expecting any change, but only a few days later, she asked me to bring my girlfriend for dinner again. When Katrina entered the house my mother apologized to her and pretty much reduced her to tears. Katrina hugged her and said that she wished her own parents could be more like her and find a way to forgive. I had seldom been more proud of my mother than I was in that moment. Her love had saved the day.

So all in all, apart from a chronic sore throat, my life at the time was a very good one. Unfortunately the cause of sore throat was tonsillitis - three different doctors had had told me that I needed a tonsillectomy – but I had some serious misgivings about the operation that I couldn't quite place. But I knew my family doctor well and after I had seen the surgeon he sent me to I had total confidence in the decision to operate. After this little bump in the road I would begin work on the renovations for our new restaurant. The procedure was to take place at the Doctors' Hospital in Toronto, and when the day came I was completely at ease. The surgeon and I even exchanged a few jokes before I passed out from the anaesthesia. Nothing could have prepared me for what happened next.

Even though I was fully "under" and feeling no pain, I was completely aware of everything that was going on. My vantage point seemed to be from above my body. I was simply observing the operation without any sense of panic - or even particular concern. It was very similar to a dream. It was then that I noticed a lot of commotion going on around my body. I couldn't tell what was wrong, but the next thing I saw was my body in what was clearly an intensive care unit with a male nurse sitting next to it. Mine was the bed closest to the nursing station and I could see my mother and girl friend Muriel sitting close by - both of them looking pretty grim. I found myself wondering whether or not I should go back into my body when I had a very strong feeling that I still had plenty of experiences to enjoy. Within a fraction of a second I had returned to my body, now feeling tremendous fear. I woke up extremely agitated and almost jumped out of bed. The poor guy assigned to me yelled for help. My mother rushed over immediately, Muriel right behind her. I tried to say something to them and panicked when I wasn't able to form intelligible words. My mind seemed to be in shock. It turned out that the surgeon had had to perform a tracheotomy to save my life, and as soon as the nurse plugged the hole in my throat I was able to speak again.

In answer to my mother's question about how I was feeling, I replied, "Lousy." Then as if to prove my point I vomited blood all over the bed. Apparently I had swallowed a lot of it during the surgery. My mother and Muriel were sent away while everything was cleaned up. Then I was plugged into a drip that almost completely immobilized my body but seemed to have the opposite effect on my mind - which seemed to be firing in all directions. I didn't sleep at all that night and I had lots of time to try and explain in logical terms what had happened. How could I possibly know that I had been dead three times with no heart beat for long periods, and still come back to life? It was later explained to me that a simple half-hour surgery had taken six hours. My first tonsil was removed easily, but the second turned out to have a large blood vessel running through it which led to the blood vessel being cut along with the tonsil. The result was a sudden fountain of blood. Initially the surgeons couldn't reach the rupture from inside the neck, so they had to remove two little neck muscles in the left side to get at the site. That of course took time and I lost a lot of blood in the process. I was saved by transfusions and I owe my life to the blood donors.

I still have the scars on my neck and every so often some brave soul would ask me what happened. I was always happy to explain the physical facts, but my experience of watching the surgery from outside of my body I kept to myself. I didn't want to find myself being admitted to a psychiatric ward somewhere. What puzzled me at first was how, if the body was dead, even if only temporarily, could I still be conscious? And how on earth was I able to witness events from *outside* my body? These were hard facts to swallow for the committed atheist that I was at the time. The events sent me on a search for answers to these troubling questions.

So for the next few months I did a lot of soul searching (even without really knowing the meaning of the term). And then one day in the Yorkville area of Toronto I passed a book store called the Omega Book Store and my curiosity drew me inside. The store offered a wide variety of books on spiritual and occult subjects. Most of the items held little appeal for me, but I somehow screwed up the courage to ask one of the staff if he would be willing hear about my recent experience and perhaps recommend a book that might help me to understand it. He was kind enough to agree and when he had heard me out he immediately told me that I had had an "out of body" experience. He went on to say that such experiences were quite common and that some people deliberately sought them out while others, like me, had them more or less accidentally. He suggested a book about the famous American psychic Edgar Cayce. Perhaps something in it might resonate with me. The book was called The Sleeping Prophet and the author wasn't Casey himself, but Jess Stern. Most of it left me puzzled but I was fascinated and the ideas seemed truthful to me in some way. Still, my old beliefs remained more or less intact, at least for the time being. Yet over the coming years an enormous transformation took place at the subconscious level.

CHAPTER 6

Making a Small Print on the Toronto Scene

B ut as interesting as these new ideas were they weren't going to help me set up my new business and that had to be my main concern at the time. We had leased the place in Rosedale for a song – one hundred and eighty dollars a month for ten years. We would even get an automatic renewal at the end of the lease at a rate to be negotiated at the time. So when all was said and done we had been able to set up our new enterprise with very little expense. We decided to have a big opening party to celebrate. The food preparations were done in our existing Millwood location and once we had organized a display of the products (all made by my mother and myself) we opened our door for the first time. It was the spring of 1971. And unlike the Millwood fiasco, the place filled up with customers in what seemed like no time at all. What a beautiful feeling!

Unfortunately I had forgotten one very important thing – money. I had forgotten to go to the bank so when people asked to pay for their purchases I couldn't make change. Still, openings are always prone to mistakes, so I decided to give them the items for free. I made a joke of it, suggesting that they could decide whether or not to pay if they came again. Some smiled, but a few also looked at me with suspicion, not knowing what to make of it all. This went on for an hour until there had been enough customers with exact change to keep us going for a while and I was able to send my helper to the bank for change. When I finally had a few minutes without customers I called my mother to tell her all the wonderful news. She didn't care if the people ever came back to pay or not, the fact that that food was going so fast was a great relief. We had definitely found the right location. And in fact everyone came back to pay, most of them the same day. We made friends with so many beautiful and faithful people. Later some of them confessed that they had doubted that someone so careless about money would be a success, but they allowed as I clearly knew what I was doing after all. It seemed that my desperate decision to make payment optional on that first day had actually won me many customers. It made people trust us and feel happy and confident about us.

And we did our best to deserve that trust. Our prices were always fair and if we had food left over from the previous day it was always sold at half price. We also took great care with the staff that we hired. Of course they needed to be efficient, but we also hired people who were congenial and shared our beliefs about providing superior service. If they had been unhappy in their work it would have affected the ambience, a key element. Obviously the food must be good or even at times excellent, but it is at least equally important that there be a feeling of harmony and good will. The buying experience that we offered our customers was an essential element in our continued success.

I haven't mentioned location as a prime condition for success as it is not a straightforward matter. It's important to be close to an important centre but not necessarily at a prime spot with the highest rent. If your product is an excellent one, your customers will be willing to walk a bit farther or go around the corner to find you. In such a location the savings in rent can be passed on in the form of fairer prices. In the very best locations, such as the ones favoured by coffee outlets, the high rents demand a huge turnover. The result is usually poor wages paid to a staff largely made up of young part-time workers – not a formula for truly satisfied patrons.

Our location on Yonge St. at Rosedale quickly became more and more active as new operators with a flair for attracting the area's sophisticated residents began to set up new businesses. A store called the Pack Rat opened beside me. It offered a range of furniture and decorative items that had not been seen before. Shortly after that, two young and enthusiastic entrepreneurs came in with their girlfriends to ask us our opinions about the area and our clientele. I remember being very enthusiastic about their project. I told them about the fiasco of our first location and how great our present one had turned out to be. I told them that if their products were interesting it would be impossible not to succeed. They apparently agreed and set up the first Roots store on Yonge Street. The year was 1973. Many others followed. This was a time when large chains were short on creativity and smart individuals had a chance to secure a living with their talents. Today's offshore manufacturing and subsequent low prices have created a situation where the creative individual needs the backing of one of the large companies in order to succeed. Despite the overall situation it is still possible for someone with a truly superb idea to create a small niche market, but profitability is far more difficult to achieve than it once was. And that's assuming that some large corporation doesn't steal the idea before it is even realized – an all-too-frequent occurrence.

But the ethically-challenged corporate world is only part of a larger pattern, one where there seem to be very few absolutes, only competing systems of belief. And while that may be a dismaying thought to most of us, there is a sense in which moral relativity has always been a fact of life. Apart from actions which are covered by the criminal code I have come, with time, to believe that there is no such thing as right or wrong, only perceptions of them. To make this idea work in practice we need to be very observant, extremely tolerant, and completely aware of why and how what is right for you may be wrong for me. As Walsch notes in *Conversations with God*, "No one acts inappropriately given their model of the world." To grasp that concept means that we must make a serious effort to be objective about our *own* belief systems and desires – not just everyone else's. And in turn, all of the above is rooted in the ultimate polarities - love and fear.

I hope that you'll pardon the brief digression, but the above are only some of the ideas that came out of the search initiated by my "out of body" experience. In addition to new ideas about morality, my understanding of God and other core concepts changed as well. And my discoveries not only changed my views, but also the way that I lived my life. So even though I had to get on with making a living, my spiritual quest continued – and still does.

Le Petit Gourmet continued to thrive, but with that success came an unexpected side-effect: I discovered that I was allergic to flour and even with the help of a great baker named Noel who worked for us part-time, I couldn't avoid it completely. So I decided, with a French friend, Jacques, to open a restaurant in downtown Toronto. My mother agreed with my decision and was happy to keep the Rosedale location going on her own. She did very well and Le Petit Gourmet became a very popular place for the locals to gather and chat while enjoying my mother's wonderful food. In fact on one occasion, it became a kind of refuge for a very famous person.

One day in June of 1974 I was at Le Petit Gourmet visiting my mother when she pointed out a very handsome young man in the restaurant's garden. He had been there all day and the previous two days as well. Something clicked in my mind and I took a careful look at him. Could this possibly be the great Russian ballet star Mikhail

Baryshnikov? If so, he was the very one who had recently defected when he was performing with the Bolshoi Ballet at Toronto's O'Keefe Centre (now the Sony Centre). What made the idea even more credible was the fact that he was speaking Russian to his companion. I mentioned my suspicions to my mother, adding that if it were indeed Baryshnikov the KGB was undoubtedly looking for him. The whole idea had great appeal to the old resistance fighter in my mother. She was certain that she would recognize a KGB agent should one come to Le Petit Gourmet. The next day she spoke to the couple and learned that the young man was indeed Baryshnikov, so she arranged a signal to warn them should any suspicious-looking Russians appear. She gave them an escape route that involved them going out the back way and then hiding at her nearby house. Not only that, she also refused to charge them for their food and drink. A short time later, when the famous dancer was granted official refugee status she felt very honoured to have played even a small part in the drama. But of course international intrigue was not the norm in our hardworking lives.

By that time we had gotten rid of the Millwood site, so after managing to get an extended lease from our landlord (at twice the existing rent), we set up a kitchen in the garage of our Rosedale premises. We also convinced my brother to come and help our mother. Although he was a plumber by trade (and knew very little English) he hated his job and was happy to become part of our success. Surprisingly it all worked out well. He was able to retrain himself fairly fast and the extra help was a huge relief to my mother. In fact his wife Bernadette eventually joined the business as well. She began to work part-time once her two young daughters were in school. As for me, I was still looking for a place for my new downtown restaurant when I was approached by some customers and friends who were involved in real estate. They suggested that I buy a place on Temperance, a little street in the centre of the financial district.

The only problem with the suggested purchase was that I couldn't even afford the downtown rent let alone the cost of buying a building. So I decided on a middle course. Before signing the very expensive lease, I asked the owner to give me an option to buy at a pre-agreed price when the lease was up. I did this intuitively, but I secured the deal by promising to improve the building, something that would benefit us both. My own thinking was that if I was successful I would be able to reap rich rewards. The arrangement was agreed to and when prices skyrocketed in later years it worked out very well for me. But before I could realize my dream of catering for the business community there were still serious obstacles to overcome.

The first one turned out to be the street itself. I had assumed that getting permission to open a restaurant with a liquor licence would be a mere formality. I couldn't have been more wrong! When I submitted my application to City Hall, with accompanying plans, it was refused. Surprised and alarmed, I inquired as to the reason for the denial. The clerk asked me if I knew the meaning of the word "temperance". I answered that I thought it meant avoiding excess. While that may be true in general, where Temperance Street is concerned it turned out to mean that no alcohol whatsoever is allowed to be served on the street. When the street was deeded to the city by the Temperance Union over a century ago, it was with the stipulation that it remain "dry" in perpetuity. As a result, I was told, the Liquor Licence Board would be certain to deny me a licence. It seemed impossible to me that such a thing could happen in the downtown Toronto of 1972. I refused to accept that such an anachronism could exist in the modern world.

My friends were sympathetic but held out no hope that the gods of the LLBO could be persuaded to enter the twentieth century. That would probably have remained the situation had I not, by chance (or not), run into an old customer of mine. After some casual pleasantries I told him about my situation. He listened with interest and when I was finished, suggested that I see two young lawyers who were just setting up their practice. He revealed that one of them was closely connected to the family of the then current head of the LLBO. He cautioned me to behave as though I knew nothing of the relationship and not to mention his name. I did as he suggested and met with the young lawyers the next day. We had a very cordial talk and set up a very reasonable fee to do a title search. I also mentioned my intention to register my business as a limited company and apply for a liquor licence in the future.

Their work was fast and amazingly efficient. A day later they called to ask me to come to their offices. They had good news for me that they wished to explain in person. It turned out that my building once belonged to an old timer who had long ago refused to sell his portion of the street to the Temperance Union. By sheer luck I had found the only location on the street that wasn't dry. We had a good laugh about it and then began to discuss how to proceed. They went to work on my liquor licence and managed to secure one in four months, when the average waiting time was more like two or three years. They also arranged for a greatly reduced "voluntary" contribution to the party in power at Queen's Park – a quaint third world custom of the time. It was only years later that I realized that I had been their first client. Our association (one which continues today) expanded to include all of our family affairs and those of many friends as well.

I opened "Maison Basque' at fifteen Temperance Street on the twenty-seventh of March, 1973. To introduce ourselves and get the ball rolling we made sure that we had a proper opening, inviting not only our friends and the people who built the restaurant, but also the press and important personalities. To make sure that the evening went well, we provided lots of good food and drinks. Also, we added some glamour by inviting a few "beautiful people" - those who were congenial enough not to create dissension or mischief. All this activity, coupled with the renovation costs, added up to some pretty heavy outlays and we were running out of money. Nonetheless we were able to persuade our bank manager to give us a large enough line of credit to cover what we had already run up and to take into account the fact that we would be operating at a loss for a while.

Business was good early on - despite the fact that being on a side street we were not immediately visible. In fact, being a little out of the way worked to our advantage as we became a kind of secret hideaway that was worth the search. But location aside I stuck to my formula of excellent ingredients cooked well. My long-time suppliers from my previous businesses were keen to see us succeed as I continued to pay them on time and never argued about price as long as the quality was high. They all made sure to provide us with the freshest products they could. Some popular items were super fresh calves' liver and thick, lean veal chops long before they were generally available. I was also one of the few to serve free range chicken with its wonderful flavour. And when it came to seafood, being from a seaport and the son of a fisherman, I quickly established a rapport with the owners of the many Portuguese fish stores in Kensington Market. I was serving fresh grouper, monk fish, haddock and cod long before most establishments. Nothing had been previously frozen. I was also able to get fresh supplies of skate, tuna and snapper. And Maison Basque was one of the first restaurants to have fresh fish flown in. One supplier went so far as to get us out-of-season fresh, wild Atlantic salmon through contacts with a native fishery. (Their season started somewhat earlier than that of the large commercial outfits.)

Our coffee turned out to be another draw. At a time when drip was the norm in Canada we had an espresso machine as well as a press – but only for the staff. (All of us were either European or South American and we were passionate about our coffee.) These exotic appliances were a source of some curiosity to our customers – especially when they saw the steam created when we were making cappuccinos. Soon they began to ask for these strange coffees themselves. We of course obliged, but watered them down a bit - guessing that the full strength version would be a bit overwhelming. As a result of these innovations, in 1974 Toronto Calendar Magazine declared our coffee to be the best in downtown Toronto. Alas, wonderful coffee was not all that our diners wanted to drink with their meals and before Maison Basque became fully established its doors almost had to close.

We kept hearing the same comment from our customers: "We had a great time and your food was excellent. We'll come back when you have your liquor licence." And I always answered the same way: "Please keep coming so that we stay alive!" The methods of payment in those days were much slower than they are now. There was no Visa where you get your money as soon as you deposit the slips. The prestigious card of the day was American Express which charged us five per cent and took five or six weeks to pay. With our financial survival at stake that was a very long time. So even though we were doing reasonably well in the circumstances, it was the bank that was keeping us going. So you can imagine my alarm when I received a phone call from the "new" manager at our bank branch and so learned that our old friendly bank manager had been moved to another branch. I suspected that his replacement had been getting up to speed on the various accounts and was now calling the "delinquent" ones. It made me realize the risks that our old manager had been taking for us. The phone call from the current holder of the office was to set up a meeting as soon as possible. This meant trouble as I knew that I couldn't come up with enough money or even adequate security to satisfy his demands. And trouble there was. He told me that he was considering closing me up on the spot. But without even thinking, I found myself politely pointing out that having to write off as bad debt all the money I owed was not going to impress his superiors. Why couldn't he give me another month to come up with the money? He seemed shocked by my bluntness, but agreed to a two-week extension.

I was very relieved for the moment but there was no obvious source of new money that I could see. Both my parents were in tight financial situations so help from that direction was out. My staff and I had jobs for the time being but I had to ask them to give me a break and accept a pay cut with the understanding that I would compensate them with bonuses later on. Luckily, most of them agreed. My landlord was also very accommodating and let me delay paying rent for a couple of months. Now if only the liquor licence would come through we might find our way out of the woods. But a miracle was in the making from a very different direction. A dear friend came to eat with a young food critic from a major Toronto newspaper, the Toronto Star. Her name was Joanne Kates. A review appeared in the Saturday edition which described our little restaurant in extremely complimentary terms. Almost immediately we went from averaging about a dozen and a half customers a night to almost a hundred! It felt like a revolution and we were filled with joy, but now we had a new problem – how to cope with our new instant fame.

We had no way of telling if our good fortune would last, but we made the decision to continue stressing quality and service. And over time we were able to keep up our high standards in both areas. But this sudden change in our fortunes required a lot of time and attention, so much so that I nearly lost the restaurant again. I had forgotten about the new bank manager. On a Friday afternoon about two forty-five we had just finished serving lunch when the phone rang. The caller (from the bank as it turned out) asked to speak to me personally. I was told that as I had not made the agreed-upon deposits, my loan was being called in. The Sheriff would be notified shortly. And in those days, banks closed at three o'clock. I begged for ten minutes to get to there as I had quite a bit of money to deposit. Whether or not they believed me I don't know but they agreed to my request. I rushed to the basement office, opened the safe, and literally stuffed my week's receipts into a plastic bag. I made it to the bank three minutes before closing. There I asked to see the manager and apologized for my lack of priorities in failing to honour our terms of our agreement. He looked very doubtful. But by way of explanation I showed him the Star review and then poured an avalanche of cash and credit card receipts onto his desk. By now he had finished reading the article and a big smile appeared on his face. He called in two women to process the receipts and while they were doing so he took time to chat about the menu and his food preferences. Then he congratulated me. In less than an hour the threat of closure had disappeared and my heart rate finally began to return to normal. I invited him and his wife to come to the restaurant whenever they wished. It took him a while, but he came and was happy about his experience.

Another unexpected twist took place when my former bank manager came to the restaurant for lunch with some senior executives from the Bank of Nova Scotia. He first came into the kitchen to tell me about how hard they had been with him, refusing any breaks or concessions for many of his customers. But the joke turned out to be on senior management as none of my ex-manager's clients had defaulted on their loans, but a few high fliers, approved at the highest levels, were given loans purely on the basis of reputation. These guys ended up cheating the bank out of a fortune. As we finished our chat he suggested that I sit down with him and his bosses after lunch and let him tell them my story. After that I could answer their questions.

As they ate, they couldn't help but notice the presence of many famous people around them. That was because I charged more or less the same for lunch and dinner, reasoning that my expenses were the same for both meals. The indirect effect of that policy was to ensure a lot of lawyers, politicians, executives and similar types eating lunch at Maison Basque. So the bankers were not only impressed by the food but also by the blue ribbon lunchtime crowd. All the buzz gave my ex-manager lots of ammunition to settle scores with his superiors. He was happily using my success as a demonstration of how short-sighted they had been with their lack of trust. And of course we did our best to help him. I made sure that they had all that they needed and my dear friend and Maitre D' Hugo gave them impeccable service. At all of my restaurants we worked as a team with no one individual being responsible for a table. Everything was everyone's responsibility, so when I say that the service was impeccable I mean exactly that. So when I finally sat down with the bankers, I was feeling pretty confident, but it was clear that something was in the making, what, I didn't know. It turned out that they wanted me to go back to working with my old manager at another branch. They apologized for their previous mistakes and assured me that if I needed more money for expansion or some other purpose that it would definitely be approved. The timing worked out perfectly as the business upstairs was closing due to retirement and that space would shortly be available to us. We were having to turn people away due to our lack of tables so it made perfect sense to expand the premises. And with the money already promised, this time the rest was easy.

At that time, Toronto had the wind at its back. Quebec was bitterly divided and the demands on business by the provincial government under the Parti Quebecois were becoming increasingly onerous. Not the least of these was the law demanding that all business be conducted in French. Even more extreme measures were feared. As a result of this atmosphere there was a huge movement of corporations and people from Montreal to Toronto. Boring and conservative Toronto began to be transformed by this influx of newcomers as they set up many different and exciting businesses. It didn't take long for a snowball effect to develop, helping to transform the city into the vibrant multicultural centre that it is today.

We continued to do well and were often asked to expand. One of the ways we did this was to help my brother set up a downtown business called Café du Marche. Since he was a plumber by profession and not a chef, I showed him how to prepare a simple menu consisting of a variety of omelettes, quiches and roasted free-range chickens cooked in ways that were simple to do. There were also several different types of salads and - of course all the croissants and assorted pastries that he had learned to make while working with our mother at Le Petit Gourmet. It also occurred to us that it might be a good idea to expand this new enterprise into the St. Lawrence Market, the only true farmer's market in Toronto at the time. There was nothing available to lease so we approached our butcher, who had a large stand there, to see if we could buy some space from him. He agreed, and even though the market was open only on Saturday at the time, my brother sold more baked goods on that one day than he moved during the whole week at his regular location on Colborne Street.

So life was smiling on me in those days. And on top of being successful I was dating a wonderful girl named Judith who was manager of the famous Vidal Sassoon hair salon near Yorkville. We were both fairly busy and life was full of happy occasions with our circle of friends. Unfortunately at one point believing that I needed to be a good entrepreneur, I expanded our business into three new locations. The scale of the expansion necessitated taking in some partners, and I had to take on the role of overall manager of the establishments. I tried to simplify the food as much as possible to try and maintain our high standards. I also continued to deal with the same trusted suppliers who had been with me all along, so there were no problems in that area.

My fatal mistake was to involve some of my younger partners in day-to-day operations, naively believing that I would have their total cooperation. That trust turned out to be misplaced as a great deal was going on behind my back when I wasn't there. Two of the three locations were doing badly and the third one quite well. Coincidentally the third place didn't have any of my partners helping to run it. In general, my policy was to put my faith in my staff, pay them well and treat them with respect, a policy that had always worked extremely well for me in the past. At the two troubled businesses there were too many bosses and the staff was constantly changing. In addition, sales were not picking up and the ambience was uninviting. So to find out the reasons for the poor performance I took to "dropping in" at different times of the day. It didn't take long to pinpoint the roots of the problem in erratic service, sloppy work and an aloof attitude towards the customers. To make matters worse there seemed to be a pattern of closing early - more or less whenever the "bosses" felt like it. So I asked for a meeting of the partners and when it became clear that there was no agreement on either the nature of the problems or their possible solutions we parted amicably. This decision turned out to be the best possible one. I wasn't enjoying the position of cop/bookkeeper, constantly checking up on and directing people. And when the atmosphere is bad in a restaurant the effort involved in training staff is mostly wasted as they will move on at the first opportunity. The alternative is the fast food formula: hiring kids and preparing all the food in advance. That was not a solution that I would ever have contemplated. So with great relief I gave up on franchising forever.

Which brings me to what it *does* take to run an excellent restaurant. To serve authentic food from traditional sources you must have highly qualified chefs with well-trained assistants - all of them eager to perform to the best of their abilities. No carelessness can be permitted, nor are big egos welcome as they tend to boss others around, not lead by example. Such inflated egos believe that craziness is leadership, screaming at those working under them and calling them names. No one can learn under those circumstances and such authority abusers would do well to remember that they are only temporarily more knowledgeable than their employees. Such behaviour also leads to a divided workplace, everyone separated by false beliefs that give the more experienced chef the right to be above treating others with decency and respect.

The true teachers - and I have been blessed to work for some - somehow sense that all of us are divine and that no one should ever be bullied or mistreated. And as I became increasingly experienced in the restaurant business I realized more and more that creating a positive working environment was the key to having my leadership respected. In fact in such an atmosphere I was relieved of the need to feel that I had to be perfect all the time. Mistakes are much more likely to be treated as unimportant when there is a willingness to be honest and admit them. Such straightforwardness creates the opportunity to create even greater cohesion by asking for help with a problem. By establishing a workplace of that kind I was able to relax and do my work to the best of my ability. If something went wrong we would work together to fix it - and probably laugh about it afterwards. I always paid my staff well, and more often than not there were additional bonuses when sales or volume increased. At Maison Basque I had my servers work as a team and share their tips. I also included the kitchen staff in the arrangements: they received fifteen per cent of the week's total. Any waiter who objected to the scheme would quickly regret resigning, as my staff made a very good living and no one else ever quit.

I should make clear at this point that none of this harmony would have been possible without some very careful hiring in the first place. Before I even ask about a potential employee's skills (and restaurant workers are better educated than ever before), I want to be sure that the candidate has sound values. I make clear that I will demand total honesty, trustworthiness and transparency. If I sense any hesitation at all I don't even bother to ask about qualifications. I do recognize that not everyone is comfortable taking on that kind of commitment, and that's fine, but for the way that I run my businesses it's essential that I have complete faith in the individual. I make clear that nothing is ever locked up in my restaurant and to do my own job effectively I can't be constantly checking up on everyone. I explain that we will work as equals: eating the same food, even sharing a couple of glasses of wine after work. And if anyone wants to take something home, I will only very rarely deny the request if it is a reasonable one. This model of employee relations has worked very well for me over the years. The number of negative experiences has been so small as to be barely worth mentioning. And the roots of this philosophy lie in the huge gift given to me by my Basque grandmother. I felt so empowered by her absolute trust in me that I vowed that I would pass her example on to others. In doing so, I have consistently gained the respect and trust of my staff - who typically stay with me for years. They, in turn, pass this wisdom on to others, certainly in their professional lives, and possibly in their personal ones as well.

In contrast, most of today's food establishments operate on the basis of constant surveillance. It is assumed that no one can be trusted to be a responsible human being, so all must be forced to comply with endless rules and regulations. Every item must be accounted for and if there are drinks after work the employees must pay for them – at a discount perhaps, but pay they must. Managers of such workplaces become glorified policemen and accountants rather than true leaders. Nor do such places reward employees for obeying all these strictures; they are hired and fired - not according to economics - but at the whim of the latest business model. The fiercely competitive, modern business environment allows little room for spiritual values, but it is still possible to treat employees with fairness and respect, keeping as many employed as possible - and not only succeed, but flourish.

And the businesses that were run by my mother, my brother and I were indeed flourishing. The next logical step, for some, would have been to undertake a massive expansion and perhaps to become rich in the process, but that was not the way that the three of us saw things. We decided that we were all making a very comfortable living, and that that was enough. We couldn't have cared less about the standard American and Canadian business view that an organization had to expand or have the competition gobble it up. Instead we focused on the things that we did well. It was decided that my brother would concentrate on making the various kinds of dough for all of us. This decision was prompted by the fact that outsiders were keen to learn how we made things. A few unscrupulous people came to work for us only long enough to discover our "secrets" and then quit. So we developed a policy of paying people well and training them properly but with the condition that our family recipes were not to be shared. Anything else they were welcome to. But that was many years ago and we have long since given all of our secrets away.

With matters thus settled, I would have been happy to focus exclusively on my own enterprise, but there was still a remaining business left over from the partnership agreement to be attended to. Luckily my staff at Maison Basque was excellent and quite capable of running the place without me. Their abilities left me feeling secure about the place so I was able to focus on rescuing the new business, also called Le Petit Gourmet like my mother's place. Situated at Yonge and Eglinton it had not been doing at all well. As a family we had agreed that I would be totally in charge of running the place with my mother keeping a half share and my brother opting out completely. The goal was to get the restaurant in good enough shape to sell it, thus freeing me to concentrate on Maison Basque. When we eventually found buyers, part of the arrangement would be to train them in running things before they took over.

The rescue operation got off to rather bad start – with a huge disagreement with our accountants. They tried to persuade us to make the operation "more profitable". (This confrontation was occasioned when our ex-partners decided that our way of doing things wouldn't produce high enough returns.) Our highest priority was pleasing people and making sure that they liked the whole concept from the minute they passed through the front door up to and including the meal that they ate there or took out. The accountants wanted us to meet very specific targets on food and labour, and all other costs. The minimum profit was to be between fifteen and twenty per cent. Now while the guidelines were meant to be helpful, they were impractical for us and we pretty much ignored them all. That said, the profits exceeded all expectations every day of every week that we were open, the reason being that our focus on pleasing the customers produced such a huge volume that the other things really didn't matter much. With our success the accountants never again tried to tell us how to do things.

The core of this operation was a fast turnover of food at very reasonable prices, including a variety of fresh salads. In a daring move for the time, I applied for the first cafeteria liquor licence (to serve only beer and wine) and thanks to my hardworking and efficient lawyers, the application was successful. The size of the place required more people than were working there initially, so I trusted the existing employees to pass on the offer of employment by word of mouth and most of the new staff were found in this way. To all of them, old and new I stressed the importance of a spirit of cooperation and the necessity of creating a pleasant ambience. In keeping with this idea, I insisted that the kitchen never refuse a customer's little extra request. This was in keeping with my belief that service is the responsibility of the entire team, not just the servers. The result of all these efforts, as I have noted above, was an extremely successful business. And the basic principles involved in the way that I have run all my businesses have relevance to the larger world as well. Integrity, equality, fairness and mutual respect are transformative values on whatever scale they are applied.

To give the reader a more complete picture, the restaurant was located in a huge basement with seating for over a hundred people. The proposed cafeteria model seemed the only practical way to cater for large numbers of area workers. I decided on a bright décor with peach-coloured walls decorated with paintings or prints representing beautiful natural scenes or attractive arrangements of food. To further augment the "natural" feel there were plants located throughout the room. On the floor were large red Mexican-style tiles. The space was well-lit but there were no neon lights anywhere. Maple-topped tables with assorted chairs completed the overall colour scheme. The focal point was a long modern counter with all the wonderful-looking food out on display. To get people in the right mood, all the freshly-baked pastries, wine and beer were available at the start of the line. Both hot and cold foods were offered at the most reasonable prices possible. The set-up worked so well that any number of women told me that placing the very tempting baked goods first was "wicked". I always replied that the pastries were worth the calories. I would also helpfully suggest that they could compensate for the desserts with one of our many salads or light dishes.

We didn't make much money at first, but we were counting on increased volume to become profitable. And within about two months word of mouth had made our operation very lucrative. There were many businesses nearby and the customer volume was increasing every week. We had two full-time chefs and many excellent assistants, some of whom went on to open their own restaurants. Once we were established we had the good fortune to have a visit from Judy Laine Fine, another food critic, and she gave us a very good notice, after which our numbers picked up even more.

Part of what made the business so successful consisted of things that the customer would never see. One of those was the design of the kitchen. Drawing on my years of experience, and consulting with those who would be working there, I drew up plans that would maximize the efficiency of the space. I also made sure that we had all the modern equipment available, and to assure adequate storage I included a cool room that was truly immense. Specialized kitchen architects weren't common at the time, and later when they did arrive on the scene in greater numbers, many of them asked to see our set-up. What all this careful planning made possible was the ability to produce a large quantity of inexpensive, fresh and nutritious food (including daily specials that depended on what I was able to find or was offered by my suppliers) for six hundred to eight hundred sittings a day - not including take-out.

After a few months, with the restaurant well-established, my mother and I agreed to pass on the business to three Swiss brothers, two of whom were excellent chefs. They had little money, but we decided to trust them and give them time to pay us back. Our trust turned out to be more than justified as they never missed a payment. They also did very well with the business, although they did eventually go their own ways.

CHAPTER 7

Time for a Break

Around this time I began to feel an urgent need for a break. I had covered for both my brother and my mother while they took some time off and now I felt that it was my turn. Maison Basque was going well without me and I had no debt apart from mortgage payments which were easily managed. So one day I sat down with my girlfriend and convinced her to come on a trip around the world with me. The idea was not only to have a holiday, but also to fulfill a desire to see some faraway and intriguing places. I thought that these new experiences might refresh and renew us. It took a few days to come up with a set of destinations to discuss with our travel agent. Some slight modifications had to be made in order to meet the requirements of our around-the-world flat-fee ticket. In those days you could stop off as often as you wanted on your journey as long as you kept moving in the same direction – no backtracking was allowed. A few days later, it was with a wonderful sense of anticipation that we went to the travel agency to pick up and pay for an unbelievably large bundle of tickets.

Our first destination was to be Rio de Janeiro in Brazil. From there we would go on to Buenos Aires in Argentina and then Cusco in Peru. From Cusco we would travel to Machu Picchu. Lake Titicaca in Bolivia would be next and then back to Argentina to take in all the wineries around Mendoza. After some leisurely wine tasting we would take a plane over Aconcagua, the second highest mountain in the world, to reach Santiago de Chile. From there we would continue on to the Pacific Ocean and Easter Island, the first of our planned exotic destinations. We intended to visit many more islands as well. That was the plan at least. But there was an unexpected hitch even before we were able to begin our journey.

I am rarely sick but just two days before our departure I spent a feverish night with pain in the side of my belly. I thought it unimportant and didn't even wake Judith up. But by morning I was a little more worried and admitting that I was unwell, went to the nearest hospital - Women's College. Luckily a kind doctor was available right away and he looked extremely alarmed at what he found. Within fifteen minutes I was in an operating room having my appendix removed. All went well, and the surgeon, Dr. Fish told me that the appendix had been very close to rupturing and flooding my body with poisons, resulting in a potentially fatal condition known as peritonitis. As a result of this health crisis we had to cancel part of our trip, delaying our departure by three weeks. But I quickly realized that the incident had been a blessing in disguise. Had I become ill in a foreign country I might have attributed the pain to different food or strange bugs. I might well have waited too long to get treatment. The delay could have led to my death.

So we cancelled the trip to Peru and Bolivia and when the morning of our new departure date arrived - in December of 1976 – we headed for the airport in the middle of a snow storm. We were booked on an Aerolineas flight to Rio de Janeiro in Brazil, where we planned to spend two weeks. From Brazil we were to go on to Argentina. But in the immediate moment our challenge was to first get to the airport in the middle of a blizzard. Somehow we managed, but now we worried, needlessly as it turned out, that our connecting flight to New York wouldn't be able to take off. When we reached the departure area the check-in clerk looked at our large bundle of tickets and couldn't resist exclaiming, "once upon a time". He said that a trip like ours was a dream of his, and wished us all the good times possible. And in those days of easy air travel, even the U.S. customs official wished us a pleasant time.

Our arrival in Rio was a shock. When we left Toronto the temperature was minus eight degrees, whereas in Rio we were greeted by a steamy forty-one degrees Celsius, a temperature that leaves you feeling wet pretty much all of the time. The weather was just one challenge; the political climate was another. When we got to passport control we had a strange feeling that we were being greeted with suspicion. We had to deposit our documents in a drawer - at which point they disappeared. Facing us was a kind of grey mirror that I strongly suspected had police or customs officers looking at us from the other side. They kept us waiting for some time and Judith was becoming very uneasy and agitated. I whispered urgently to her that she had to keep absolutely quiet and that I would explain later. Finally we got our passports back and after that the customs inspection was relaxed and easy. There was even free coffee for tourists being offered at a nearby kiosk. Now we felt human again, and even welcome. The real side of Brazilian life – many smiles and kind gestures – was taking over. When we had finished with the formalities, I took my girlfriend aside and explained to her that when you enter a totalitarian country such as Brazil was at the time, the authorities would always do their best to impress on you that they were in total control.

Having lived near the border of Franco's Spain for so many years I knew how these things worked. The last thing you wanted to do was show annoyance at being treated unfairly. If you gave into those feelings you would quickly find yourself facing a barrage of malicious questions designed to find some excuse to hold you. When I was a young man still living in France, my father had so impressed on me the dangers of trips south of the border that I decided that drinking expeditions to Spain, despite its lower prices, were not worth the risk. Those risks were demonstrated dramatically on one occasion when my brother returned from Spain with two friends - one fewer than he had left with. The absent friend, after too many drinks had gotten into an argument with a Spanish officer. He told the latter that Franco's laws and rules were "fucked up". That comment led to his immediate arrest. The others were warned to leave immediately or face detention themselves. The parents of my brother's friend were deeply worried, knowing well the harsh Spanish courts and the general inability of the French government to wring any concessions out of the fascists. Their fears turned out to be well-founded as the hapless young man was sentenced to three years in jail for "Offence to the Head of State". Luckily the Spanish jailers were completely corrupt and the boy's father was able to secure lenient treatment for him, including being allowed to smuggle in food. And the sentence itself turned out to be flexible as well. With the help of friends in Spain and another bribe, the youth's father was able to get the time served reduced to eight months.

I told this story to Judith at the beginning of our trip as our next destinations were Argentina and Chile. Like Brazil, Argentina had military rulers, and in Chile, General Pinochet had just ruthlessly assassinated the democratically elected President, Salvador Allende. I wanted to make sure that she understood that we couldn't afford to do anything at all controversial while travelling in this part of the world. We were not equipped to play at being Che Guevaras.

Our stay in Brazil can best be described as a mixture of beautiful scenery, easy living (if you stuck to affluent areas) but also terrible, grinding poverty – often in close proximity to the wealthy neighbourhoods.

The vast majority of the poor were decent people who somehow were able to accept their difficult lives, but there definitely were many who could not. There were some whose rage led them to robbery, mass looting and even murder. Such horrific living conditions as those experienced by Brazil's poor in those days could easily produce a mindset that accepted crime as permissible. As a result, some Brazilians saw any vulnerable person as "prey" - and tourists certainly fit into that category, so we had to exercise great caution while we were there. Fortunately economic circumstances for ordinary Brazilians have improved since the seventies, but at the time of writing, 2009, there is still immeasurable suffering in much of the world. The rich countries too are criminals in their own way, making off with the resources of poor countries on unconscionable terms. And desperation responds in whatever way it can, from Somali pirates to militant groups of one kind or another. Economic inequality makes violence inevitable.

With the conditions I have described we became somewhat disenchanted with Brazil, so we shortened our stay and moved on to Buenos Aires. We not only had a very dear friend there, Hugo, who had worked with me in Toronto, but we also had an invitation from our Argentinean wine agent to visit him so that he could show us around the vineyards. That offer came about because of my selling so much Argentinean wine in my restaurants. When we arrived at the airport in Buenos Aires it turned out to be a very good thing that I had briefed Judith on the nature of military regimes. Even I wasn't prepared for the huge army of armed men that seemed to be everywhere. Clearly the military regime, under General Videla, was taking no chances. Nor was their presence limited to the airport: we saw soldiers patrolling every key area that we came to. Their ubiquitous presence was all the more alarming as those were the days of the "disappearances", when anyone judged to be a threat or even thought to have dangerous beliefs, could be kidnapped and pushed out the open door of an airplane flying over the estuary of the Rio de la Plata. The water was always muddy and the flights invariably at night, so there was little or no chance that any trace would be found. Similar methods were widely used by General Franco as well. Just ask any Basque.

So our first impressions of Argentina were very bad ones. We began to wonder if we had made a stupid mistake. But, eventually we discovered that, as in Brazil, most people just wanted to get on with their lives, doing their best to ignore the oppressive atmosphere. Our mood began to lift even on the bus ride into the city. Buenos Aires looked very much like certain parts of Europe, but with brighter colours and much more easygoing attitudes. The traffic was pure madness with everyone seeming to follow individual rules – if there were any at all. There was a constant cacophony of blaring horns and shouts exchanged between drivers. While still in Rio we had tried to phone Hugo, but the phone lines were very inefficient in those days and we couldn't reach him. So we went straight to our hotel, a nice place located just behind a very famous street named Nueve De Julio (9th of July). We were very tired from our journey so we went to bed and fell asleep right away.

By the time we woke up it was one o'clock in the morning and we were sure we'd missed any chance of supper. All we had was some water which we hoped would keep us going until morning. But as we were discussing the unavailability of food I happened to look out the window where I was very surprised to see the street still filled with people. None of them seemed in any rush to get home; they were walking and chatting as though they had all the time in the world. So we decided to join them. It was summer there and everyone was dressed in light clothing. There was a nice breeze which made us feel very comfortable after the heat of the day. All this activity late at night was surprising enough but the sight of open restaurants and people still eating made Judith and I look at each other in wonder. I stopped someone on the street to ask what was going on. (I speak fluent Spanish so this was a much easier task than it would have been in Brazil where my very inadequate Portuguese would not have been up to the task.) My informant, who had been to North America, laughed as he replied, "Senor, this is not Toronto or Chicago; you are in Buenos Aires, the city that never sleeps."

We picked a restaurant whose entrance looked in on a glass-walled room containing a huge barbecue. It was designed to attract customers with the spectacle of meat and other goodies grilling over a charcoal fire. In one area, entire sections of meat were cooking gently on the side of a huge fire. They were being grilled on skewers like giant brochettes. I had never even imagined such a place. Brazil had smaller versions of this barbecue heaven, but in Argentina, where meat was plentiful and cheap, the scale of the operation was unlike anything I had seen before. And this staggering display of plenty was still available to diners in the middle of the night. So even though I was and still am mostly vegetarian, the sight of all these delicious offerings was too much to resist. I decided then and there that as long as I was in Argentina, I would happily go with the flow of the local culture. It turned out to be a good decision as their food was prepared with great expertise in a variety of wonderful ways.

We finally got in touch with Hugo the next day and learned that he had arranged a better hotel for us – one situated in a beautiful section of the city where all the embassies are located. And in this area there was an even greater profusion of exotic restaurants to choose from, places where the prices were surprisingly reasonable. I remember, on many occasions, inviting Hugo and his friend, also named Hugo, to meals at these fancy restaurants and never having to pay more than the equivalent of fifty dollars Canadian. And it wasn't just the restaurants that were a bargain; our luxury hotel offered rooms starting at only thirty-five dollars when we first checked in, and rising to forty-two by the time we left. The increase was due to runaway inflation of two hundred per cent a year – a rate that would have been unthinkable in first world countries. At a local bank I was even offered interest of sixteen per cent a month if I deposited some of my travellers' cheques. A rate like that appeared to suggest that you could deposit money that you had saved, travel the world on the interest and still have money left over. There had to be a catch.

And there was. Our plan was to stay about a month in Argentina, during which time we intended to visit Mar del Plata, Mendoza, St. Rafael and some spots in the Andes. At the end of our time there, our next destination was to be Easter Island. There was an element of guesswork operating here as our going to Easter Island depended on there being an "opening". Such an opening could take as long as three months, but I had asked a local travel agent to book the first available opportunity and was hoping for the best. When I was quoted a price for the next stage of our journey that seemed too good to be true I began to look a little more closely at the idea of depositing some of our money in a local bank. The idea of travelling for free seemed distinctly possible. But when I investigated more closely, I discovered the downside of those incredible interest rates. If we had decided to stay in Argentina we would have been fine, but we could only withdraw our money in Argentinean pesos - a currency accepted nowhere else in the world. So to go anywhere else, we would have had to convert our savings back into dollars again. The result? A return less than our initial investment!

So we held on to our travellers' cheques and returned our attention to where it belonged – having a great time in Buenos Aires. It was certainly much easier to do that with Hugo's local expertise available to us and that blessing was apparently pure luck as our visit happened to coincide with his coming to Buenos Aires, the city of his birth, to visit family. Hugo had been my Maitre D at Maison Basque in Toronto and as a gay man in 1970's Toronto, he was extremely cautious. Even though he could see that I was very accepting of gay friends and customers, he was afraid to tell me about his sexual orientation. That fear was demonstrated dramatically when he tried to bring his lover to Canada. The latter was deported within forty-eight hours. But even in this case of extreme bigotry and injustice, he was still afraid to ask for my help. Later on, when he finally told me what had happened, we managed to get a proper immigrant visa for his partner. And while today Canada is much more tolerant than it was then, there are still risks in transparency if your nature or your views are unpopular.

But the dangers in 1970's Argentina were of course of a whole different order. While Hugo's father was not a supporter of the military government, he was very careful not to speak openly. Even some other members of Hugo's family were in favour of the government's policies, believing in the need for strong leaders to deal with "troublemakers". An opinion carelessly voiced in the wrong company could easily lead to one's disappearance. But what many Argentineans could agree on was their fondness and nostalgia for the days of Juan Peron and his charismatic wife Evita. I listened politely to their tales of the "good old days" but I couldn't help mentioning that someone named Peron had extensive property holdings in San Sebastian in the Spanish part of the Basque country as well as in other areas of Spain. Odd behaviour for someone supposedly dedicated to the welfare of ordinary Argentinean citizens. But the Perons were only part of a long line of corrupt leaders who in thirty years managed to reduce a country that was once the richest of all the nations, from Mexico south to Chile, to one with a worthless currency and a paralyzing climate of fear. This despite a well-educated population and agricultural conditions second to none. Sadly, at the time of writing global corruption, if anything, is even worse. Small elites continue to exploit not only their own citizens, but often those of other nations as well. Honesty and transparency continue to be elusive goals.

But despite the chilling atmosphere in Argentina, Judith and I were far more interested in our love for each other than in local politics. (So much so that one day on a walk we went into a very nice jewellery store and bought a beautiful engagement ring.) But I don't want to leave the reader with the impression that all else was doom and gloom in Argentina. The representatives of the local wine industry greeted us with great warmth, arranging our hotel in Buenos Aeries and taking us to many great eating places where we were not allowed to pay for anything. They even insisted in covering our hotel charges as it turned out. In addition, visits to a number of wineries were arranged. All this hospitality was the result, not only of my importing large quantities of Argentinean wine, but of importing them before anyone else. The wineries we were to visit were in the Mendoza area.

The first one we saw was called *Peñaflor*, supposedly the largest winery in the world, so when we arrived and saw only a small office building, a kind of shed and a metal ramp going down into the ground, it was something of a letdown. But all this changed when we were taken to an elevator that served three underground levels. These underground floors turned out to be large enough to store hundreds and hundreds of oak barrels, some of them extremely large. But even more surprising were vast reservoirs called "piletas" – each holding five million litres. And the reason for all this wine being stored underground was to protect it from the searing heat of the area, thus allowing it to be kept at the required uniform temperature.

After seeing this mammoth operation up close, I naturally had to ask where it was all going. The answer turned out to be that most of it was consumed domestically, only twenty per cent being exported. Argentina was at the time the fourth largest wine producer in the world, most of its production was being consumed by a population of fewer than sixteen million people. But the longer I was in the country the more those figures made sense. I was surprised to see wine in restaurants or homes being served with ice cubes or even mixed with soda. Once I got used to the idea it seemed perfectly sensible, and far healthier than Coca Cola or any other soft drink.

Continuing our explorations we took a ride to St. Rafael, to the excellent Bianchi winery where I wanted to buy some wine privately. Mr. Bianchi the owner greeted us personally and gave us the royal treatment with an excellent lunch and then a visit to the vineyards, a cool oasis in the middle of dry and arid land. There I was puzzled by the sight of a T-shaped metal net over the vines. When I asked the reason he told me that it was to protect them from hail. While hailstorms were rare, when they did happen the hail was the size of golf balls and could destroy an entire year's crop. I also wondered how the vines were kept so well-watered in such forbidding terrain. The answer was under my feet. All the water they needed was underground, and not very deep down. I was struck by the enormous skill and effort needed to run a successful winery. First off, a huge investment is required. Then the varieties of grapes must be carefully chosen before the extremely complicated process of creating good wine can even begin. I was so impressed by the place that I made a commitment to Mr. Bianchi to buy two varieties from among his many great wines. Not only did I not argue about price, I even suggested that he make sure not to charge me too little. And to make sense of that statement I must explain to my readers, as I did to Mr. Bianchi, the strange workings of the LCBO.

I told him that the Liquor Control Board of Ontario would be the ones who decided what I had to pay for the two crates, or about eighty cases containing almost a thousand bottles. At the time of purchase I was working on the understanding that the provincially-owned corporation would not charge me more than two hundred per cent above the buying price to cover taxes, insurance, and delivery to the various LCBO store locations. Mr. Bianchi and I agreed on a price of five US dollars per case (at the time, the Canadian dollar was worth more than the American one) which worked out to around forty cents a bottle. However, when I returned to Canada and put the whole thing in motion - and at the point when the wine was already on the docks in Buenos Aires – the gods of the LCBO decreed that they would charge me *four dollars a bottle*. A mark-up of *ten* times the original price. And to add insult to injury I had to pay half the amount in advance and then wait five months to get my wine.

Two years later Mr Bianchi visited us at Maison Basque and asked to see our wine list. We were charging just under ten dollars for a bottle of his wine (our policy being to take no more than four or five dollars profit per bottle). The pricing seems rather quaint today where the sky is the limit. When Mr Bianchi saw his wines marked up over twenty times he almost choked. He could barely speak, and when he recovered himself he accused me of being a thief. At first I didn't understand what the problem was, but I quickly realized that he felt highly insulted and was holding me responsible for the outrage. Fortunately Hugo swung into action and after considerable effort seemed to appease him. To further smooth the waters I took his assistant, who was also his bookkeeper, to my office and showed him my books. He too came to understand the bizarre workings of a government policy seemingly designed to punish the sellers and consumers of alcoholic drinks – a policy that allowed the LCBO to relieve me of ten times the value of my purchase. Later in the conversation, the bookkeeper told me of the LCBO's crowning insult. They had waited eight months to pay poor Mr. Bianchi which, with Argentina's two hundred per cent inflation, resulted in substantial losses. He vowed to never sell a bottle of his wine in this country again. And we call Canada a democracy!

To return to the trip, our tour of the Argentinean wine country was coming to an end and we came back to Mendoza in order to fly out the next day. Due to a cancellation, we had been fortunate enough to get a flight, at the end of December, 1976, from Mendoza to Santiago De Chile. There, on January the second, we would board the only plane flying to Easter Island. The time period here is significant, as it was during the years of the murderous Pinochet regime. We were arranging things so as to spend as little time in Chile as possible.

The day of our flight out of Mendoza dawned bright and sunny with superb visibility. Our plane took off mid-morning but as I was enjoying the view, it struck me that we were travelling east, rather than west. When I asked one of the flight attendants about this she smiled and told me that I wasn't the only one wondering. She explained that the plane had to circle the way an eagle does in order to gain enough altitude to fly over the famed Aconcagua, the highest mountain outside of Asia, which was just north of the city of Mendoza. Once we gained altitude we had a spectacular view of both the mountain and the Andes range of which it is a part. All the mountains looked gigantic to me. And once we had crossed them we began to spiral, as we had on our ascent, only downwards of course, to land in Santiago.

Santiago presented a startling contrast to the uplifting scenery of our flight. The taxi ride from the airport to our hotel (which was in one of the established older districts) seemed overly expensive, but this was a place where it would not have been wise to complain about anything. As we drove through town we saw a broken people, no one smiling, on streets where shops that were boarded up, barred and even completely covered with metal, were an all-too-common sight. The few businesses that weren't fortified in some way had been smashed up and stripped of their contents. There was little traffic and the few vehicles on the road seemed to be mostly military ones. When we got to our hotel we were relieved to see that it was a good one, and that the staff was doing its best to be pleasant and polite. I asked the desk clerk, in Spanish, if it was safe to go out and he warned us to go only to areas where tourists were allowed. Otherwise we apparently risked being roughed up or even robbed by undisciplined soldiers.

We didn't go out the first day, but on the second one we took a tourist bus to Valparaiso on the Pacific coast and got back in time to celebrate New Year's Eve at a restaurant near the hotel, one that had been suggested by the management. Supper would be late, starting at nine p.m. The walk there was an easy two blocks, but somewhat dispiriting as none of the people we passed smiled or spoke even a single word. Our hotel had made a reservation for us and we ended up seated by ourselves at a small table facing a small stage. Clearly some kind of entertainment would be part of the evening's festivities. The meal was a fixed price which included as many "pisco" drinks as we wanted. At somewhere around one hundred dollars Canadian, it was a lot of money for the locals, but somehow the room filled up. It seemed that the customers had managed to find the money for this special occasion. The whole evening was alive, fun and cheerful, with food that was good, if not memorable. Unfortunately the pleasant mood dissipated quickly when it came time to leave!

It was impossible to get a taxi so we faced walking back – a very dangerous proposition as it turned out. The hotel staff, assuring us that everything would be safe, had neglected to mention the military-imposed ten p.m. curfew. We started our walk back in almost complete darkness as the street lighting was virtually non-existent. Suddenly out of nowhere we saw an armoured car racing towards us and as it stopped a few metres away, its guns swung around to point in our direction. Judith was paralyzed with fear, but I managed to tell them – in Spanish of course – that we were tourists on our way back to our hotel. At that an officer came out of the vehicle, asked me a few more questions and let us go - even wishing us a happy new year. In another gesture of good will the armoured car drove behind us, illuminating the way until the hotel was in view. At the time I saluted the soldiers for their courtesy, but once we reached the safety of our room, we began to realize that we could very easily have been shot and killed with no questions asked. As it happened the military turned out to be human, even quite helpful, but that was not something to be counted on. The experience has made me glad of the efforts made in both Spanish and Chilean courts to call Pinochet to account. His death in 2006 left the efforts in limbo, but an important principle was established. But all this legal activity was long after the fact. At the time it was a great relief to leave Chile behind.

Only LAN Chile (as it was then known), the national Chilean Airline, is allowed to fly to Easter Island. As we approached the island after a five-hour flight, I realized that something was wrong. I was looking out the window, trying to get a picture of the island's topography, when I noticed that the plane was coming in so low that we were almost touching the surface of the ocean. Then almost immediately we came down hard on the runway and I could feel the aircraft braking as the pilot tried to slow the plane before it overshot and ended up in the ocean on the other side. There was no room for error as the strip was barely long enough to allow the small jets to take off and land. It was no wonder that LAN Chile was the only airline allowed to use the airport.

Once off the plane, we were greeted, not by the sight of a modern airport with a control tower and proper facilities, but only that of a small shed holding a few basic instruments. The impression was not one that inspired confidence. More reassuring was the sight of locals bearing little crowns of flowers. They would approach with the offer to host you on your stay and if you accepted, the flowers would be placed on your head. We ended up staying with a sweet family whose home lacked modern conveniences but was filled with warmth and kindness. Our clothes were a source of great interest, and they would have readily bought everything that we had. There was only one small shop on the whole island and what sticks in my mind is that the price of a bottle of pisco, an alcoholic drink similar to tequila, cost less than half that of a bottle of Coca-Cola. There was no food for sale, and with only very marginal subsistence farming possible on this volcanic island, life must have been difficult.

Our host family had an old jeep, very rusty from the salt air, but still serviceable, so we were able to get around. There were also rental horses available. And while the scenery is quite spectacular, of course the main reason people come to Easter Island is to see the moai, the famous statues. There are eight-hundred and eighty-seven of these remarkable works, in a variety of sizes. They were carved over a period of a thousand years yet all follow the same design. But the greatest mystery is how these huge stone statues were taken from the quarry to their present locations. There were no trees to provide logs for rolling these behemoths and certainly nothing with wheels. According to the locals, the Islanders of old had the ability to concentrate as a total group and move matter with their minds. And whether the ancients had such abilities or not, science has been unable to come up with a satisfactory explanation to this day.

Our stay there was for five days and the food provided, while adequate, and likely plentiful by local standards, certainly made it impossible to get fat. There was an abundance of langouste, or spiny lobster, which suited me perfectly. In fact a German lady staying with the same family was happy to trade me her share of the langouste (which she was unable to eat), for my portion of any meat dishes. There was only one choice per meal, so depending on what was served, one of us ate almost nothing and the other ate a double portion. But overall it was a very pleasant stay and as we settled our account with our host family we gave them some of our clothes as a way of thanking them for their hospitality. During our stay we had been struck not only by their simple way of living, but also by their complete transparency where their feelings and desires were concerned. While life on the mainland was undoubtedly sad, here in this remote Chilean territory things seemed largely unchanged. As we waited at the airport for our flight to Tahiti, the next stop on our itinerary, I made a point of carefully watching the very precise landing. I would be on board to observe the takeoff for myself - assuming that we survived it.

Landing at the airport in Papeete, the capital of Tahiti (also known as French Polynesia), was quite a culture shock. There were two huge hotels close to the runway with all the amenities that you might expect in a large city, and in the town centre, the streets were busy with traffic. On the sidewalks you could see local women wearing *pareos*, colourful and elegant sarong-like garments consisting of a single cloth wrapped around the body. There were many nice shops to choose from, most featuring the work of local artists. And the visual delights of the town centre were evident on the sea shore as well. A French colony, planning in Tahiti is governed by the French aesthetic. France is a very visual culture so Tahiti does not have the tall oceanfront rabbit cages of Hawaii or Florida, but instead the hotels facing the sea are built on a human scale, with the tops of the buildings being no higher than the surrounding trees. The prices were not cheap, but they were reasonable, which is all that you can ask.

I have stayed in hotels all over the world, and they all offer the same basic things: a comfortable bed and a clean bathroom. The distinctions between them are often just a creation of marketing and the huge differences in price are frequently hard to justify. The only factors that are important to me are architecture, décor, location and service. These are palpable things that I'm happy to pay for, but I refuse to pay top dollar for some marketer's fantasy. As I have already stressed earlier in these pages, the key to sound and moral business practice is transparency. However outrageous profits made on the basis of cheap foreign labour and unconscionable mark-ups are practically the norm today. I was once in conversation with a young man who seemed to be doing very well for himself. He explained that he sold surgical instruments whose high prices provided him with excellent commissions. When I asked if the high prices were the result of the devices being manufactured in Sweden or Germany, he said no; they were cheap knock-offs made in Pakistan. That manufacturing source, he explained proudly, allowed his company to charge the unsuspecting hospitals ten times the manufacturing costs. The incident again brought to mind *Conversations with God*, where Walsch suggests that if you wanted to change the world overnight, the easiest way would be to make every single human transaction totally transparent. Imagine buying shoes whose label told you that only ten per cent of the price could be reasonably explained!

Luckily, Tahiti in the seventies was largely free of such extreme business practices. The locals were not very materialistic and services were available at pretty fair prices. A popular method of transportation was a small pickup truck with a low back with benches on each side. If you needed a ride you flagged the driver down and paid a small fee, usually to his wife who would be sitting beside him. These vehicles were quite numerous and constantly circled the coast road that circumnavigated the main island. As long as it was daylight you never had to wait very long, but at night you had to take the more expensive taxi. A further benefit of these informal buses was the chance to have pleasant conversations with your fellow travellers. We always found them to be courteous and welcoming and we never felt threatened in any way.

But while Tahiti was idyllic for tourists, the situation for the indigenous population was considerably more complex. The French military, while trying to keep a low profile, nevertheless maintained a strong presence in Tahiti because of undersea nuclear testing that they were conducting at the time. To somewhat compensate the locals the French government provided generous social benefits and restricted residency by French nationals to five years. Nonetheless, foreign domination was still deeply resented by the natives. Another source of anger was the large population of Chinese immigrants brought in to do labour spurned by the locals. The Asians had ended up owning the bulk of prime real estate and most businesses as well. Their presence was very evident in most work places. In one conversation that we had with some native Tahitians they made their anger at outsiders very clear. They accused the Europeans of inventing the whole idea of "work", a strange concept for peoples who had once lived entirely on the bounty of nature. The Tahitians had seen their way of life poisoned in less than a century.

While in Tahiti we had the good fortune to connect with the sister of one of my chefs who, with her husband, was teaching there on a temporary contract. As we didn't want to be a burden we waited until a few days before the end of our visit to go and see them. The delay was unfortunate as we quickly realized that we had many things in common, not the least of which was our shared *joie de vivre*. They told us a great deal that we didn't know about Tahiti and in addition, they had a wonderful boat to take us around the many beautiful islands. The husband was also an avid fisherman, and he lamented the fact that we had waited so long to get in touch – as did we. Just as we were starting to have a really good time and beginning to explore this huge archipelago it was time to leave.

Our next destination was Tonga, once British-ruled, but by that time an independent nation. It was a place that Judith had long wanted to visit, since as a child she remembered her church sending donations to this faraway place. And Tonga did not disappoint. The people were very sweet, the powerful-looking men dressed in long skirts, the women mostly large also, but some having slender bodies similar to those of Tahitian women. The weather, mostly torrential rains, was a disappointment, but we amused ourselves by sending postcards to our friends. The local stamps featured the island's fruit, butterflies and fish – the last cut up to beautiful and amusing affect.

After a few days on Tonga we moved on to Viti Levu (Main Island), the largest of the Fiji Islands, where we had made plans to spend a week and do a little sightseeing. Viti Levu is a very big island (over fifteen thousand square kilometres) and at the time of our visit there it was developing rapidly. The population consisted of indigenous people, Indians, Pakistanis, a few Chinese and a tiny minority of Europeans. Rather than a hotel, this time we chose a bed and breakfast in the city of Suva. It was a colonial style house overlooking beautiful Suva Bay and the city's harbour. We had an amazing view of the large cruise ships which were frequent visitors there. In our unit, we had a small but well set-up kitchen, and as I had already spotted the daily farmer's market, I was eager to do some of my own cooking now and again.

But we made sure to sample the local food as well. It was strange to us, but it was a feast for the eyes as well as the taste buds, as it included some extraordinarily colourful species of fish. This was my first exposure to Indian or Pakistani food, not to mention the wonderful dishes that were part of the indigenous tradition and we regretted that our time in Fiji was so short. My only disappointment on the culinary side was the almost universal use of ghee made from a butter derived from buffalo milk. It was nothing like the butter we're used to in North America and Europe, having, at least to Judith and me, an almost rancid taste. Everything that we bought seemed to be saturated with ghee, so we began to do our own cooking more and more of the time. The local produce was excellent and available fresh daily, and we cooked it with peanut oil as olive oil was not available.

But of course we didn't just eat; this was after all a place where the natives were reputed to have the ability to walk barefoot on hot coals. So to see some of the local wonders we leased a car for a week, but returned it after only a day as the roads were so dangerous. There was no paving outside the city and the country roads were so dusty that it was almost impossible to see. Further, there were many dangerous ravines and such a constant stream of slow-moving truck traffic that passing was hopeless. In a whole day we managed to travel only sixty tortuous kilometres. So we never managed to see the fire walkers. We had seen films that assured us that this ritual existed but we had to take the filmmakers' word for it. For the rest of our stay we travelled only to places that could be reached by bus or on foot.

From Fiji we went on to Auckland, New Zealand, for a few days. Auckland is a beautiful city with wonderful ocean views. As on Tonga, cars drive on the right side of the road, and the cars themselves are a bit of a curiosity as you can see many very old English cars, still in perfect running order. Auckland is a windy city so when we looked out to the ocean there were always sailboats to watch and admire, but the water itself turned out to be shockingly cold. We were reminded that New Zealand is not very far from Antarctica whose icy waters cool the surrounding seas. The upside is that those same seas provide New Zealanders with a rich variety of seafood. We were able to feast on huge mussels, abalone, langouste again, as well as deep sea fish and an assortment of other interesting species. And when we travelled out to the countryside it was to a lush and gentle landscape very reminiscent of Ontario - but of course with a difference. We saw the famous kiwi birds, enormous ferns and *kauri* trees with trunks larger than anything I had ever seen.

From New Zealand we flew west, first to Melbourne - its aridity a shock after lush New Zealand - and then via a connecting flight to Hobart, the largest city on the island of Tasmania. (Now part of Australia, Tasmania was named for the Dutch navigator Abel Tasman who in 1642 was the first European to sight the island.) The first permanent settlement was established, by the English, in 1803.) We had come to Hobart mostly to spend time visiting Judith's brother Jeffrey, an architect who lived there with his young family. Jeffrey was waiting for us at the airport and after introductions we crammed into his Austin Mini Cooper and headed home. The scenery was beautiful, but everything seemed very dry there as well. (However we were assured that with the arrival of winter, in May, the rains would come and the landscape would turn green.) Our trip to his house involved some backtracking as the bridge crossing the mighty Derwent River had been struck by a cargo vessel and collapsed. As a result we had to travel to a more northerly bridge in order to cross.

We arrived at a cozy and comfortable home overlooking the Derwent estuary with a view of the open sea off to the right. We met his wife Mona, and his children, Charles and Olivia. They were a delightful family and immediately made us feel at home. Although it was summer, they had made a fire of eucalyptus wood which gave off a wonderful and unforgettable scent. The need for a fire, we learned subsequently, was the result of Tasmania's extremely changeable weather: apparently it was not unusual to experience four seasons in a single day. This was a fact that we frequently experienced for ourselves in our travels throughout the island. We visited many wild and beautiful places that seemed untouched by modern life. It was as though we were seeing a long lost world. The virgin lands were bordered by natural harbours and endless pristine beaches with names like Seven Mile Beach or Nine Mile Beach. Coles Bay was a wilderness gem of pure, endless coastline with not a single person in sight. Later on we chartered a small plane and were able to see far more of this awe-inspiring place. I felt that the very core of my being had been touched as never before in a moment of pure grace. It was, I imagined, how a mountaineer must feel at the summit or an astronaut looking for the first time at the earth from space.

Sadly however, even here there were the scars of clear-cutting on the land. They felt like blows. I know there are powerful economic arguments for such activity, but at that moment it seemed a terrible aberration. Forests that had taken millennia to develop complex ecosystems were being destroyed in days. And with their loss came and continues to do so the degradation of the very air we breathe. Why doesn't the world look to more sustainable practices? In Italy fast-growing poplars are grown as crops and harvested. Hemp is a viable alternative to wood for paper manufacture, yet we continue to destroy irreplaceable wonders for the sake of a few dollars in savings or to satisfy powerful lobby groups. And no one really knows the long-term effects of such destructive practices. We are stealing the very birthright of future generations.

I was reminded of a similar lack of foresight in my native country of France. There, when I was growing up in the forties and fifties there was no planning or regulation of the fishing industry. At the time, the waters around St. Jean de Luz teemed with fish. I have mentioned that my father was a mechanic on a tuna boat and at times I went fishing with him. The tuna were plentiful and immense in size, especially the "thon rouge" or yellow fin: weights of three or even four hundred kilos were not at all unusual. Later came fishing for albacore which while smaller in size was prized because it didn't darken when canned like the yellow fin. As most of the catch was canned in those days, the lighter colour of the albacore made it more expensive. Compared to today, the price of all fish in those days was very low.

The already poor returns for fishermen were further exacerbated by out-of-date contracts with processing plants which compelled them to process as much fish as possible – further depressing prices. The net effect of these factors was chronic over-fishing with less and less reward. Cutthroat competition between the competing groups of fishermen (French Basques, Spanish Basques and Portuguese) was inevitable. The animosity would lead to disaster. One night my brother and I heard our parents having a furious argument in the middle of the night. We were extremely puzzled because we knew that my father had to get up very early in the morning for his work. In the morning we learned the cause of their disagreement. The streets of the town were covered with cut-up tuna sprinkled with diesel oil to make it inedible. The reasons for the horror were primitive at best. Something along the lines of making sure that the other guy didn't get it first. The insult to the town of contaminating the fish was beyond comprehension. My mother later told me that if it hadn't been for the argument with my father that I would have had to go out with him on this insane mission. And this was only the microcosm of what was happening on a larger scale: better technology and techniques leading to larger and larger takes in an oversupplied market. The failure to bring the warring parties together and work out some kind of agreement has led to today's situation where fish stocks have been reduced by ninety-five per cent. This is what happens when an absence of ethics and spirituality is combined with utter contempt for nature. And the destruction of tuna stocks in the Bay of Biscay is only one small example of a much larger problem.

In an age where we can travel to the moon or send space craft to distant planets, scientists have still been unable to discover where tuna reproduce. Young "bonitos", young tuna only a foot long, are caught and then grown to commercial size in tuna farms - large sea ponds in the Mediterranean or off the coast of Australia. Other fish, such as salmon, tilapia and other species, are farmed through the whole life cycle but tuna can only be raised once they are wild caught. Not surprisingly, sparing no tuna, no matter how small, has led to a situation where the tuna fishery is dangerously close to unsustainability. According to marine scientists unless international agreements can be reached to stop tuna fishing for a few years, the species will be virtually extinct in less than a decade. And the strangest thing is that the very countries who consume the most tuna are the ones actively blocking agreements that might save the food source for the long term. It seems that nothing has changed in fifty years. Like most human problems, the destruction of fisheries is another example of people unwilling to trust themselves or others. It is easy to find examples from all over the world of injustice and suffering that stem from those very same factors. Would that the planet could start to apply the principle that my friend Laird Orr suggests in his book, *When Love Has Won*. There he suggests that all significant policy decisions by business and government should be made with a thousand-year time frame in mind. What a difference that would make!

But I have strayed from my purpose, which was to describe the joys of our Tasmanian visit. The Tasmanian clear cutting, while upsetting at the time, was only a small blot on an otherwise spectacular visit. Not only was the wilderness scenery fabulous, but the food, from the great produce to the abundant fish, was cheap and plentiful. And the people were so welcoming it was hard to believe. We were introduced to many, many nice people who invited us into their homes for great barbecues and dinners. The wine too, although the industry was just starting, was quite excellent. When it came time to leave Tasmania, as much as we had enjoyed our visit, we still wondered how people managed to live so far from the mainstream of big cities and their many amenities. We assumed that we would never return, having not even the slightest inkling that within five years we would make Hobart our home.

From Hobart we returned to Melbourne, planning to spend a few days sightseeing there. Our first stop was the zoo. We thought we had a good idea of Australian wildlife from our time on Tasmania, but the diversity of species on display was truly mind-blowing - almost more than we could absorb. In a general way, the city reminded us of Toronto, as Melbourne too had many streetcars and a similar city centre full of modern office buildings. And when it came to restaurants, not only was there a large variety of ethnicities to choose from, but also fabulous produce, much of which was unfamiliar to me. The city seemed much more business-oriented than Hobart, but it also offered the tourist the chance to see great houses with beautiful gardens, and endless beaches that were close by and very accessible.

Our last Australian destination was Fremantle in Western Australia, and from there we flew on to the Seychelles Islands in the Indian Ocean. It was on the beach in Fremantle that we saw our first sharks, which were enough of a problem to clear the beaches from time to time. Far more numerous and more troubling were the mosquitoes which made a special net over our bed a necessity. Almost as plentiful, but a delight rather than an annoyance, were the innumerable fireflies with their magical lights. Our first expedition was to an amazing island called Praslin. To get there we chartered a beautiful boat owned and skippered by an Australian man. We shared the cost of the charter with a couple of French nationals from Madagascar. The captain's girl friend was on board as well. During the crossing, which took all of a warm and breezy night, we lay on top of the boat under an eerie sky watching multitudes of stars. When the sun appeared above the horizon it was a revelation. We all felt a great sense of the glory of life.

The day was to offer some additional excitement before very long. Two fishing lines constantly trailed the boat, and part way through the morning, we were told to look astern. Some distance behind the boat we could see that a sailfish had been hooked and was desperately trying to free itself. The Captain's girlfriend became very upset and insisted that the fish be freed. He refused her as he planned to sell the unfortunate creature to a restaurant. It took another hour and a half before the exhausted fish could be pulled close to the boat, immobilized with a blow to the head, and hooked in the gills. Not quite dead, it moved in the water from time to time, its skin reflecting a rainbow of colours. We were in awe of its beauty, but the skipper seemed uninterested in anything but getting the huge fish on board and asked for our help in doing so. Working with him brought back memories of fishing for tuna in the Bay of Biscay so I could empathize with both with the captain and his girlfriend. For the Aussie, the catch constituted a valuable windfall which would probably go to someone else if he failed to make use of the opportunity, while to the girlfriend the fish was part of something sacred. She saw its capture as a despoiling of a natural order that should have been treated with reverence.

By now we were near the coast of Praline Island, a true gem set in beautiful, clear, turquoise water. With its multitude of plant and animal species much of the island was under government protection as a park. You were strictly forbidden to interfere with nature in any way – even collecting sea shells was against the law. I was taken ashore in a Zodiac, a safe, inflatable rescue craft. Judith didn't accompany me as she was not a swimmer, and the journey to the area in an open boat had been test enough of her courage. There were many wonders to see, but the coco-fesses, a species of coconut that grows only on the islands of Praline and Curieuse in the Seychelles sticks in my mind. It has giant flowers and leaves, and its fruit, weighing between fifteen and thirty kilos is the largest of any plant species.

Back onboard our regular boat, we were taken to an exquisite hotel, Chateau des Feuilles, the best hotel on the island, where we had decided to treat ourselves to a bit of luxury. We had booked a package that included dinner and lodging. Staying at Chateau des Feuilles was such a memorable experience that I vowed to create my own version one day. The aspects that I hoped to emulate were the beautiful, natural surroundings, very fresh local food, and warm and genuine human contact. The overall feeling was one of sharing a love of life. Such places are not cheap of course, but they do not rip their guests off, as is often the case with luxury resorts such as the ones I mention above. There is a difference between paying for real amenities, as opposed to paying for an artificially- created image.

From Praline we returned by boat to the Seychelles International Airport where we boarded a flight to Nairobi, Kenya where we experienced some pretty extreme culture shock. Our goal in going to Africa was to see wild animals in their natural surroundings – which we eventually did, but first we had to deal with life in Nairobi. There we saw a degree of poverty that nothing in our lives had prepared us for. The most basic amenities that we take for granted in the industrialized world were denied to much of the population. Beggars were everywhere on the streets and our ignorance of the local conditions almost resulted in tragedy. When I saw someone asking for money I made the very serious mistake of giving it. Some of the beggars were horribly disfigured or crippled, a fact which naturally evoked our compassion. But I learned later that many of these disabilities were self-inflicted to increase the likelihood of being given money – a revelation that was incomprehensible to us. In any event, my misguided generosity led to beggars being attracted to us from every corner. We tried to take a side street to avoid them, but they all followed us and we ended up surrounded and trapped against a wall. It was clear that we were in extreme danger, so I took out the money in my pockets and threw it into the crowd. Of course they began to fight over it and in the confusion I was able to push two guys out of the way and grab Judith. Then we ran for our lives until we reached a street where things seemed normal again and by this time our hotel was in sight. The next day we went on a week-long, organized, sightseeing trip to a national park. There we were rewarded with some wonderful experiences - at times even getting very close to lions and other wild beasts. But we still felt safer than we had on the streets of Nairobi. I hope things have changed there since 1977.

Returning from our safari we prepared for the next step on our journey, which was to be a night flight to Cairo, via Air Egypt. But when we arrived at the airport there was no sign of a booth for our airline. Luckily someone explained to me that the airline booth would open before flight time and then you had to make a rush for it as there was no guarantee you would get on the airplane – even with a reservation. Apparently they habitually overbooked the flights and would accept money on the basis of first come, first served. I was shocked that the usual rules of civilized travel didn't apply here. At this point we had been almost around the world and we had never encountered a similar situation. Further, weight limits seemed not to apply to people who showed their passports with money inside. Nonetheless we were grateful to get on board at all, but the plane was packed and there was a definite problem with the air quality that led to a long delay.

When we finally took off it was into the teeth of a storm which led to a shaky and bumpy ride. I was seated next to a priest who was sweating profusely due to his anxiety. But having spent many hours gliding as a youth I wasn't too troubled by the weather conditions and I was able to calm him down a bit. Later, when the storm subsided we had a good chat. On arrival in Cairo we debarked into very cold temperatures and after the heat and humidity of Nairobi it was quite a shock. However I knew from our Australian experience that when the sun rose things would warm up quickly and by mid-day it would be hot. So it was a relief to get inside the warm terminal.

The feeling didn't last as we encountered the same kind of customs hostility that we had experienced in South America. With my Canadian passport I got through quickly, but Judith was travelling on a British one, a very unpopular document in Egypt where there was still bad feeling over the 1957 attempt by Britain, France and Israel to seize the Suez Canal. Judith seemed to have been taken away somewhere and the longer I waited, the more worried I became. My sense was that the "boys" were showing her who was boss. Eventually all the passengers had passed through except for Judith, so I meekly asked an official if he could find out what had happened to my fiancée, handing him my passport with thirty US dollars inside. I offered to help in any way that I could. Not even ten minutes later, Judith appeared and she was definitely not happy. She said that she had been left alone in a room with a two-way mirror, knowing that she was being watched. So while I was keen to stay in Egypt for at least two weeks, to see the pyramids and the like, Judith wanted to get out of the country as fast as possible. The situation was not improved by the fact that the hotel refused to honour

our reservations, probably having given our room to someone more important.

So there we were standing on the street outside the hotel trying to figure out what to do when we were approached by an Egyptian who spoke excellent English. He offered us a half or full day tour to the most popular tourist destinations. I asked his price, understanding that a little haggling was a normal part of business dealings in the Arab world. But the figure he gave us was so reasonable that I agreed to it right away. However, I did add a condition: that he find us a place to stay. After looking at places for nearly the whole morning - some okay, others feeling rather sinister - we finally settled on a Russian-speaking place. We had planned to leave our luggage there while we saw the sights, but we were also asked to surrender our passports, a request that made us more than a little uneasy. What if they took our belongings and papers and pretended that they had never seen us? We consulted our guide and he assured us that this was a normal practice, so we did as asked.

Over the course of the morning we came to be on very friendly terms with our guide. It turned out that he lived in Buffalo and came back to Egypt every winter to avoid the cold weather in the US northeast. Our relationship with him was really cemented when he learned that we were from Toronto. In that very winter of 1977, ploughs from Toronto had helped to clear away the snow after a huge blizzard in Buffalo. Those ploughs turned our business dealings into a friendship. He became much more enthusiastic about helping his "neighbours". As a result, we ended up keeping him as our guide through our whole time there. Just one of those sweet surprises that life offers from time to time.

Now with just half of our first day left we invited our guide to join us for lunch at a place of his choice. After eating, we planned to go to the bazaar district. That was a very appealing destination to Judith who was starting to lose her initial feelings about Egypt. In fact however, the bazaar was very ordinary and we quickly lost interest in it. Instead we chose to finish our day at the famous Cairo Museum, place to so many dazzling treasures that it would take a whole book to describe them. We arranged to meet our guide the next day to continue our adventures.

Back in our hotel we had the opportunity to get to know a bit more about Russia and Russians. And contrary to all the negative reports in the western media of that time, we found them to be very courteous and polite. After all these were Canada's northern neighbours so perhaps it wasn't so surprising that we got along well with them. They spoke no English and we no Russian, so while communication was pretty limited, we all did a lot of smiling. However as positive as our relations were with the Russian, the huge cockroaches that overran our hotel were another matter. The first night I pretended not to see them and turned the light off fast, but on the second one Judith spotted one of the ugly beasts and that pretty much ended any hope of an extended stay in Egypt. In the morning I went to TWA to arrange a flight to Athens for the next day and later, when we met up with our guide, I asked him to take us to see the Sphinx and the Great Pyramid of Giza. If time permitted we might see a little more of the area as well. Seeing the Great Pyramid had been an ambition of mine ever since I read about it in the book about Edgar Cayce, *The Sleeping Prophet*, mentioned above. It presented such a radically different view of history from what I had been taught that it gripped my imagination. To think that the Great Pyramid might have been the work of a highly advanced civilization predating the known ones by thousands of years was an extraordinary idea to me. Now of course, as Cayce's information about ancient Egypt and its predecessors came through trance channelling it was not, and probably never will be accepted by historians, but nonetheless I found his insights challenging and illuminating. It struck me that we need to teach our young people that the conventional history of the world may only be a small part of the real story.

In any event, it was with tremendous anticipation that we approached the pyramid. It was clear from the outset that going inside was not going to be a picnic. People were emerging sweating and puffing, stopping frequently to catch their breath. When our turn came to go in we were surprised by the need to bend very low at first in order to be able to access a steeply rising passageway. A wooden walkway with an easy-to-grip covering, and a rope to hold onto made the process a little safer and easier. Once inside there was no turning back as there were people both in front of and behind us. After a time we came out of the tunnel into the King's Chamber, a huge, empty chamber flawlessly constructed out of immense blocks of limestone. The surface is highly polished and appears to have been carved from a single massive piece, but as I ran my hands along the stone I was eventually able to find perfectly straight and barely detectable joins. How did the ancients manage to lift and precisely cut these huge blocks of stone, each weighing in the neighbourhood of two to twenty tons? This massive structure, visible from the moon, was designed with a degree of mathematical precision and ability to move extreme weights that is barely within the capabilities of the most modern technology. And the Great Pyramid is not only the most sophisticated of all the pyramids, but also the *oldest*. Perhaps Edgar Cayce was onto something. (For those interested in knowing more about this famous American psychic, there is a bibliography at the back of this book.) After emerging from the pyramid we spent some time admiring the Sphinx, which also had a very powerful effect on me. It appears to be guarding its surroundings, but the enigmatic look on its face also suggests that the whole area has a hidden purpose.

Early the next morning, our wonderful guide arrived at our hotel right on time to take us to the airport. After many goodbyes and promises to meet again Judith and I passed through the gate of no return, but unlike our terrible arrival experience, this time everything was civilized and easy. Once on the plane, Judith and I looked at each other in wonder at the charming flight attendants and impeccable service. After the corruption we had encountered in Egypt it was a joy to experience such a high standard of service.

Arriving in Athens we were relieved to see that the dictatorship there was of a much milder variety – almost invisible - so we were able to look forward to seeing the many attractions of Greece without worrying too much about the country's politics. We enjoyed the many monuments and amazing white marble sculptures. And in addition to the marvels of the ancient world, there were many pleasures to be found in present-day Greece as well. The food was superb and the narrow streets filled with fascinating sights and sounds. One curious fact was the presence of an improbable number of jewellery stores every place we went. Adding to our tourist experience was the ease of communication there. Pretty much everyone spoke English, a fact that is commonplace in much of the world. It struck me as curious that while people from small countries often speak three or four languages, English speakers seldom seem interested in learning other tongues.

From Athens we flew on to Rome, yet another beautiful city. At the airport, as we had done in a number of places, we made use of the tourist information office. There we were able to inquire about possible destinations and receive helpful directions. We were also helped to find a hotel that fit our budget and even to book a room. We took the bus into the centre of the city, but we still needed a taxi to travel the short distance from the bus terminal to our hotel. We knew the appropriate cost, but our taxi driver started out in the opposite direction from the hotel. I protested in my very basic Italian but he completely ignored me and took us for a long drive around Rome. I complained again, but he clearly intended to take us for a ride, quite literally. When we finally reached our destination the fare was of course outrageous, so I went into the hotel and asked for the person in charge so I could explain what had happened. Luckily the owner was there and I complained to him that people like the taxi driver were hurting Rome's image. He asked me to give him the equivalent of ten dollars, and told me that he would deal with the driver. As we took our luggage out of the car we witnessed a fierce argument between the two. I felt sorry to have been the cause of so much drama, but if the taxi driver had been prepared to do an honest day's work there would not have been a problem.

We spent the remainder of our time in the Eternal City taking tours, enjoying the great variety of food, and even socializing a little with the locals when opportunities presented themselves. All in all it was a very pleasant stay and we resolved to return some day. We also made plans to include Greece and Turkey on our next trip. So it was with some good memories that we went on to Madrid. Strange as it may seem, even though I grew up near the Spanish border and knew Spain almost better than I knew France, in all those years, I had never been to Madrid. The logistics of the flights made it necessary to fly out of Madrid in order to get to San Sebastian, which is only a few kilometres from my family home, but we wanted to spend some time in Madrid first. And we made good use of our three days there. We took things easy, enjoying leisurely walks along the many interesting streets, and making good use of the attractive shops and restaurants. We also enjoyed the many terraces, little oases that are magically created out of streets and plazas during the summer months. There we enjoyed wonderful food and music in a tranquil atmosphere. Another highlight was the Prado museum which we visited twice and barely scratched the surface of the exhibits.

But the three days had come to an end, and as much as we were enjoying our time in Madrid I was eager to see family and friends again. We flew into the small airport of Fuenterrabia very close to the Franco-Spanish border, where we were met by my dear friend Jacques. There is nothing greater than a reunion with an old and dear friend, where every single moment is treasured and the air seems to vibrate with joy. No matter what the length of the separation it is as though time has stood still: the reconnection is instantaneous and overwhelmingly powerful. This was what I experienced in seeing Jacques again. He had helped me during the first two years at Maison Basque, but had then returned to France and I had not seen him since. So we had a lot of catching up to do and made plans to spend as much time as possible together.

But of course we also had to make time for my extended family who were understandably eager to see me and meet my fiancée. Everyone had made an effort to be at home for us. (Unfortunately those present did not include my mother, father, brother and sister who were still busy working back in Canada.) While it was wonderful to be back in Saint Jean de Luz where I had grown up, one's home town is also full of memories, both good and bad. So my time there was not only one of joyous reunion but also a period of reflection on my life in every area: things savoured, things I would rather have forgotten – even meditations on my spiritual life - which as you may recall started rather uneasily with a highly conflicted relationship with the Catholic Church. I began to see that old enemies can, over time, turn into good friends. With the perspective of distance I realized that with good will and honesty nothing can ever be a failure in the long run. Sometimes a so-called failure can plant a seed that bears fruit much later, and a vital part of using the experience of adversity is the willingness to say, "I'm sorry." Not in the way that it is used in the English language, casually, indifferently, but with utter sincerity and a genuine desire to change the behaviour or make amends in some way. And finally I saw even more clearly the importance of not taking sides in life's little dramas, whether friends or family are involved. I was reminded that remaining a neutral observer - no matter what the pressure to take sides – is the best way to be of service to all concerned. Acceptance and tolerance, I vowed, would continue to be my watchwords.

CHAPTER 8

Opening My Heart to a New Vision

But of all these philosophical musings perhaps my beliefs about my spirituality, the ones I held and, for the most part, continue to hold, were of the greatest significance, for it is the search for greater significance that had played the most important role in defining me as a person. In a small town, especially in the fifties, gender equality was a long way off, and that bias infected religion as well as every other area of life. So many religions narrow the idea of God or gods to reflect outdated injustices. Why is divinity still so often portrayed as masculine when so many great sages have tried to teach us that God is all there is? The designation would seem to have more to do with culture than religion.

The culture that I grew up in was overwhelmingly Catholic, so I not only had to try to wrap my head around a masculine God, but one who was three in one – an almost completely incomprehensible concept. But the words still had to be said, understood or not: "In the name of the father, son and holy ghost," - and said endlessly. Another meaningless ritual was making the sign of the cross. This gesture was apparently suitable for almost any occasion and again I could not have begun to explain why. As a child, the most important thing was to avoid getting into trouble. I may have thought that these adult-imposed gestures were insane, but I sure wasn't going to share that thought with anyone. No, the safest thing was to follow the crowd, lie low and receive my first Communion when I was twelve. After that, as I have said, my family had given me permission to follow my own conscience where church attendance was concerned. Shortly thereafter I made the decision to be a non-believer rather than continuing to worship like an automaton. I was convinced, at least at the time, that there was no reality beyond the one I experienced with my five senses. But things turned out to be nowhere near that simple. During the course of my life since then I have had a number of wake-up calls, experiences that led me to realize that there are greater realities than mere physical ones. The first of these, as I have already described, was a near-death experience during a tonsillectomy that went terribly wrong. It was not to be the last.

But in the years before that life-changing moment I continued to wrestle with the big spiritual questions. Compared with the mindless dogma of the church, the views of atheists (my father and many of my friends were ones) were very appealing to me. Much of their thinking was very intelligent and they did a good job of debunking silly beliefs. I had much more faith in the power of reason than I did in the words of the priests. I understood what they were trying to teach us, but their approach wasn't working for me. And it wasn't that I didn't want to know God; in fact it was my most cherished wish that I would somehow become sure of his presence. I didn't even reject the teachings of Jesus whose message and example were inspiring to me. The problem was that in everyday life I couldn't see much of his spirit in action. I mostly saw people paying lip service to the gospels, not living by them. So while I agreed that the world would be a much nicer place if Jesus' teachings were more generally followed, when I was at my most pessimistic, the messiah seemed about as real to me as Santa Claus.

However over the years things gradually changed and Jesus became more and more real to me. But my influences were not primarily the mainstream church but rather the work of mystics who followed teachings that were given to them directly by spirit, not mediated by religious institutions. They taught me to see Jesus not so much as the son of God (we are all sons or daughters of the divine) but rather as an amazing big brother who loves us totally without judgement of any kind. I learned that Jesus gives completely of himself and that anyone who is open to him (and to the other great masters) can receive extraordinary gifts.

One of my mystic guides on my way to that realization was my dear friend, author of many books, and gifted musician, James Twyman. His book, *The Art of Spiritual Peacemaking* has been a great influence on me and I strongly recommend it. As a curious aside, I should also mention that Twyman has the ability to psychically bend forks and spoons. I once touched a spoon that he had just finished bending and it was blazing hot. Neale Donald Walsch, whom I have already described as an important influence has also been a mentor to James Twyman.

So gradually the cracks in my atheist armour began to grow larger. Others whose writings helped me along the way are Edgar Cayce and

Seth (channelled by Jane Roberts) as noted earlier. I was also given valuable guidance by A Course in Miracles, and the work of Louise Hay and Ruth Montgomery. In short there was an explosion of information available to me. I just had to figure out what to make of it all.

However my life was not devoted exclusively to spirituality and Judith and I returned to Canada. A few months later, in September of 1977, we were married. We had a small but beautiful wedding at the house of a dear friend, the offices performed by a non-denominational priest. This was a title that I had never encountered before but as we had friends from different religions it worked well, especially as the half-hour ceremony was not religious. In place of traditional religious texts, we used poems and other quotations from authors that served the purpose of helping us proclaim our love for each other. The dinner was exquisitely prepared with great care and artistry by my different chefs working together in perfect unison. The result was a magnificent feast which was accompanied by wines that my father and I had selected together. It was all in all a joyful and memorable day.

And as a further addition to our happiness, a dear customer and friend had given us a honeymoon gift of two nights at the beautiful Millcroft Inn, near Orangeville – a lovely gesture that would turn out to have a profound effect on my life. This friend remains a part of my life today and is now one of the owners of Langdon Hall, the wonderful country house hotel near Cambridge, Ontario. During our time at the Millcroft Inn we decided to go for a drive in the country and visit a friend, Floreal, who had once worked for us. Since that time, with my mother's help he had opened a very successful Café Patisserie called Café Flore in Elora, a beautiful village just north of Guelph. As we drove into town we saw a sign advertising a stunning stone property for sale. We drove around the block to see it from every angle, agreeing that it would sure be nice to live in such a lovely place. But putting our musings aside for the moment we went on down the street to join Floreal and his wife Rita at the café for a late lunch. In the course of our conversation I mentioned the property we had seen and Floreal said that it had been on the market for two years and there hadn't been a single offer. He added that he thought the price was too high given the work that it needed and the added expense of keeping up an old property with large grounds to maintain. I told him that I could see the place as an exquisite small inn with a nice restaurant for tourists. There would be the additional advantage of abundant local produce in the summer months. He didn't seem convinced. After lunch we said our farewells and got into the car to return to our hotel, but first I had to have one last admiring look at the wonderful stone house. And even when we were back in our room Elora remained very much in my mind.

Eventually, even though we had only been married for two days, I suggested to Judith that we consider buying the property. What if we were to come to the country, have a family and enjoy a quieter rhythm of life? She wasn't sure about it all at first, but agreed to at least investigate, so I called the agent to arrange to see the property. As we lived so far away we wondered if we should extend our stay. The extension turned out to be unnecessary as once we got see the place we both fell in love with it almost instantly. Now the burning issue was finding the money to buy it. I had only two thousand dollars in my personal account – not a great start with a one hundred and ninety five thousand dollar asking price. I had plenty of assets but little in the way of available cash. But ever the optimist, I told the agent to give me two days to work on raising the money to make an offer. Unfortunately my bank manager couldn't extend his limits and his superiors, although they trusted my reliability, couldn't get their heads around putting money into a project in the middle of the country. My last hope was my ingenious lawyers who had performed so many near-miracles in the past. And they did in fact have some ideas, but needed time to look over the paperwork and do some research first. Luckily one of them had studied in Guelph and had a good relationship with one of the local banks. The Guelph bank agreed to approve mortgages on the property. I was getting closer, but I didn't have enough for an adequate down payment until my mother and brother came to the rescue. Still and all, the absolute maximum that I would be able to offer on the property was one hundred and fifty-five thousand – forty thousand short.

I called the agent and gave him the news, holding out little hope that such a small amount would be accepted. Nevertheless he said he would present the offer and get back to me within forty-eight hours. But many days went by without a call and I was beginning to let go of my dream. In fact it was a full month before I received a call from him asking if we were still serious about our house. I assured him that we were and he told me that the owners had had a major argument, one agreeing to our price, the other not. But the fact was that it was the only offer they had received in two years, so they eventually agreed to accept it, even though I attached a condition concerning municipal permission to build a small inn. After reconfirming that all my financing was in place we signed on the dotted line. I continued to trust in my initial vision for the place and fully intended to bring it to life.

But first I had to win over the people who I hoped would soon be my neighbours. I paid many visits and talked to a great number of nearby residents, but despite my efforts opposition to my project was starting to gain momentum. Sadly it is a fact of life that in small villages like Elora there is a tendency towards extreme conservatism. For those who hold such opinions the best change is no change at all. While they may fly in the face of modern world reality it can't be denied that such views exist. At least I certainly couldn't ignore these beliefs as it quickly became apparent that I wasn't going to get the needed planning permission. But I wasn't too discouraged. We were still making a good living in Toronto so we decided to buy the place anyway and put our dream of building an inn aside for the time being. Instead of running a business there, we would use the place in Elora as a country retreat. It would be our Muskoka or Lake Simcoe. After all, it was and remains an extremely picturesque community set in the heart of the countryside. Not surprisingly then, there are many farmers' markets close by, each offering a rich supply of the wonderful produce so dear to my heart.

Still, our life in Toronto remained as happy and congenial as before, but we now needed a place to live. As luck would have it two old houses went up for sale next to my mother's place. We bought and renovated them combining them into a single house so we would have room for a family. And indeed fortune smiled on us and gave a beautiful baby boy, Olivier, to bring even more joy and delight into our lives. It seemed that our blessings would be endless. But life being what it is clouds had begun to gather.

At first we had the sense that something wasn't quite right with my mother, but she wasn't one for doctors, so we didn't push her to seek help. As time went by however, it became clear that her health was failing so I insisted that she let me take her to see our family physician, the one who had delivered Olivier. After the examination, my mother was referred to the Women's College Hospital to see a specialist - who turned out to be the surgeon who had operated on me when I had appendicitis. When he had finished with my mother the doctor took me out for a private chat. I could tell from his face that the situation was grave, and my worst fears were confirmed when the diagnosis turned out to be advanced colon cancer. And as my mother's English was limited and the doctor spoke little French, he asked me to translate his words for my mother. She took the news courageously, and we talked about the coming treatment and even spoke somewhat optimistically about the possibility of her recovery.

My next task was to break the news to the rest of the family, all of whom were anxious for news. We gathered at my mother's house, and once I had brought everyone up to date we tried to be as optimistic as we could about her condition, doing our best to minimize our fears. But the masks were quickly dropped in the phone calls that I received afterwards. My brother and sister quickly made it obvious that they held out little hope for our mother's recovery. They seemed to feel that I hadn't told them the whole truth. I couldn't convince them that I had simply repeated the doctor's words - no more and no less. And yes it was hurtful to have my integrity questioned in such a way, but Judith somewhat minimized the impact of their words by suggesting that my siblings were likely just speaking out of fear, not sure what to believe themselves. But my thankless job as bearer of ill tidings was not over yet. By this time my father had returned to France so I had to break the news to him over the phone. He didn't sound as though he was reacting much one way or the other, but most of us struggle to find words in such situations so I didn't attach too much meaning to his seeming lack of response. Often it is only much later that we think of those loving and comforting words that have eluded us in the moment.

That night I was reflecting on the abilities of Edgar Cayce and thinking how wonderful and helpful it would be to know someone who possessed such gifts. If I knew such a person I would be able to ask if my mother was going to survive, and if so, would she have to deal with a colostomy bag, something she dreaded more than the surgery itself. And those questions would be just the beginning; I would have many more about life and its many mysteries. And while I didn't expect a Cayce-like figure to magically materialize on the spot, life had taught me that God hears and answers such cries of the heart, that prayers are answered. I had too much experience of such grace to doubt it.

So two days later, I was surprised and not surprised by an ad in a magazine on display in my local health food store. I often went there to buy the almond paste and whole meal raisin bread that I enjoyed having with my breakfast. But this time, quite uncharacteristically, I picked up a magazine from the display rack and began to leaf through it. Right on the inside cover was an ad for "psychic readings" given by a woman named Doreen Bennett. I later learned that it was the first time that she had ever bought advertising space. Naturally I bought the magazine along with my other items and as soon as I returned home phoned and set up an appointment with Doreen the next day.

What followed was pure bliss. I went at the appointed time and met what turned out to be two very nice ladies. After the usual pleasantries we got right down to business. Of course my first questions were about my mother's surgery and I was told that she was going to be fine, and that there would be no need for the dreaded colostomy bag. Further, it was important that my mother stop working so hard and learn to relax. It was time for her to enjoy the fruits of all her years of hard work. I was also given a suggested diet for my mother that would help her to recuperate and quickly regain her strength. (Thankfully, all of the information about my mother's condition later turned out to be spot on.) And since the reading was an hour long I was able to ask a number of questions about my own life as well. The answers resonated with me immediately and I had no doubt that they were true. I left the two gifted women with a promise to set up another appointment and return with more questions.

Doreen and I quickly became friends and have remained so to this day. In fact, a few years later I began working with her. She does her readings, like Cayce, in a trance state and my job was to induce the trance, make sure that all was well during the reading, and then bring her safely out of the trance. Doreen, now in her eighties, is still very vigorous and from time to time we still do readings together. But the most important gift that I received from Doreen was being forced to accept the existence of larger realities than those of the senses. I had long resisted the possibility that such things were possible but now I felt that I had no choice. Inspired by this experience I began my search for the elusive God, with a greatly enlarged perspective. At the time my understanding was still very limited and many things didn't make sense, but the journey was now underway.

Like so many others before me I began to tackle the age-old questions. My first big hurdle was trying to understand the esoteric meaning of good and evil. I once asked in a reading why there was evil. How could a God of Love permit the many iniquities of the human race? The answer that I received was simple and direct. I was told that free will is the prime medium through which we experience life, and that every choice had consequences. When I wondered about how to be a decent human being, one who desires to know God, I was given the instruction to make a "light" of myself.

When I sought clarification the presence replied that if, "… I am but a small light unto the darkness there can be no such thing as total darkness." I found this concept difficult to grasp as well, but years later in Australia I had a powerful experience that made the meaning of the words crystal clear. I will come to this story shortly.

Good and evil have always been part of human history. The Judeo-Christian tradition teaches that evil originated with the fall of Adam, and other traditions have similar stories. When I first read *Conversations with God* I was very taken with Neale Donald Walsch's position that there was no such thing as the Devil and his views reminded me of the debates that had taken place in my parents' home years before. On one side were the atheists, on the other the religious - and wonderful discussions they were, ranging across all the important issues. Concerning the Devil: if God is all-knowing why would he allow an entity with powers as great as his own to compete for his kingdom and the souls of humanity? Surely, such a blunder tells us that God must then not only be imperfect but lacking absolute knowledge as well. The pious would respond to this irreverence by arguing that God gives human beings free will and this means that the outcome of life's journey can't be known in advance. Evil is always one of the options. The sceptics would have none of this, insisting that our imperfect world demonstrates that God can't possibly be perfect in the way that religion claims. Then would come the clincher. The non-believers would point to the excesses of the Old Testament and joke that a rebellion against such a crazy and paranoid God was inevitable. They applauded Lucifer for his courage. "Who needs a God like that?" they would ask.

The gap between the two belief systems was unbridgeable, as both sides were entrenched in their respective positions. But there were never hard feelings and the interchanges were always amiable ones, usually punctuated with much laughter. The main purpose of the gatherings was after all social, and if discussions of religion or politics got a little too heated the subject would be quickly changed to something less controversial. Each of these old friends was capable of great kindness and each brought something very special to our table. I loved and respected them all.

When I look back on those days, it seems to me that in some ways the kitchen table discussions were a microcosm of the world, and remembering those conversations makes me wonder why we can't have an idea of God that unites the planet rather than dividing it. All religions and even humanistic systems seem to share core ethical messages so it should be possible to find common ground that will benefit the whole. But all too often religions seem to forget their similarities and focus instead on their differences. Many believers, of whatever stripe, too readily fall into the pattern of condemning those who do not share their views. Old myths of punishment and sin get translated, even in the modern world, into dangerous intolerance that frequently turns into violence. And ideas of divine judgement can drive even the faithful to torments of self-doubt, even self-loathing. Even the revered Mother Theresa suffered in this way.

But in my case at least, my previous atheism had led me to lose the fear of God that had informed so much of my Catholic upbringing. That particular lack was an enormous advantage as I continued on my quest for greater spiritual understanding. I was free to pursue the direct experience of divine love unhampered by dogma that give lip service to Love, but in reality demonstrate anything but. I had no intention of living my life in thrall to some terrible unseen force, or of holding any belief that separated me from the rest of humanity. I needed to find a God who united us all, who was oneness itself.

Around this time I encountered another wonderful book that proved enormously helpful. It was called *The Law of Attraction*. The authors were Jerry and Esther Hicks and it served to reinforce and extend the ideas that I was struggling to give shape to. It speaks of a generous and loving God, one who wants us to enjoy happiness and fulfillment. It teaches that much of what we experience is within our control and that we are co-creators of our own lives. So what you think becomes extremely important as your thoughts help to shape what you experience. I found these ideas to be extremely liberating.

Well, where has all this ferment led to at this stage in my life? Now I can say truthfully that I believe in God, and very much so, but not in a way that has a lot to do with formal religion. I have, very slowly, and only *experientially* found a way to live my own particular "God reality," my expression of the particular aspect of God that is Roger Dufau. I have come to the view that once we find a way to God that we truly begin to flourish as human beings. How we get there doesn't matter, only that we do. And if we simply can't, no matter how hard we try, we can at least strive to find common ground with others in searching for much-needed solutions to the world's many problems and inequities.

In fact, in his recent book, *Happier Than God: Turn Ordinary Life into an Extraordinary Experience*, Neale Donald Walsch argues convincingly that we don't need God. While on the surface the idea seems blasphemous, in reality it is anything but. He writes that whether we believe in God or not, because the whole that is God is one and indivisible, it is impossible for anyone to be separate from God. However if you consciously draw on God's power and use the gifts that God so freely offers us, you can live a life that is infinitely rich and fulfilling, one that offers limitless opportunities. Even modern science confirms at least part of this view: one definition of quantum physics is that it puts forward the idea that all possibilities exist at once. So why not choose the path that makes your soul sing?

Of course we use the Source of all things on a constant basis in co-creating the lives that we lead, but can we always be sure that our choices are in harmony with the whole? In my view, we are most likely to achieve that harmony if some notion of the divine comes into our reasoning. Once again I turn to *Conversations*, where Walsch references the New Testament (Mathew 28:20): "And surely I am with you always to the very end of the age." When I first read this familiar, comforting quotation in Neale's book its meaning struck me with great force – more so than ever before. It dawned on me in that moment that nothing can be separate from God and that therefore all things are manifestations of divinity. What we see and experience as life is God manifested as physical reality. Further, if we can, like the poet William Blake, ("Auguries of Innocence") "...see a world in a grain of sand," we may also be able to know ourselves as microcosms of the divine. If God is absolute love, perhaps we can see something of that in ourselves. It may also be true that the closer we come to that ideal, that Source of all creation, the more effective and powerful we can be in our lives. To me, this is the true meaning of our being made in God's image, of trying to live the psalmist's (82:6) words, "Ye are all Gods." Sadly, while some version of this teaching is present in almost every religion its wisdom seems to have been observed more in word than deed.

Another important biblical teaching (Matthew 7:7) that seems to have fallen on deaf ears is, "Ask and it shall be given you; seek, and ye shall find; knock and it shall be opened to you." Now this is admittedly a difficult concept to accept as, religion aside, we live in a world which is not much given to trust – in God, or anything else for that matter. Nevertheless, when I look back over my own life, those ancient words of wisdom make perfect sense to me. When my desires were motivated not only by my own needs, but also by concern for others, sooner or later, they were realized. I have learned that consciously or not, we create our lives by the choices that we make and the beliefs that we hold. I have been able to exercise my free will, but more than success, I have always chosen love to be my guide. And interestingly, my life has been blessed with great abundance.

I have always wished that the world as a whole were also able to trust in a loving creator. Instead what we see in the news is perverted religion, tyrannical rulers, exploitative corporations, and divisions of all kinds keeping humanity in a constant state of war with itself. And as I noted above, some of my earliest spiritual questions were about good and evil. But when I find humanity's failings overwhelming, I turn, as I have mentioned repeatedly, for clarity and wisdom to the words of Neale Donald Walsch. In the second book of the series, *Conversations with God, Book 2: An Uncommon Dialogue*, Walsch states (page 49):

> "All events, all experiences, have as their purpose the creating of opportunity. Events and experiences are Opportunities. Nothing more, nothing less.
>
> It would be a mistake to judge them as 'works of the devil,' 'punishments from God,' 'rewards from Heaven,' or anything in between. They are simply Events and Experiences – things that happen.
>
> It is what we *think* of them, *do* about them, *be* in response to them, that gives them meaning.
>
> Events and experiences are opportunities drawn to you – created *by* you individually or collectively, through consciousness. Consciousness creates experience. You are attempting to raise your consciousness. You have drawn these opportunities to you in order that you might use them as tools in the creation and experiencing of Who You Are."

Neale's words have always kept me centred when facing the crises that life seems to provide on a regular basis. Whatever happens, I try to take responsibility for it and learn what I can from the experience.

And I have heard some of the core elements in the *Conversations* books echoed in the words of others as well. In the course of my life I have had a number of opportunities to hear very gifted channelers: psychics who speak from a place of deep inspiration. Perhaps in another time the best of them would have been called prophets, a word much abused in the modern world. What has always struck me most about such people is that the information they convey is remarkably similar in content, never insulting to one's intelligence and it always appeals to the very best in us. Of course the messages are influenced by the speaker's personal history, culture and so forth, but they are almost always presented as gifts to do with as we choose, not dogmatic instructions to be followed no matter what. I wish that more of this spirit of open-minded exploration was present in mainstream religions; the strict

Catholicism of my childhood accepted no truth but its own. In fact a healthy curiosity about other faith traditions could result in excommunication from the church. It was this rigidity that drove many of my friends to prefer humanism or science to such tyranny of thought. It also led to more extreme views.

In the forties and fifties when I was growing up, many of the socially conscious people of France were searching for an alternative to the iron grip of the Catholic Church and found it in Communism. At that time the world was largely unaware of Stalinist atrocities and the economically liberating ideas of Marx and Lenin held great appeal. When I was in my teens, one third of French voters supported the Party.[1] So you can well imagine that I had many Communist friends, and I couldn't help but agree with their liberal views on medical care and education. But my personal interest in the Party completely disappeared after the Soviet rape of Hungary in 1956. Ironically the rule of Soviet Russia turned out to be dramatically worse than the strictures of the Catholic Church. For this and many other reasons my life would be focused much more on my spiritual journey than on the battlefield of politics.

And so it has remained. Without pretending to be an expert of any kind, I would like to share a few more of my "discoveries" on the road to peace. I have found that if you can minimize the "noise" of the ego (there are many spiritual paths to this state) you become ready to embrace any experience, to greet even difficult events with acceptance, instead of denial or anger. You also open yourself up to a kind of knowledge that is eternal and free of illusions. The belief that death is to be feared is washed away, along with many other false notions. And in the process you will find that your mind has become sharper, more focused, and also that you have developed an *inner* moral guide, one that makes it much more difficult to consider unethical or negative behaviour. Now the focus of your life has become, as the *Conversations* passage above advises, to simply know and experience being. And as Walsch point out in the same work, your realizing this state of being is how you can come to fully experience your God nature. Just some thoughts. I hope you find them helpful.

And if you will bear with me a moment longer, I would like to see the parameters of mainstream science expanded to include serious

---

[1] In fact communists were members of three different government coalitions - in the forties, eighties, and from 1997-2002. After a very poor showing in the 2007 election they joined with the Greens and other left-wing politicians to form the Democratic and Republican Left.

research into what is now ghettoized as parapsychology, or religion. Do such things as telepathy and psychic healing have solid foundations in energies that we do not yet understand? Is there a whole aspect to human experience that we ignore at our peril? What if there are possibilities for medical cures that can embrace wisdoms ancient and modern? Perhaps if we could even begin such a process young people might become slightly less cynical about the older generation. They might begin to consider the possibility their elders may be willing to abandon the practices that have left humans alienated from nature and from each other. Such are my thoughts on the state of things, both spiritual and material. I will now return to my narrative with tales of wonder from Tasmania to Elora.

But first back to Toronto where my siblings and I were telling our mother that it was time to relax and enjoy life without the need to make a living. She had worked hard all her life and now it was time to retire to France. My brother and sister and I would make sure that she had enough money to secure her future. But before she left I took over Le Petit Gourmet until we could sell it. It was good to go back in time, to again be involved in the place that had first made our name. And there was also the pleasure of interacting with my mother's loyal customers, all of them keen to know about her health. When I told them about her decision to retire they were extremely supportive - even though they would sorely miss her - and wished her a happy life. To see such affection for my mother and witness first-hand the impact that she had had on so many people was extremely humbling, a real display of the power of love in action.

And when it came to the sale of the Le Petit Gourmet, fortune smiled on us. Hubert, a Swiss national and one of the chefs at our Yonge and Eglinton location expressed interest in buying the business. He was highly skilled, very personable, and a very hard worker. In addition, a recent inheritance had provided him with the funds to make the purchase without any need for our assistance. He ended up bringing an even greater measure of conviviality and good cheer to the place and the regular customers were delighted with him. I was finally able to turn my full attention to Maison Basque again.

And the first thing that I had to do there was to deal with an unexpected crisis. One Sunday, when we were closed, a pipe broke in The Grill Basque, our upstairs dining room, and ended up flooding the one downstairs. So on the Monday morning when the mess was first discovered, I had to cancel many reservations before I could even begin to organize the clean-up. But the setback made me think about creating a new menu for the downstairs. My idea was to keep the offerings in The Grill Basque just as they were to keep our regulars happy, and to introduce a new menu downstairs. Unfortunately I made the mistake of not announcing my experiment, naively believing that my regular customers would trust me enough to try something different. I was wrong. So while the Grill was normally full with many waiting for tables, the new menu was available in a room that was largely empty. I decided to gradually break down resistance by inviting those who were waiting to instead come downstairs and try the new menu. Initially, only a few adventurous patrons responded, with the majority preferring to continue waiting, but over time the word went out that the more challenging menu was worth trying, and eventually both dining rooms were working at full capacity. I was relieved to see that I hadn't lost my touch and I further encouraged customer loyalty by continuing my usual policy of not only charging very fair prices, but also promising to redo or refund the cost of any item that hadn't satisfied the customer.

One evening this latter policy led to a very challenging experience when a customer pushed my patience and customer satisfaction policy to the limit. I was trying to process a large number of orders when my Maitre D., Hugo, returned a veal chop that a diner had found lacking. I replaced it without argument though I could see nothing wrong with the original one. A short time later Hugo returned with the second chop - also apparently deficient in some mysterious way. I asked Hugo if he thought the guy was playing some kind of game but with misgivings I sent out yet a third chop, hoping that it would pass the test. Again Hugo returned with the unsurprising news that the third chop was also unsatisfactory. By now the rhythm of our work was being thrown off and I was starting to get angry. The way my staff was looking at me I could tell that they were wondering if I was going to blow up. I didn't, but instead consulted my Inner Self which instantly advised me: "Go and ask the customer to show you how to do his chop. Tell him that you are always eager to learn new things." I smiled at the brilliance of the advice. Then I put on a brand new apron to look smart, picked up the veal chop and went out to where he was sitting. All eyes were now focused on the two of us, and since I was smiling and apparently not upset at all, the dining room began to fill with laughter. As I had been directed, I told him that I would be grateful if he would join me in the kitchen so that I could learn how to cook a veal chop properly. From the look on his face it was clear that he was hoping the earth would swallow him, but that having failed he decided to keep the third chop. And strangely, when he had finished his meal he insisted on buying me a drink after which (according to Hugo), he went home happy. The whole episode was a source of great relief and considerable amusement to the staff. Hugo was asked to tell the story to a number of our regulars who enjoyed it as much as we did – especially the ending. It became one of those anecdotes that gets told over and over again – and always to much laughter.

Well spring comes eventually – even in the restaurant business – and in June of that year my brother-in-law came from Australia to visit us. We took him around Toronto and also to Elora. The weather was pleasantly warm and the surrounding countryside was lush with green pastures and an explosion of flowers. The trees too were at their best, seeming particularly majestic. It all reminded him of his native England. For us, this was an opportunity to repay the extraordinary kindness that he had shown us on our visit to Tasmania. Jeffrey was great company and it was a sad day when the time came for him to return home.

With the coming of summer I received an offer for my Maison Basque site from The Cadillac Fairview Group which was planning a development - but the amount on the table was so low as to be insulting. Considering that I first had to buy the building and even though the price, originally negotiated back in the seventies, was very low, with the figure the developers were proposing I would not have been left with even enough money to build a new restaurant. With great effort I managed to bite my tongue and simply told the representative that the property was not for sale. However I added that if I were ever to change my mind I would need to see a much higher offer, one that included the provision of a place in the new building for my business. I also insisted that I occupy the space rent-free, simply sharing common expenses. I heard nothing more from them and pretty much forgot about it – especially as we were looking forward to a vacation in my old hometown, St. Jean de Luz.

We had a joyful visit, staying in my mother's house. My mother had adapted well to retirement and her joy in life was very gratifying to see. And of course my mother being my mother there were many wonderful meals with friends and family – including on a number of occasions, my very dear friend Jacques. Another great pleasure was the town's wonderful beach which our son Olivier was now old enough to enjoy. And in the time honoured way, he was also extremely happy to be spoiled by his grandmother on every possible occasion, a fact which gave us a bit of freedom to socialize. We were thus able to spend time with Judith's sister Jennifer and her partner Stroud who had come from

A Fun Evening: My mother, me, Olivier and Judith in
St. Jean de Luz. (1981)

England to see us. There were also many visits from my mother's large extended family. It was a happy time indeed, but one that would be interrupted tragedy.

Continuing on our trip, we had left France and were staying in England for a few days prior to returning to Canada when we received news that my father had been in a terrible accident. There had been a huge explosion on his fishing boat and he had been thrown unconscious into the sea. But that was not to be the end of the story. A short distance away, a small team of divers was about to enter the ocean. They quickly swam to where he was and found him floating under water. In a very short period of time, they were able to find him under water, quickly bring him to the surface and begin resuscitation efforts. They managed to restart his breathing, but he was unconscious. A further blessing was the nearby presence of a Coast Guard helicopter - close enough to pick him up within a few minutes and whisk him to a major hospital in Bayonne. There, a team of doctors managed to bring him out of his coma and were then able to begin treating a variety of serious injuries, including broken bones, the effect of shock from his near-drowning, and very deep bruising all over his body. He had to endure five months of hospitalization and then a full year of physiotherapy before he was once again able to walk. I thanked God for the miracle of seeing my father alive, and for all the extraordinary events that had made his survival possible. But of course my father being an atheist called it luck.

Once he was well on the road to recovery we returned to Canada and resumed our normal lives. It had been several months since I had given any thought to Cadillac Fairview when they suddenly reappeared. This time I was to sit down with the boss of the whole operation, Mr. Daniels. Our meeting had been preceded by some preliminary talks in which I had made clear that my position had not changed - despite apparent rumours that I was upping my demands. In any event Mr. Daniels came back with an offer that matched what I had asked for but it came accompanied by a prospective lease agreement that was almost an inch thick! He told me that in the interval before work started, my rent would be triple what I had been paying to the original owner. I smiled at Mr. Daniels and refused to even look at his "book". I simply stated that if I agreed to the sale, I would continue to honour the terms of my longstanding lease until the building was demolished (a proviso that turned out very well for me). But I did ask for an extension of six months before they started to raze the place, as I had promised to help my staff find work. Everything was agreed to and even though it took nine years before the development got under way, no one ever asked me to pay more rent - this despite the fact that it was an old price negotiated years before.

CHAPTER 9

Risky Swimming in Sydney, Australia

B ut life wasn't through with us yet. In 1982, only a few days after signing my restaurant away we received sad news concerning my brother-in-law in Australia. He had been suffering from terrible headaches and his doctor ordered tests for him. The result was the discovery of a deadly cancer of the pituitary gland in the middle of the brain. At that time surgery for the condition was impossible and the diagnosis was effectively a death sentence. Depending on the speed of the tumour's growth he was given a life expectancy of one to two years. We wanted to help in some way and given the distance involved we decided that the best thing to do would be to move to Tasmania for an extended period. A tourist visa would not have given us enough time there so we chose to apply to immigrate instead. As luck would have it I had excellent contacts with the Australian Chamber of Commerce as Maison Basque was the first Canadian restaurant to serve Australian wines - a fact also known to the Australian Consul. He also knew my restaurant well and had asked me to cater for many events held by the Consulate. In fact he had even asked me on a number of occasions to consider going to Australia to open a restaurant in one of their major cities. In light of all the above I was optimistic when I made an appointment to meet with him at the Consulate.

And while I was well received, my desire to secure a visa for family reasons was not sufficient grounds for one to be issued. But he knew that I had considerable cash in hand from the sale of my building and suggested that visa permission would be much easier for him to obtain if I were to take some of that money with me. I agreed that the amount involved was completely reasonable and said that we had been planning to take nearly the suggested sum in any case. However, when I mentioned that we were planning to move to Hobart he was greatly amused and joked that almost any other city would be a better choice. Nonetheless he approved the applications and they were processed over the next two months. It took an additional two months to get our affairs in order before we were ready to go and during this time Judith's brother, Jeffrey, succumbed to his illness.

We could have cancelled the move but decided that Mona and her young children would be happy to have us around to aid in whatever way we could. But I must say that my first choice of an Australian city would have been Sydney. When we travelled to Australia in 1981, I not only fell in love with Sydney itself - and especially with its vibrant Paddington area - but also with the magnificent Bondi beach nearby. The surfing there was even better than that of Biarritz in my native France. But that said the decision to locate in Hobart turned out to be right in more than one way. Our help to Jeffrey's family was certainly welcome and I was astonished to find that the business climate in Hobart was vastly more welcoming than I could have possibly imagined. The restaurant that I opened there was an instant success, much more so than any business that I had opened before.

And after all Sydney was only a two-hour flight away and we were to have many happy occasions there visiting with Canadian friends Bill and Griff. In fact even on our way to Hobart we stopped off to see them, a visit that almost ended in tragedy. On the second day of our visit we went to Tamarama Beach, not far from Bondi Beach itself. After our swim we were to visit the home of friends of Bill and Griff who lived nearby. Tamarama Beach was a great favourite of surfers and body surfing is considered a must there. The beauty of the perfect clear day filled me with awe and I wasn't at all dismayed by the rough sea. After all I was an experienced surfer and there seemed to be many others who were willing to cope with the challenging conditions. What I didn't know was that the beach had been closed all morning but since it was Sunday the lifeguards had relented and reopened the beach so that people could enjoy their day off. The reason for the closing had to do with the presence of particularly dangerous currents, something that can't be readily seen. What I could have noticed however, was the fact that few were daring to try the huge waves, choosing instead to remain on shore. But I was so eager to body surf in this lovely warm water (unlike Tasmania) that I was all but blind to the conditions. Judith was not a swimmer and Griff and Bill wisely stayed on shore as well.

But I the foolhardy one plunged in, and I did have a good hour of fun even though at times I had to struggle to keep up with the strong and wonderfully skilled Aussie surfers and body surfers. When I began to tire I decided to call it a day and it was only then that I realized that I was quite a distance from the shore. The current had already taken me behind the first set of breaking waves and while the next was some distance away and breaking up before it reached me, it was still producing significant turbulence. At first I tried to use the momentum of the water to move myself closer to shore, but I found that I was just being moved up and down. So I began ducking under before the impact - which was somewhat less tiring. The beach was in the shape of a horseshoe with only the top portion being sandy. The sides were rocky but the only part that I had any hope of reaching. I tried zigzagging to work with the current but when this got me nowhere I decided to swim straight across, choosing the weaker or first three of a seven wave pattern to make my move. But despite my efforts I had gotten nowhere and I was becoming dangerously tired - now simply doing my utmost to stay afloat. I tried waving to signal my distress, but no one saw me and with the noise of the surf, calling out would have been equally futile. It was a beautiful sunny day and I could see the people on shore having fun. How strange it would be if I were to join my late brother-in-law on the other side on only my second day in the country when I had come here to help his family. Not to mention that I had family responsibilities of my own as well. But as crazy as it seemed death was becoming an imminent possibility. There seemed to be nothing that I could do to help myself, except pray.

And that's exactly what I did. I prayed to God from my very heart, saying that I didn't think that it was yet my time and asking for His help in getting me out of the situation. And miraculously, within a very short time a surfer passed close by me and I waved to him and screamed for help, hoping that he would hear me and summon a life guard. And within minutes a huge guy came up to me on a long red surf board and asked, "Mate, are you okay?" I told him, "No," that I was dead tired. Before I knew it I was lying on the edge of the board and being swept towards the beach on a big wave. Seconds later he dumped me near the beach. I turned to thank him but he had already taken off backwards as fast as he had come in order to rescue someone else. (I didn't even have a chance to see his face and was unable to find him later.) I tried to walk to shore, barely able to fight the very weak current, but even that challenge was too much so I just floated for a bit while I recovered enough strength to stand up again. Finally I floated close enough to shore that I was able to crawl to where the water was shallow enough for me to lie down. I was so utterly exhausted that I almost fell asleep. Never in my life had I experienced such weakness in my body. I don't know how long I stayed like that but I remained there until my friend Bill discovered me some time later.

He had been looking for me all over the beach, and was both relieved and alarmed when he found me in such poor shape. I asked him to wait a while and then say as little as possible to Judith about what had happened. Griff had remained with her and two year-old Olivier who, unaware of the unfolding drama, continued to play happily in the sand. I had received a wake-up call about the fragility of life and I thanked God for my survival. I promised to be much more careful in this new country with its beautiful but treacherous beaches - especially as I had a young son to think about. When I was finally reunited with Judith I minimized the danger that I had been in so as not to create fear for the future. She was understandably upset by my three-hour absence and I couldn't help but feel that her anger was fully justified. Unfortunately, the day's drama had caused us to miss our scheduled lunch and to be truthful it had entirely escaped my mind. But luckily my apologies were accepted and the incident gradually faded into the background for everyone except me.

I was left to quietly ponder whether what seemed like divine intervention was just good luck. Back in the comfort and security of a strong, healthy body my mind was gradually erasing the more frightening aspects of my experience. The need for a belief in God began to seem more remote as life resumed its normal pace and the question of the larger significance of my near-drowning would have to be dealt with at a later date. In fact I was to be given another opportunity to consider these matters in the future and discovered for myself the truth that God never gives up on us; like a good parent he loves us unconditionally and will always help us if we ask. So it was repeated experiences rather than clever arguments that led me to my present view that not only is God as real as life itself, but that he allows us free will *without judgement* to make of ourselves and our lives whatever we choose. In Neale Donald Walsch's book *Communion with God* he explains that God is all there is, and that divinity doesn't work against itself. At the level of the individual, I interpret this idea to mean that if we choose to consciously align our lives with God-consciousness we sign on to a life that demands of us uncompromising ethics, and a love that envelops everyone and everything. Such lives are the fullest possible and looking back I can see that I always tried to glorify life in these ways even though there were times when such optimism seemed futile and out of place. But interestingly enough, recent research has shown that societies coming closest to such principles have the lowest levels of mental illness and crime. Clearly, whatever it is called, the God-centred life *works* and it is this fact that makes me optimistic about the future. It is my belief that a world based on harmony and love is inevitable and is in fact very gradually coming into being – admittedly not likely in my lifetime but inevitable nonetheless.

On our arrival in Tasmania we stayed for a short time with my sister-in-law and in the process were immediately adopted by her circle of friends. One couple even gave us the use of their beautiful house while they were away for a month. They had a son the same age as Olivier and the two boys took to each other right away. They wanted to be together as much as possible - a situation, that on the family's return, brought us all very close together. And now that we were getting settled in I could turn my attention to business again. In return for being granted immigration visas, I had made a commitment to the Australian authorities to set up a café bakery and pastry shop. I was doing this rather than opening a full restaurant as I had promised Judith that we would have time for a normal family life without the pressure of the need to work crazy hours – inevitable with any restaurant. We also needed to think about where we were going to live so as we were going to stay for a year or two it made sense to buy a home. We had brought enough funds with us to buy a small building for the business and a house as well. In those days of very reasonable prices we were also able to have some basic renovations done. How different from the present situation where people of ordinary means are gradually being priced out of almost every major city. In many places, the widening disparity in incomes is becoming a source of social unrest. So while I believe that a more equitable and spiritual way of life is coming, I certainly can't claim that it's already here.

In the Australia of those days however I had to contend with too many laws benefiting the worker, rather than too few. These regulations were so extreme as to be a real hindrance to business. As an example, every employee was entitled to five weeks of paid holidays plus an additional twelve days of public holidays. Added to these generous amounts was an additional two weeks of sick leave that the employee was paid for whether he or she was ever sick or not. And as if these benefits were not enough, the food industry with its very early starts was further penalized in many cases by having to pay double time for any hours worked before say eight o'clock am. The root of the problem lay in the fact that legislators had not made any distinction between food services and factory work. In North America it was only where powerful unions monopolized key industries that employees enjoyed conditions even approaching the ones to which every single Australian worker was entitled by law. I found all these laws to be quite oppressive but I respected them nonetheless. However as I wasn't about to charge varying amounts on different days or even at different times of day to compensate for so-called "overtime" I decided to work five days a week like the locals and enjoy the weekend like everybody else. Oh I might have led the charge against laws that discriminated against my industry but since I wasn't planning to be in the country for very long there seemed to be little or no point in becoming a crusader. But one problem that I couldn't ignore was my family's tradition of fair pricing for our services. It was a great strain to absorb all these unnecessary costs and still keep our prices at a reasonable level.

Opening of La Cuisine in Hobart, Tasmania. (1982)

Australia has changed enormously since those years, mostly as those overly protective practices made the country's industries uncompetitive in world markets. The result was a drop in the value of the Australian dollar. The whole problem was the product of intense labour conflict in the 1960's and an entrenched us versus them mentality. The unfortunate effect of this dysfunction was the unnecessary bankruptcy of many companies. Since then the laws have been changed to end the imbalance in labour relations, but the Australian story is yet another example of what happens when there is a lack of fairness in the way that a business is operated. More often the balance is tilted towards management and shareholders, but in the situation I have described, the opposite was true – a fact which may lead the reader to ask if fairness in the workplace is a hopeless fantasy or whether it can sometimes be possible. Well I can in fact provide some examples. The Mondragon Corporation, based in the Basque region of Spain, is a federation of worker cooperatives which at the end of 2008 was employing 92,773 people working in 256 companies in the areas of finance, industry, retail and knowledge.[2] In Canada alone there are 135 co-ops employing 200,000 people[3], so fairness and respect in the workplace are not impossible at all – just not as widely practised as one might like.

But whatever the laws of the time, Hobart was now my home so I needed to focus on making my new venture successful. My idea was to use the same principles that had made Le Petit Gourmet do so well. I would make a number of our classics available to my new clientele and I also planned to devote half my space to a restaurant which would open only for lunch. As I checked out the local suppliers I quickly realized that the local breads were very ordinary – unlike the rich variety available in Toronto – so I decided to also open a bakery with just a few good products available. I didn't want it to be so large that it distracted us from our primary purpose. But before I could put any of these plans into action, I first had to find contractors to prepare the space to suit my needs. Fortunately as my late brother-in-law had been an architect I had ready access to contacts in the building trades. I was introduced to a small private contractor of German origin who came highly recommended and quickly lived up to his reputation. Further aiding the process was the ready cooperation of the Hobart City Council and their inspectors. I threw myself enthusiastically into the renovations as I had lots of experience in this area and I knew exactly what I needed to make things functional. And while the construction work was in progress I had plenty of time to scout the local produce suppliers and was delighted with the variety and quality of what was available – especially where seafood was concerned. To give you an idea of the cost and availability of fish products were in the early eighties, here are some examples: scallops, already shucked, were extremely plentiful and sold for three to four dollars a kilo or just over two pounds. Orange roughy

---

[2] Wikipedia
[3] Canadian Worker Co-op Federation web site

and trevalla, both deep sea fish with their white flesh and nice texture, were about the same price and offered the additional advantage of being easy to prepare in a variety of delicious ways. Langouste, known as Florida lobster in the U.S., was just over five dollars a kilo – and that price include cooking in sea water if you wished. They were also available alive. And that list is by no means a complete one. Plenty of other varieties including stripy trumpeter, tuna, and flat head, while slightly less abundant were also available at similar low prices. And some of what was on offer was downright cheap. These latter included abalone, conch and sea urchin. Having grown up in a fishing port, I was in heaven being able to prepare these wonderfully fresh and delicious fruits of the sea. (Sadly, I must add that on a recent visit to Tasmania I learned that there too the plague of over fishing has decimated once-abundant marine life.)

But at the time that I opened my first business - a café,-bakery-pastry shop - we had to invent some new menu items to make use of this astonishing variety of reasonably-priced seafood. Among the choices we offered were flat rolls made of croissant dough and filled with scallops, crab meat and fresh herbs. These were so popular that we expanded the line to include ham and cheese, vegetarian, and one stuffed with sausage made of veal and pork. Each of these varieties was big enough for a lunch and we sold them all for a dollar. And of course we also had to cater to the Australian love of pies. These included seafood, lamb curry and beef - the last made in the Canadian "tourtiere" style. But there was more yet. We also had many types of freshly-made soups, quiches and salads – also priced at a dollar. Finally, our patrons could round out their meals with pastries, natural juice and fresh coffee. When all was said and done the price of a whole lunch was four or five dollars. And if you wanted some nice wine, Australian law allowed (and still does) restaurant patrons to bring their own bottles. So naturally we encouraged the practice at La Cuisine as well - not even charging corkage!

Leading up to the big day I only encountered one problem of any significance: I was let down by a supplier of French-made dough-rollers who failed to deliver the machine until three months after we opened. Lack of the device meant that our work was much more labour-intensive and tiring and our output significantly less. But in the end the renovation was completed on time and we were able to open right on schedule – something unique in my experience. Everything had come together so quickly that our only advertising was a small sign in the window reading, "La Cuisine opening soon."

The demands of opening a new business might well have produced some strains at home, but luckily my mother had offered to come - both to look after her grandson and to see something of our new country. At first she couldn't resist helping me in the café, but eventually we made a deal that she would only work at the shop in the very early hours of the morning - before we were open - to help prepare the food. She would then spend the rest of the day with little Olivier. This arrangement allowed Judith to look after our customers. My role, with two helpers-in-training, was to produce all the food. We also hired a girl to serve in our small dining room.

Before opening day we had the traditional party to showcase our extremely attractive shop, the work of top architects. Of course we invited the architects to the festivities, as well as our contractor and workers. Also attending were some suppliers, and a few new friends and neighbours. The first day that we opened for business - at 8:30 in the morning – we put out a modest display of hot croissants, brioches, raisin buns, apple turnovers and Danish-style apricot swirls. There were also a few dozen other items, including our famous gateaux Basque, some beautiful French pastries, and freshly baked fruit tartlets made with colourful seasonal fruits – all displayed in a brand-new, stylish refrigerated display counter. On one side were the baked goods, and on the other, in a separate section, the salads, pies, quiches and rolls. There were a few other things as well, but we hadn't made large quantities of anything as we had no idea what to expect. We also offered cold drinks of various kinds displayed in upright glass refrigerators. Among the available selections were the best available fruit drinks and assorted waters. There were no unhealthy drinks, a policy that I had always followed in my various enterprises. We were the only business with this kind of menu so we had nothing to compare ourselves with in terms of the likelihood of success. In fact we were so uncertain that Wendy, a friend of ours, had offered to come to lunch with a few friends to make the place "look busy". So you can imagine my delight when we were completely sold out by 10:00 am. Never in my life had I experienced such immediate and overwhelming demand. But along with the joy there was some embarrassment as well, as I had to spend the rest of the morning apologizing for being empty-handed. And there was yet another problem to deal with.

Knowing that our friend Wendy was coming for lunch and given that I had promised others as well, we had a great deal to do over the next couple of hours. My mother had gone way beyond her scheduled four hours, but was having a wonderful time going flat out and I was more than grateful for this amazing beautiful workaholic. Without her, as our staff was still very inexperienced, I would have ended up doing almost all the work myself. I thanked God for her presence and promised her that I would not ask her to work such long hours beyond the first ten days. Despite the hard work my mother was in heaven at our instant success as she well remembered our failure at the Millwood address in Toronto. When all was said and done we managed to produce enough food to serve a meal to a few people at least, and all the morning's disappointed customers were promised that our production would increase over the next couple of days. In fact I had to double my staff to be able to produce large enough quantities of food to meet the huge demand.

On the customer relations side, Judith turned out to be a great asset. Her manner was very welcoming and she gave the place a happy feeling. She promoted our products tirelessly, claiming that Hobart now had the opportunity to match any of the major world cities in the availability of classic cuisine. She patiently outlined the ingredients and flavours of our different products and answered many other questions as well. And in fact, a few days later, it was Judith herself who was the focus of an article in the local paper, The Mercury. The female journalist praised the shop itself but seemed to have been taken even more by Judith herself. She was much impressed by Judith's international cachet and the bulk of the article was taken up with a description of her work with Vidal Sassoon hair salons. It described the progress of her career, starting with Judith's time with Sassoon in the United Kingdom followed by her setting up and managing new salons in New York, Toronto and California. What seemed to interest the writer most about Judith was the fact that such a cosmopolitan executive would choose to come and live in little Hobart. Describing Judith's successes was a way of pointing out to the patriarchal Australian society that women should be taken more seriously, even that their pay should be equal to that of men.

So it goes without saying that Judith's presence was another very helpful element in our rapidly expanding business. Another factor has always been a part of the way that I do business. As I noted earlier, we always set our prices at the lowest level that can be managed using the best ingredients, ensuring quality workmanship and paying good wages. And of course there must also be a small margin of profit. I have never felt the need to charge what the market would bear, or to raise prices in an effort to reduce workload. No, it has always been important to me to make our food available to as many people as possible within the limits stated above. Our prices seemed so reasonable to the residents of Hobart that they could scarcely believe them and they responded accordingly. But to me it was just another example – one of many in my life - of the truth of St. Paul's words: "As you sow, so shall you reap." And in saying this, I'm not just referring to business practices; I'm talking about all of experience.

CHAPTER 10

Starting Anew Down Under in Hobart, Tasmania

At this stage in my life, my idea of spirituality was evolving rapidly. I was starting to see that *every* moment of one's life is spiritual. We can choose to act in petty and false ways or we can live in a manner that constantly affirms God's presence for us. And by His presence I mean having a palpable sense of the meaning of the words "limitless love". No matter how many religious or "new age" rituals we may practise, all that effort it is in vain if we do not offer of ourselves in love. We may give our entire lives over to spiritual disciplines of one kind or another, but without love all this effort will be as "sounding brass." How we give that love will be different for each person. Some of us are blessed with material abundance and we may choose to share that, while others may have gifts or talents that bring encouragement and joy to others. Even something as simple as a smile, one given with pure love, will open doors in wondrous ways. Again the bible (Matthew 6:33) affirms what I have always found to be true: "Seek ye first the kingdom of God ... and all these things shall be added unto you." I think the idea here is that once you surrender yourself to serving love, then life's needs will take care of themselves. In sum then, despite the negative ideas of God and religion from my youth, I have come to trying to live a God-centred life as a result, not of words, no matter how poetic, but rather of seeing God in action, of witnessing for myself that it is love that binds us and makes us one. I have come to see that love is the glue that keeps all of creation together and the power that makes it possible.

And while many books and teachings tell us that the only way to experience the infinite at work in the finite is to live in the moment, in the eternal now, most of us struggle to avoid the endless distractions that life provides at every turn. So while I can't pretend to be an expert on spiritual matters, I can tell you what has been helpful in my own practice. What is essential in my view is setting time aside for renewal and quiet reflection. Without consciously shutting out the endless chatter of the modern world it is almost impossible to be aware of the subtle urgings of spirit that are always within us. Initially we may just choose to reflect on our lives and their challenges - perhaps taking a longer view of things than we are likely to do in the middle of the fray. Out of that longer view may come insights into how well or not we are honouring our most basic ideals and beliefs. And if we are unhappy with what our meditations reveal we may be encouraged to try and live life differently. Perhaps we will decide to employ some of the techniques that are now widely available for consciously changing one's personal reality. I refer the reader to the works of Wayne Dyer, and Deepak Chopra as well as the Seth books, first published in the 1970's and since reissued. And there are many other books of this nature as well. But out of this process will gradually come the awareness that if we put aside fear, even for a little while, the boundless creative power within will find a way to help us recreate ourselves in ways that best serve both us and those around us.

So what exactly is this "boundless creative power"? I have come to believe that it is an aspect of the divine working in and through us to help us become what we truly need to be – a light both to ourselves and to humanity. In using the process that I have described above we gradually begin to hear the quiet voice within us, the one that is never afraid, the one that loves us without measure, the voice whose guidance never fails us. In one sense these are our own words, but not those of our physical selves. Instead they are a source of knowledge that has always been with us - even before birth. The wisdom offered is that of the higher self, a kind of super-consciousness that is not God, but is inseparable from God. It allows us to experience God-within - the means by which we are helped to become what we were always meant to be. And as we come to deepen our understanding, to see ourselves as aspects of God, we start to realize that the whole world is divine and to hear, as if for the first time, St. Luke's words, "For nothing is impossible with God." We discover too that as we begin to succeed in changing ourselves, we start to alter everything around us. And finally, as people all over the planet begin to see that in God we are all one, every aspect of religion, politics and economics will begin to shift in the most radical way imaginable. We will all, with utter certainty, experience every living thing as an integral part of our very selves. These are, in my mind, the characteristics of the new world that is starting to emerge. And when this new planetary culture does come into being, it will be after a long struggle with the dark and dysfunctional forces in this deeply troubled world. But make no mistake; it will come.

The above ideas have helped me with every aspect of my work and personal life and always will. Now with my new venture in Hobart (my sixteenth) successfully off the ground I had more time to practise what I preach and made time for a little reflection of my own. In all my businesses, as elsewhere, I believe that over the years, I have been (unconsciously at first) following principles that Neale Donald Walsch describes as key to not only living and working successfully but also doing it in a way that allows us to fulfill life's true purpose: "...to evolve to become grander versions of ourselves."[4] To do so we must live in a way that serves others as well as ourselves. He names three core elements of a life that allow for such evolution. These are *functionality* (in my case providing the best quality products that I could - for a reasonable price); *adaptability* (honest observation of what works and doesn't and the necessary adjustments to improve); *sustainability* (what not only keeps us alive but feeds us, so that we always have new energy to devote to what we do). And these concepts can be equally valid for our bodies or indeed our actions in general as we relate to the world of which we are a part. It's all about living creatively and acting out of clear intention, not simply reacting to events. Every success in my life is owed to living these principles and making them my own.

I believe that there is a great hunger in the world for a genuine spirituality, one that will give people the means to morally elevate themselves and the world. I think we will see more and more institutions of learning placing a greater emphasis on the teaching of ethics. One of the greatest teachers and exemplars of living in service to such a higher good is the Dalai Lama. His ethical views are free of dogma, religious or otherwise. As Donna Seaman writes in her review of the Dalai Lama's book, *Ethics for a New Millennium*, on Bookbrowser.com:

> Stating bluntly that it is far more important to be a good human being than to be a religious believer, the Dalai Lama encourages his readers to act out of concern for the well-being of others rather than indulge our habitual preoccupation with self. This may sound simplistic, but there is nothing superficial about the Dalai Lama's argument or the ethics he defines.

---

[4] Conversations with God" a fan site.

I had the pleasure of hearing this remarkable man in Tasmania in the early eighties at the beginning of a world tour. His loving kindness was apparent and his sense of humour and wit were a delight. At the time, as his English was limited he spoke through a translator, but he was extremely inspiring nonetheless. His wisdom and very presence made a lasting impression on me.

And when I reflect on my time in Tasmania as a whole, I see it as another period of great experiences. What at first seemed like the end of the earth, an isolated and forgotten land, quickly won our love. Admittedly the isolation didn't have great appeal for our Canadian friends and very few came to visit, but we compensated by travelling a great deal ourselves, both around the world (many times) and throughout the Australian mainland. Australia is a wonderful country filled with amazing beautiful places and with a population that not only seems mostly joyful, but is also very hospitable and always up for a party. Australians also have a passion for the outdoors and a famous love of sport that is characterized by a sense of fair play and respect for all players who do their best, regardless of who wins or loses.

When I returned to North America I was shocked to hear commentators glorifying winning competitors and barely mentioning the losers. And I have to say that such stress on winning is not only the antithesis of spirituality, but also seems to consign all but the most gifted to the sidelines. Great athletes are idolized, yet forced to be one-dimensional slaves to their sports, while the average person has few opportunities, even in school, to learn the pleasures of teamwork and fitness. And needless to say, with poor conditioning and the resulting compromised health come low self-esteem. The epidemic of obesity may well have something to do with these distorted values - and not just where sports are concerned but in almost every other area of North American life we celebrate the successful and mock the so-called "losers". So from earliest childhood Americans and Canadians are taught that the many exist to admire the few - hardly a viewpoint conducive to a healthy and enlightened society. In fact, virtually brainwashed by the mass media and their tiny handful of inconceivably powerful corporate owners we have become passive slaves to the latest gadgets and fads. Even the natural world has become commercialized and reduced to a vehicle for selling beer and cars.

But I have never seen the world situation as hopeless. In the last few decades, there has also been a growing awareness of the dangers of our way of life. Countless individuals and organizations work tirelessly for change. One example is that of Greenpeace whose members constantly risk death to expose abusers of the ecosystem, but Greenpeace is not the only such organization doing valuable work. There are NGO's all over the world not only striving to save the environment but also bringing aid to those wretched human beings in so many parts of the world that are living testaments to our selfish and violent ways. And at a more subtle level, there is also a growing spiritual awareness of our mystical connection to the earth and all living things that is gradually inspiring a change of attitudes in the world. It is all these things and more that give me hope for the future, a future in which my son Olivier and perhaps one day his children, will greet the dawning of a very different day for this planet.

As the years passed in our new country my son was growing up fast as were his cousins Charles and Olivia. They really enjoyed each other's company so we tried to spend as much time as possible with Mona and her children. We were able do so readily because of the weekend closing of our business that I mentioned above. Free weekends were a revelation to me, making possible a much more active social life than ever before. On my fortieth birthday I was treated to a wonderful surprise party on the beach. Our many friends had gotten together to provide an amazing feast. My birthday is in December, which is a summer month in Australia, so to be able to spend a beautiful day swimming and eating while surrounded by our many friends brought tears of joy and love to my eyes. It was a day that I will never forget.

Hobart and Tasmania continued to fill us with joy and as time went on we explored more and more of the island, doing our best to see as many of its wonders as we could. Meanwhile our business began to attract more and more attention. We were asked to participate in a number of discussions with business leaders and give our opinions in many areas. Of course we were asked about food specialties and other related matters, but also about broader issues like products for niche markets. At an early stage in its development we were small investors in the Pipers Brook winery. I was also involved in the work of a hospitality school called Drysdale where I was invited to speak on a number of occasions. Unfortunately my ideas didn't fit the mould of their philosophy so my time as advisor was cut short. It took ten years and new management before I was not only invited back but also much appreciated and actually taken seriously.

In the political world of Tasmania in the eighties there was bitter division between conservationists and promoters of big hydroelectric projects that would have forever closed the beautiful and wild Gordon

River. Mercifully the construction didn't go forward, something that turned out to be a blessing. First off, the dams turned out to be unnecessary and in addition, unforeseen events would have bankrupted the state of Tasmania. Shortly after the controversy the Australian dollar collapsed and as the debt for these massive undertakings would have been in U.S. dollars, the result would have been a financial catastrophe.[5] And further, the environmental damage was headed off in both the short and long term when the whole area was declared a World Heritage Site.

Meanwhile at home we had to make a decision about where to send Olivier to school. I was intrigued by the fact that there was a Quaker school in Hobart – the only one in Australia, but I knew little about the beliefs of the religion. However, as I investigated further I decided that the school would be a perfect fit with my own spiritual beliefs. It stressed individual dignity and responsibility and further, taught that all human beings are equal in the eyes of God. An additional plus was the fact that the Friends' School also turned out to be one of the finest in the country, its students consistently winning top honours for academic achievement and music. They were never the best in sports- with the exception of rowing – as for some reason athletics didn't seem to be a priority. Once our son was established in his new school, I often marvelled at his happiness there. I wondered if it was his natural character or if the school itself was responsible. I gradually learned that the institution had a very enlightened view of discipline, applying it firmly but gently in a way that left the student wanting to contribute more to the group rather than continuing to act out. The fact that it was a coeducational school also helped to bring a measure of civilized behaviour. Another benefit was the practice of altering the mix of students each term so that the students became adept at making new friends. In determining the makeup of classes, the staff made sure that there was always a range of abilities in each one. All pupils were expected to meet the same standards eventually, but slower learners were given more time to reach them. Whatever their abilities, all were honoured for their unique gifts and respect was given to everyone.

One day at my work I faced a situation that was very different from the happy interactions at Olivier's wonderful school. I received a visit from a former employee, Jack (not his real name), who had presented me

---

[5] The dollar's collapse also affected us personally as our investments in Australian currency were hit hard. Luckily, over time, they more than recovered their value.

with some challenges. At one time he had been a very good worker, but he began going on alcoholic binges and the day came when he didn't show up for work at all. He had been in a few days earlier to pick up his pay cheque but on his next scheduled work day he failed to appear. We tried to contact him but were unsuccessful. The day that he appeared was several weeks after those events so his reappearance was quite unexpected. He asked to speak to me privately so I took him to our small office. Once we were alone he suddenly took out a gun and pointed it at my forehead, laughingly asking me if I was scared now. And to my own surprise I realized that I wasn't – not at all. Something was keeping me completely calm and I heard myself saying that I didn't believe he was a criminal and that if he wanted or needed something from me all he needed to do was ask. I invited him to sit down and tell me what was troubling him so much that he thought he needed a gun to prove something to himself or to me. Then, calling him gently by his first name I asked what I could do to help him.

Jack slowly put the gun back into his jacket, sat down and began to tell me what had been going on in his life over the previous few weeks. He had been facing some difficulties and had gotten himself into trouble. My role, it quickly became clear, was to be a sort of priest who would hear his "confession" or perhaps even serve as a kind of father figure who would admonish him for his failings. Mostly it seemed that he just needed me to listen and all that I needed to contribute was the odd word of encouragement. Eventually I persuaded him to accept help, assuring him that he was inherently a good person who was well worth saving. I also told him that our lives are determined by the choices that we make and that I trusted him to start making better decisions. I even promised that the police would not hear of the incident and offered the additional incentive of finding work for him once he had demonstrated that he could be trusted again. Now of course the man needed more than assurances so I also told him that I would arrange for him to spend time with a psychologist friend of mine who would help him to understand the reasons for his destructive behaviour. He left rather shaken up and very meek compared to his manner of only an hour earlier. After he was gone it struck me with great force - not only how narrowly I had managed to avert tragedy - but also how the words that had saved me, words that were always exactly right, seemed to have come out of nowhere as though some unseen presence had handed me a script to follow.

I didn't tell any of the other workers about what had taken place, but I shared the events with Judith and she was extremely upset. She insisted that I call the police to report what had happened. I tried very hard to persuade her that keeping my word was very important to me and also that I truly believed in Jack's intention to keep his promise. I understood my wife's concerns but I chose to trust even if doing so flew in the face of common sense. As things turned out Jack did in fact attend the therapy sessions and I never felt the need to report him to the police. The treatment was successful and he has lived a good life ever since – even joining Alcoholics Anonymous and helping not only himself but eventually others as well. He later married a sweet girl who knew of his problems (although not of the gun incident) but chose to trust him anyway. Two years later they were blessed with the birth of a son. Jack and I have stayed in touch over the years and I know that there has never been another incident of the sort that occurred on that memorable day. Beyond Judith, I have never mentioned what happened in that office to his wife or anyone else. And the principle that I followed that day (or more accurately, that the "script" chose) namely that love can often be far more effective than punishment, remains as true today as it was then. In fact, where I currently live, in Elora, Ontario, there is a farm belonging to a country-wide organization called "Portage" (from the French word meaning to carry or support) where youth who are dealing with substance abuse are made part of a loving therapeutic community that seeks to re-socialize and rehabilitate rather than punish them. There they are able to continue their schooling and learn to deal with the issues that created their problems in the first place. Since opening in 1985, the Elora centre has treated over four thousand adolescents. Love instead of more super jails seems like a good idea to me.

CHAPTER 12

Mother Passes Away

B ut I'm getting ahead of myself. At this point in my story (winter of 1985) I was still in Tasmania where I had just received the news that we had long feared: my mother's cancer had returned. This time she was refusing surgical intervention, making it clear that she was ready to go. But in the short term she wanted us to take her back to Canada to see her kind doctor one last time. She flew on ahead to Toronto while we made arrangements to join her. This meant that we had to make a number of decisions very quickly. Arranging for Olivier to miss school for a while turned out to be easy to do and we also readily found someone to live in our house while we were away. The business was a more complicated matter. We couldn't afford to let the continuity of our customer relations suffer so we asked each of our two key workers to manage an aspect of the business. The idea was that each individual's strengths would complement those of the other. We helped them by carefully working out a schedule of tasks that had to be completed during the day. All this organization took about two weeks and at the end of that time we boarded a flight to Toronto via Honolulu.

As soon as we touched down we went straight to my sister Valerie's house where my mother was staying. Her condition had become much worse in the intervening weeks. The urgency of the situation allowed me to make an immediate appointment with Dr. Fish, the kind doctor who had operated on her twice before. After he examined her he took me aside and gently warned me that her death was imminent – within the next two or three weeks. He suggested that I take her home, make her comfortable and give her anything she wanted to eat or drink, but in small quantities. He also stressed that someone should always be with her to show her that she was loved and to make sure that her needs were taken care of. It was then that I told him that she had asked to be taken back to France and I wondered if she would be able to make the trip. He said it was possible but we would have go as soon as a flight could be arranged. Just to make sure I asked my friend Doreen, my psychic friend mentioned above, to do a reading. She confirmed all that the doctor had said and also added a few suggestions to make the trip more comfortable. As my sister was a travel agent at the time, tickets were no problem. The three of us flew Air France as Valerie had a good relationship with them and because it was the only airline that would accept a seriously ill passenger. I soon came to see why.

Even as we took off my mother was only able to stay conscious for brief periods, but at least we were flying first class and so she had the greatest amount of room and comfort possible. And as it happened we were the only passengers in that section which not only gave us a lot of extra attention, but saved us from worrying about the other passengers if something went wrong. Over the middle of the Atlantic her breathing became laboured and she didn't seem able to tell us what was wrong. Our kind flight attendant asked the captain to inquire if there was a doctor on board. A young woman who was a fourth-year medical student came to see if she could assist but quickly realized that the situation was beyond her expertise. Then the Head Steward brought oxygen to see if it would help - and it did, to a small degree. There was at least enough improvement to calm everybody down. I took her hand and the contact seemed to be exactly what she needed as she immediately fell into a deep sleep. It was so deep as to seem unnatural to me, but this time I didn't bother seeking for help as we were close to landing. However I did ask that medical attention be available on our arrival and was told that a request had already been sent. And indeed as soon as the plane doors opened that morning (May 24th, 1985) on my mother's beloved France, a medical team rushed on board.

They knew exactly what they were doing and after a quick examination put her on a stretcher and into a waiting ambulance where I joined her. While en route I could see frustration and despair in her eyes but she wasn't able to speak. A few minutes later whatever she had wanted to say remained unsaid as on our arrival at the hospital they whisked her away. I was asked to wait in a special room where someone would come to brief me on her condition. After an hour or so, a doctor in his forties came to tell me what they had determined and to make some suggestions about how to proceed. He said that her situation was grave and even if they used every available method it would only be possible to prolong her life by a week at most. I asked if it was necessary to treat her so aggressively and he replied that if it was important to me to see her live a few more days with little chance of regaining consciousness, they would respect my wishes. I said that I only wished her free of pain and asked him to let her go naturally. He understood and I was taken to her room where I now found her comatose. The kind staff had provided an extra bed and invited me to remain with her until she passed away.

Valerie joined me a little later and together we passed the hours sitting and talking with her, even at times pretending that she was aware, but of course there was no response. But in the late afternoon she suddenly regained consciousness and sat up in bed. Her eyes were very expressive and shining with an eerie light. She began to speak in a strange language that neither my sister nor I had ever heard before. It was not Basque, not Spanish, and certainly not French or English. What was even more extraordinary was the fact that she seemed to be having her conversation, not just with us, but with unseen presences in the room as well. Valerie and I looked at each other in astonishment. I took my mother's hand and gently asked her to speak to us in French. She immediately switched and we were finally able to understand her. She said that she wanted to go to Sare, the home of her youth and the sooner the better. I promised to take her but told her that she would need to rest for the night, and that I would remain to watch over her. She spoke a few loving words to us, said goodbye, and seemed to go into a deep sleep. However when the nurse came in a while later she told us that our mother was in a coma and would probably not regain consciousness. I told my sister to go to her hotel and get some rest. She agreed and promised to return before lunch time the next day to see how things were going.

I tried to get some rest myself, but it took me a long time to relax. I was seeing life with my mother in little scenes. They were like videos of our relationship over the years and the memories just kept coming, one after the other. Some made me want to laugh, others to cry, but each and every one of them was infinitely precious. I knew that life would be very different when she was gone, and our parting now seemed very close. Finally I fell asleep, but only a short time later, about 2:00 in the morning, the nurse woke me up to tell me that my mother had passed away, suggesting that I wait until morning to make arrangements. I kissed my mother goodbye and asked God to take good care of her. I felt certain in that moment that this was not an end but a transition: she was returning to the spirit world where she belonged. There was grief of course, but also profound joy. By the time the orderly came to take my mother away I was ready to let her go.

Sleep was now out of the question and I couldn't wait for morning to see my sister so I decided to get a taxi and try to find her. The problem was that I didn't even know the name of the hotel, let alone the address. I remembered that the place was in the outskirts somewhere, but I couldn't remember which direction. However some instinct told me look in the northeast. The driver told me there were two small hotels and one motel in that area. Somehow I picked a building and as it happened, two of the units still had lights on. I was convinced that Valerie was in one of them, but there was no reception desk open or even a concierge available. My only option was to knock on one of the doors. The taxi driver offered to wait a few minutes until I knew if my search had worked out. The rooms were accessed through a long open balcony visible from the road, the two with the lights were on the same floor, so we arranged that I would signal him whether to stay or go. I paid him well and went to knock on the first door - this despite the fact that my intuition was telling me to try the farther door first. But at the time I was filled with doubt and fear, so I rapped on the first door. A guy in his underwear answered and not surprisingly was not happy at being disturbed. I quickly explained about the death of my mother and how I was trying to find my sister to tell her. I apologized for picking the wrong room. Then I tried the next door and it was indeed the right one. When my sister answered the door she was already crying and hugged me even though I hadn't said anything yet. Valerie told me that she already knew my mother was dead as her spirit had come to see her. I looked back and saw the guy whose door I had knocked on, now dressed and coming to make sure that I was legitimate. Once he saw Valerie and me together he knew that what I had said was true and offered his condolences before returning to his room. I waved my thanks to the taxi driver and my sister and I went into her room to talk and support each other. She started by describing my mother's appearance to her. At around 2:00 am Valerie had been in bed, but awake when she suddenly saw my mother standing at the foot of her bed. Somehow, despite the fact that no words were spoken, she knew that our mother had come to say goodbye. We talked all night, including praying a few times, as we remembered our lives with this wonderful woman. And by the time a new day dawned we felt better prepared to make the many decisions that awaited us. We fully accepted our responsibility to take care of the remaining earthly matters.

The formalities at the hospital were straightforward, and the cost almost nothing. Because my mother was French we benefited from the amazing medical system there. Despite all the expensive tests and procedures that had been done the total bill was thirty dollars – and that was for the extra bed for me. Everything else had been covered. The next step was to transport my mother's body to the Basque region for her funeral and burial – and this is where our troubles began. The process of taking a body from one region of France to another, despite the French Revolution, remains pretty much as it was under the feudal system. Apart from the actual cost of transportation, each time a new region is entered an outrageous fee must be paid - just for the privilege of driving through. It's no wonder that the French have developed a whole series of clever stratagems for moving bodies in secrecy. We couldn't decide whether to be outraged or amused, but nonetheless paid what was demanded.

We held my mother's funeral mass in Sare at the beautiful seventeenth century Chapel of St. Martin and St. Catherine, the church of her youth, where the lives of all her family had been commemorated before her. The chapel was full - the village coming to honour her not only as a respected member of the community but also as one who had left a legacy of heroism stemming from her role in the resistance during the war. And despite my feelings about the Catholic Church I was able to appreciate the importance of shared ritual in the expression of a community's grief. At root, such rituals are expressions of love for both the deceased and remaining family members.

She is buried behind the little church where, in typical Basque fashion, no ostentatious displays of wealth –only modest stone carvings - are permitted. The cemetery is owned by the city and a family is allowed to purchase a plot large enough for nine graves, at cost, as long as proof can be provided of a lineage connected to the village.

The last earthly matter to be seen to was my mother's estate. She had made me executor and trusting my sense of fairness had left much to my discretion. The resulting vagueness in the will would, I knew, make the task of carrying out her wishes very difficult, so to minimize the chances of conflict I immediately involved my brother and sister as equals in the decision-making process. But nothing is ever straightforward where wills are concerned as long-buried emotions tend to resurface. It would have been folly to assume that loving cooperation would be the rule of the day. So to say that I was extremely stressed about the whole business would have been an understatement. My back - which had obviously been paying attention - decided to create a physical metaphor for the "weight" on my mind, and with little or no movement or strain on my part, I was suddenly faced with a dislocated disc. As I have said repeatedly above, we are the creators of our own reality, and in this case it was relatively easy to sort things out as stress had already given me a crippled back a few years earlier in Hobart. In any event, one morning I simply couldn't get up. But with previous experience to guide me I knew that I needed to make a renewed effort to settle the outstanding estate issues as quickly as possible. Luckily peaceful agreement among all parties was achieved without too much difficulty and with the medical profession doing the rest my back was restored to health.

CHAPTER 13

Time for New Ventures Again

By the time we returned to Tasmania a whole year had gone by and Judith and I were somewhat concerned about how Olivier would manage after being away from his school for so long. But we needn't have worried as he was happy to reconnect with his many friends and quickly began catching up his missed work. One thing that helped greatly was the fact that his teachers asked him to share his experiences in France. Their encouragement in this and other ways helped him reach grade level in time to move on with his class at the end of the year.

There was similar good news when it came to our business. For the most part it had carried on pretty much as though we had still been there running it. But the very fact that things had gone so well created a problem of another sort. My return would, on the face of it, mean that I would again be in charge and the two workers would return to their former roles. That scenario promised no end of resentment and trouble so I made the decision to discuss setting them up in their own businesses. The three of us met, and after thanking them for all their hard work and congratulating them on their success, I made a proposal which offered each of them the chance to run his own show while putting in very little money up front. They would make payments to me over five years at a very low rate of interest and at the end of that time they would be sole owners of independent enterprises. Other details of the suggested arrangement included the understanding that if they chose to continue using the La Cuisine name we would agree on common standards and a simple code of business ethics. I also offered to train additional staff as necessary. Finally, I said that I would include clauses stating that the investment was not transferable and that in the event of non-payment I would take over the running of the business that was in default. We agreed to meet again in two weeks.

One of the men, Hasan Guzel, seemed very excited by my offer, but the other, Stephan Baranski, remained pretty much mute during the discussion, so I began to wonder about the wisdom of getting into a financial arrangement with someone who appeared to have no faith either in himself or the proposal. I knew that his background was anything but entrepreneurial so I met a second time with him alone and stressed that I would be there to help in whatever way he needed. When the two weeks were up and we all met again Stephan had overcome his doubts and we decided to proceed as discussed originally. I should mention here that one of the reasons that I could offer them such generous terms was because an inheritance from my mother had made our life even more secure and it made sense to me to use some of that money to reward those we trusted and who had worked so hard on our behalf.

Stephan was the first one to open his restaurant and almost right away I could sense trouble in the making. Of course he now had the power to hire whomever he pleased and in his case that didn't prove to be an advantage. In an effort to please his family he hired two of its members even though they appeared to know nothing of the industry. Had they been qualified it wouldn't have been a problem at all, but as this wasn't the case, he had immediately put the success of his business in jeopardy. I tried to help him as much possible by suggesting that he hire two people I knew to be very good to take care of the front of this brand new and beautiful shop. And he did take them on but with his untrained family members hampering efficiency in the back, production couldn't keep up with demand. I tried to help his kitchen team to become more efficient but he refused to make any changes. So all I could do was wait for the inevitable. Eventually the returns from his business were so bad that one day this wonderful worker but poor manager begged me to take over his business and let him return to work at the old place as a simple worker again.

Hasan, the other former employee, couldn't start his new business right away since his chosen site in a new mall was still being built. But what he at first thought would be a short wait turned into a very, very long one as the construction became paralyzed by strikes and court cases. So strangely enough, as I now had to rescue the failing new shop to protect my investment I once again left the original La Cuisine in the hands of the two workers I had intended to free by setting them up in their own businesses.

The new shop was foundering because of a lack of leadership so I had to make changes quickly. I began by letting go unqualified staff, keeping only the two skilled workers who had been hired at my suggestion. The shop was located in a great area and within a month we had restored profitability, and with our steady clientele spreading the word our volumes increased steadily. The success was all well and good, but my intention had simply been to expand - not to have an even greater load on my back. So I tried to convince Hasan to forget the mall location and take over his colleague's former business instead. As it happened the timing was excellent as he had just received an inheritance and was in a position to buy the place outright. The only problem was that he came from a culture (Turkish) that valued haggling over prices. Unfortunately I hadn't thought to take this factor into account and had immediately offered him my bottom price. The amount, fully accounted for and not even allowing for a profit, would have simply returned my investment, so I was puzzled when he asked for a week to think about it.

When Hasan and I met again as arranged, I knew immediately that something was wrong. He seemed uncomfortable and it took quite a while before he came out with what was on his mind. He explained that he had two options: the first involved buying an old bakery north of Hobart, the other was of course buying me out of Stephan's former shop. I replied simply that either option seemed good for him and that I would be fine with whatever he decided. For some reason my answer didn't satisfy him so I asked him what it was that he really wanted. Well apparently what he was looking for was a much lower price to take over my business. Naturally I pointed out that I wasn't willing to sell at a loss – especially as I had restored the business to health and all that he needed to do was maintain the standard. I tried to understand where he was coming from and not take things personally but I wasn't about to change my position – and neither was he. Apparently his need to bargain me down was more important than getting a thriving enterprise at a rock-bottom price.

Hasan was clearly disturbed when he left and eventually decided to buy the other bakery. But if imitation is the sincerest form of flattery then he continued to think well of us. He decided to call his store "Delicious Cuisine" - changed from its old name of "Delishus (sic) Breads". And as if stealing part of our name wasn't enough, he renovated the premises to make them a virtual copy of La Cuisine's design. Our lawyer suggested that we put a stop to his appropriations but I chose to let things be. My decision turned out to be a good thing in the long run as he did very well with his business, even adding six more shops, including –six years later – mine. Its value had appreciated in the interim and he ended up paying two and-a-half times the price that I had originally quoted him. But owning the shop where he had once been a mere employee was clearly very important to him. And a fitting ending to the story of the man's quick rise came a few months later when he hired my other ex-partner as a simple worker. The latter couldn't cope with the responsibilities of managing and seemed quite happy to return to his original status.

I have so far neglected to mention another enterprise, one that I opened in September of 1993. This was a full restaurant that I was originally planning to set up for my sister. I had sponsored her to come to Australia - a process that normally took six months to a year. In the meantime I promised not to take on any additional work and to find a suitable location for the new business. I also said that I would give her a year of my input at no cost and guide her through the process of applying for the necessary permits so that renovations could begin. Well things didn't quite work out as planned. When after six or seven months and still no Valerie I thought to ask the immigration officials - regulars at La Cuisine - if there was a problem with my sister's visa application (which according to her there was). The friendly civil servants told me that her visa had been approved months before and that she was free to come to Australia whenever she wished. Now I was beginning to realize that Valerie might have no intention of opening a restaurant with me and I phoned to see if she had made new plans. She insisted that she would arrive shortly, with as much money as she could bring, to get on with setting up the restaurant – and eventually she did in fact come.

Even though I now suspected that her heart wasn't really in the project, I wasn't too worried and simply told her that if she changed her mind I would make other arrangements. I had no intention of letting all that work go to waste and I would find other associates if need be. (Even though it would have been possible to run the new enterprise by myself that was definitely not my intention. To get involved in such an undertaking by myself would have inevitably led to my family life suffering. And I also felt that at that point in my career I had already done my bit for the local food services industry.) But when my sister finally arrived I put aside any concerns about her commitment and we set about finding a location. Her preference was for a place right on the Salamanca waterfront in Hobart. As it was a beautiful location I readily agreed and we entered into negotiations to buy the property. Valerie and I were both to have our names on the deed. Unfortunately the owners then changed their minds and refused to sell but they did agree to a long term lease at a fair rate – a fact which would give the business long-term stability. These matters settled we decided to create a bistro-style restaurant with a philosophy of freshness and a market-oriented menu. The only thing left was a wait of six to eight weeks for the approvals to come through from Hobart's City Hall. Then we could finally start construction. Alas things were not destined to be that simple.

Salamanca Market right across from Panache, in Hobart, with my sister. (1992)

By this time Christmas was approaching and my sister decided to go to France instead of staying in Hobart to wait for the permits to come through. Her decision changed everything as once back in France she soon fell in love and promised her new man that she would clear up her affairs in Hobart and return home. I wasn't upset by this turn of events and accepted her decision to withdraw. I fully reimbursed her for stake in the project, leaving me free to act on my own.

I started looking for new partners and had the good fortune to meet two young Canadians, Rick and Julie Perry, who were from Chatham, Ontario. Rick was working as a chef in a steak house and she was a hostess in the same restaurant. All they could offer was about twenty per cent of the cost of the project but it seemed that they had the ambition and ability to succeed, so I put up the balance, giving them a forty per cent share, keeping sixty per cent and promising to remain with them for a year to help them get started. We decided to call our new enterprise "Panache". It turned out to be a great partnership and one year turned into three. We have remained friends to this day.

Not about to repeat my nerve-racking experience of starting up Maison Basque in Toronto without a liquor licence, I set about making sure that we would be able to open Panache with a good wine list in place. In the Hobart of those days, approval for a licence to sell alcoholic beverages was notoriously hard to get, with long delays and near-impossible demands being the norm, so the odds of being granted a licence quickly were not in our favour. Once we had made the formal application we were given an appointment to see the judge who would make a decision as to our suitability. Rick was very anxious about the impending interview, as to a lesser degree, was I, but once we walked into the assigned room and I saw who the judge was, I smiled and whispered to Rick that I believed we would be approved. Rick looked at me in a way that suggested he thought I was delusional, but I recognized our interviewer as one of my early lunch regulars at La Cuisine.

As the hearing began we were told that a number of nearby businesses had raised objections to our application. There was no question that these concerns had the potential to be very damaging to our chances, but luckily none of the opposing owners had the courage to express his views in person and the judge dismissed the complaints out of hand. He told us that his statement on the matter would indicate that he knew the operator very well and that he would be pleased to see this worthwhile addition to the local dining scene. He added that he looked forward to dining there himself. We thanked him for his confidence in us and promised to do our best to make a valuable contribution to city life. And I believe that the subsequent glowing reviews of Panache showed that we kept out word. Afterwards Rick marvelled at the way the hearing had gone and jokingly asked me if there was anyone I didn't know.

But there was to be one more challenge before the doors could open. The beautiful modern design involved the use of a precious Tasmanian wood, huon pine, and the restoration of the original stone walls through sandblasting. We found a local company to carry out the stone work and scheduled it for a Sunday to minimize the inconvenience to our neighbours. The workmen came early and were gone by midday so it seemed that we had succeeded in minimizing the effect of the mess and noise. Then the phone call. It came around noon and we were at home. The caller was Phil, whose steak house, Ball and Chain shared a wall with Panache. (There had been some early tension between us as he had opposed our liquor licence, but things had been alright since then.) Phil was enraged about something and threatening to sue us, but the reason, despite some very colourful turns of phrase, was not yet clear. I finally calmed him down enough to discover that his restaurant, which was normally open on Sunday evenings, was filled with dust from our sandblasting. As it turned out there was a crack in the wall between the two establishments, one concealed behind a painting above his bar. The force of the sandblasting had blown it open resulting in a truly impressive mess. I asked him to give me time to clean things up. And although he clearly believed it to be an impossible task – certainly before he opened for business in a few hours – he agreed to let us try. Judith and I phoned some friends and in very short order we had a team of nine people working like maniacs to repair the damage. It took us four hours of feverish effort but we did in fact succeed in cleaning things up to Phil's satisfaction. By the end we were able to laugh about it and he invited us to stay for a drink and some cheeses. During the conversation I took the opportunity to try making him a bit more comfortable about the looming increase in competition. I pointed out that in my experience a concentration of restaurants increased business for all of them – which, over time, is exactly what happened. Both establishments thrived.

By the end of the three years I was planning to leave Tasmania before too long and with Rick and Julie's agreement I sold my shares to another partner. The restaurant was doing great business at the time and it looked as though nothing could go wrong. Sadly that was not to be the case as their new partner bought them out six months later and the whole business went into free fall. By this time, the summer of 1997, my departure for France and then Canada was fast approaching. And Panache was not the only casualty in this story as my sister's new relationship ended badly as well. Valerie too returned to Canada and now makes her living in real estate. And no, our relationship hasn't been harmed by events; we talk at least once a week.

With the end of my time in Tasmania drawing ever closer, I had to find a buyer for La Cuisine as well. Luckily a very ambitious and hardworking Czech came to me and offered to work free in exchange for being taught the business. He showed real talent from the start and we quickly became friends as well as colleagues. The restaurant continued to thrive in a by-now-quite-cosmopolitan Hobart and it continued to do so when he eventually took over. Also before leaving I was asked to be a consultant on two occasions. The first was helping set up a bakery/pastry shop in Queensland south of Brisbane and the second a much more ambitious consulting job for a large hotel in Fremantle, on Australia's west coast. The owner, an intelligent and dynamic woman had relatives in Hobart and was a regular at Panache. She wanted me to transform food services at her large and successful oceanfront hotel. Sadly her many managers and advisors didn't think that food was particularly important to the running of a successful hotel, as odd as that might sound, and created endless obstacles, so I had to limit myself to helping set up a small Panache-style restaurant as but one element of the hotel's culinary choices. That enterprise, I am happy to report, was extremely successful, but our original, far more ambitious plans had to be abandoned.

CHAPTER 14

Opening Up to My Spiritual Self

B ut I don't want to give the impression that my entire life in Hobart
was focused on business. The pleasures of family continued to
enrich my life immeasurably and I spent as much time with Judith and
Olivier as I possibly could. And of course my life-long interest in matters spiritual continued while I was in Australia, an interest that became
much greater after an experience in 1993. With Olivier and Judith I had
flown back to Canada to, among other things, spend some time at our
home in Elora. It's a large property with historic buildings so there is
always maintenance to take care of. On one memorable day, shortly
after a local electrician had replaced some old wiring, I was in the
process of cleaning the eaves troughs. Olivier was on the other side of
the large property cutting the grass with our new riding mower while
Judith was visiting a girlfriend. For my part I was perched on an alu-
minum ladder wearing wet sandals, and unaware of the close proximity
of a new wire behind my back – unaware until I touched it that is. Now
this was a wire that the electrician had assured me was completely isolated, but due to an unfortunate error on his part was very much alive.
I received a shock and was thrown off-balance. My reflexes, looking for
something to break the fall, unwisely chose both the wire and the ladder, creating a clear path for the electricity to travel through me and
down the ladder into the ground. My body began shaking like crazy
and though I could feel an electric current passing from right to left
over my shoulders my mind remained crystal clear. I knew that I had to
let go of the wire but the current kept me fused to it. I quickly realized
that my chances of survival were pretty slim and called out to Olivier
but he couldn't hear me over the noise of the mower. Aghast at the
fates giving me such an embarrassing end to my life I angrily demanded
of God that he do something about my situation. And instantly the

current miraculously released me and I fell four metres to the grass – barely missing the stone walk. I got to my feet and once I realized that I was still alive was overcome with feelings of awe and gratitude. I thanked God for hearing my cries while at the same time apologizing for the impolite tone of my request. My thanks to the deity done with I started to realize that although I had somehow survived, my body was in shock and I could feel a bruise on my back - not to mention the damage to the heroic bum that had so bravely absorbed most of the impact. With great effort, I managed to walk to the house and into the kitchen where, overwhelmed by a desire to lie down I promptly fainted.

Later on my son discovered me and tried to wake me up. I later learned that it had taken him many attempts, crying and very frightened all the while. When I finally regained consciousness I explained what had happened and asked him to get his mother who was not far away. The next thing I knew, I was in the hospital with doctors who were baffled by how I had managed to extricate myself from a live wire. As we were returning to Australia in two days I thought it best to keep the divine intervention part to myself. I wasn't keen on being hospitalized for hallucinations. I was released from hospital the next day and we were able to catch our flight but the trip was almost unbearably painful. When we arrived back in Tasmania I learned why. I immediately went to see a doctor friend who managed to extract half a litre of liquid from my behind. It had been trapped between the muscles, tearing the flesh apart and its removal brought immediate relief.

This latest brush with death had also been another opportunity to experience divine grace. I was left with a powerful desire to give back to God in whatever way I could. I shared my feelings with Judith, telling her that I felt that I now needed to serve in whatever way spirit chose to guide me. And while I acknowledged that her spiritual beliefs were very different from mine I felt that after twenty-three years together my desire to make spirituality a much more important part of my life would create more bridges than divisions between us. Sadly time would prove my optimism to be misplaced. I began to attend spiritual seminars, many taking place in a suburb of Melbourne. Even the first of these meetings was a revelation to me as I had the opportunity to experience first-hand many concepts that I had heard of but not lived through personally. After that initial exposure I became determined to attend as many of these gatherings as I could and that of course meant that I sometimes had to be away for a few days. Judith's displeasure was made very evident each time. The whole idea of non-mainstream spiritual experiences seemed to frighten her, and she regarded those involved in such things as highly suspect. I on the other hand was passionate about the opportunity to learn as much as I could. But the joy that I felt in these pursuits was lost on Judith and even served to upset her more. Gradually our differences over my spiritual life turned into a cancer in a relationship that had been an extremely happy one for a very long time. Over the next few years we grew further and further apart.

The climax of this part of my story and one of the most life-changing experiences in my life came in the latter part of 1995 as we were nearing the end of our time in Tasmania. I wanted to attend one last spiritual event before our departure and Judith was very much opposed to my doing so. However my heart was telling me even more strongly that going to the gathering would lead to the discovery of my core identity in the world. But still I procrastinated until finally a friend convinced me to go to a place north of Melbourne where I would attend a retreat lasting several weeks.

The setting was a group of roughly constructed buildings in the middle of the bush. Accommodations were Spartan: cabins with basic bunk beds, lights but no outlets or phone jacks - and thus no phones or television. Chance determined room assignments with no reference to gender or age. For nourishment we were served vegetarian food and herbal teas for the most part, with an exception being made for coffee and regular tea at breakfast. My guess is that the bare bones amenities were intended to focus the mind solely on the subject of the retreat which was a holistic approach to one's sense of self – which meant body, mind and spirit. The idea was to become free of buried "life issues" that are an impediment to growth.

As I was wondering if I had been crazy to come I heard the person next to me voicing almost my exact thoughts. We began to chat and I learned that his name was Rudy. It turned out that we were both from Europe and almost the same age. Those points of contact, not to mention a shared sense of absurdity drew us together right away and we supported each other through all that followed. Two women with similar views joined us and as we learned more about each other I became aware that all of us had issues to deal with. Attraction had nothing to do with the four of us coming together as we were all married, but there was definitely a bond formed and we have remained friends to this day. I should add that due to the artificial nature of the closeness created by intense shared experiences the facilitators actively discouraged romantic attachments.

The program was extremely demanding and very ambitious. We learned how to use psychic energy to relieve pain and facilitate healing. We were further taught methods of bringing about regression - whether to past lives or simply back to traumatic events in current life-times. And let's face it, for those around my age, the junk science in effect in the forties and fifties pretty much ensured that many of us had at least one trauma to deal with – birth. So of course these early trau-mas were a large part of the initial work, but as we dug deeper it became clear that some issues preceded the present lifetime. That kind of work meant coming to terms with the whole idea of reincarnation – even for those whose cultural and religious backgrounds denied its possibility.

We also participated in a sweat lodge ceremony where we sat in intense heat for three periods of twenty minutes each. I was so hot that I almost fainted. We followed the intense heat with a dive into very cold water – which surprisingly was a beautiful feeling. I understood how the Swedes were able to roll naked in the snow after being in a sauna. But of course the real purpose of the ceremony was not inter-esting sensations but rather to contact each person's spirit animal and to learn important qualities and values from it. A few of us had vivid dream-like images of our animal which we either interpreted ourselves or asked the teachers and facilitators to give meaning to our visions. Everyone involved was able to express important insights.

But of all the activities in which we were involved during our stay, my most profound experience came from a rebirthing ritual. I was totally immersed in a small tank of water whose temperature was slightly higher than that of my body. I wore swimming goggles and breathed through a snorkel. A young woman was in the water with me watching to make sure that I was alright, and all the while helping to direct my psychic energy by moving her hands over my higher chakras, the body's energy centres. (The higher ones are in the centre of the chest, the throat, the centre of the forehead and the crown of the head.) I floated comfortably in the water in a manner similar to being in the womb, while at the same time listening to a series of suggestions encouraging me to regress to that first stage of life. Very quickly I began recalling long-forgotten toys, faces, and events. One event that I revisited with great vividness was crawling on the floor, picking up a glass marble and swallowing it. Not long afterwards I re-experienced feeling sick and very hot. I recalled seeing my mother crying and our family doctor looking puzzled. Then it was a rubber tube into my lit-tle bum and shortly thereafter a clang as the marble fell into the potty. I could hear the adults' sighs of relief and then, completely oblivious of the whole thing I went back to playing. Later on I checked the story with one of my aunts who was still living and she confirmed all the details. Apparently I was ten months old at the time. But the journey wasn't over yet. I travelled still farther back in time and felt again the comfort and safety of the womb, the warmth of my mother's love.

I only experienced this blissful state for a moment before I found myself out of my body and travelling through a kind of mist. The mist in turn gave way to being in outer space gazing at our beautiful earth then, only a fraction of second later, to witnessing gigantic displays of fiery stars and massive nebulas. But then the celestial wonders them-selves became smaller and smaller, finally disappearing altogether. I was alone in the utter blackness of space. A feeling of panic took hold of me. Had I gone too far? And further, what had become of my familiar identity? You may recall that I had had a previous out-of-body experi-ence during my near-fatal tonsillectomy years before so I already knew that my thoughts were independent of my body and that idea was at least something of a comfort, but wherever I was there was not a single trace of light anywhere. I felt that I had somehow gone beyond the limits of the cosmos. I no longer knew what time was. Only my thoughts existed. Would anyone ever be able to find me? My fear con-tinued for what seemed like quite a while but slowly I began to accept my situation.

Now, for no apparent reason my thoughts turned to a question that I had once asked my dear psychic friend Doreen,[6] "Why do good and evil both exist?" At that time in my life I still thought of God as somehow "outside" us and was puzzled as to why he permitted human beings to do the terrible things they do. Doreen wisely answered me that if I tried to be a light unto the darkness there would be no such thing as total darkness. Still I remembered feeling at the time that the advice was not worth considering. But strangely, here in the middle of this black emptiness I was again thinking about those words from years before. Then quite suddenly a light appeared, tiny at first but rapidly increasing in size as it rushed towards me - and then the realization dawned: "That's *me*!" I said to myself. And then I began to wonder if there were other lights like mine that had just been temporarily switched off. No sooner had this thought entered my mind then the darkness was suddenly filled with an infinite number of bright lights. I was overwhelmed by feelings of awe and gratitude and also the aware-ness of being in the presence of a love so powerful that I could recall

---

[6] See page 105.

nothing even remotely approaching it in my whole life. Thoughts piled upon thoughts. I came to understand that total blackness or nothing-ness is not necessarily evil or bad, but simply a state of non-realization, where one exists, but does so in a state that is pure potential, not man-ifesting anything. Further I somehow knew that I could at any time move into a different reality and there create anything that I chose. And with that realization I found myself back in my body.

Our teacher knew that I was experiencing something very power-ful as the young woman watching over me was behaving strangely. This helper later reported that she felt great energy surging through me and also that she could also sense my fear and, ultimately, my great joy. When I finally opened my eyes and looked at the world, everything around me was vibrating. Each person was surrounded by many colours, every tree by misty shapes; the forest looked for all the world like a bank of clouds. And when I looked down I could see that the grass too had a visual atmosphere around it and the rocks were vibrat-ing with a power greater than anything around them. I could have hap-pily stayed in that state of wonder forever. My body felt very light – somehow not quite physical.

When I later reflected on experiencing myself as thought and only thought while in the midst of an infinite inky blackness, I remembered Neale Donald Walsch writing of God communicating to him not only the familiar biblical words, "I AM THAT, I AM," but the much more challenging ones, "I AM what I AM not, and it is from that I AM NOT NESS that I always return or come from." Was my experience of soli-tude in the universe something like the isolation of God before the big bang? Was my being as a light unto the darkness something like God creating the universe? Well of course I couldn't answer those questions but I was, as on many other occasions, very grateful for Neale's body of work.

After those remarkable events everything changed. I participated in the remainder of the retreat with much greater openness and conse-quently learned still more about myself before the final day. But after all that I had been through in those remarkable weeks one thing was absolutely certain: I would never try to deny my spirituality again, although it would be some time before I could readily share what I had learned.

Caution in speaking of spiritual matters was particularly impor-tant at home. Judith had no use for this part of my life and was not interested in hearing about my experiences. In fairness, she was afraid that I would end up being victimized by charlatans posing as spiritual teachers and in all too many cases that is still a valid concern. Examples of corrupt egoists wearing the cloak of enlightenment are all too readily available. Some of these con artists make a great deal of money out of the naïve trust and credulity of their fellow human beings. But I was no victim; there was no doubt in my mind that these experiences were genuine and they revealed an aspect of reality that continues to enrich my life today. And that's not to mention the benefits that I have been able to pass on to others through what I learned.

So I couldn't lie to myself or to Judith but she remained unable to accept this side of my life. We ended up drifting apart, although there was still plenty of respect, decency and tenderness. But the love that had given us a great life for twenty-three years had been irreparably damaged. And then came the day that Judith challenged me to choose between her and those activities that were making me a "stranger" to her. For a year after that ultimatum I agonized over what I should do, until one morning I woke with a feeling of absolute clarity in my mind and heart. I felt then and still feel now that no one, not even God, has the right to tell you what you should *be*. I had finally made peace with myself. I wasn't able to go on living a lie - all the while seeing Judith growing more and more unhappy - so I told her that I wanted a separation. Property division favoured me under Australian law but I had no desire to take advantage of her and we split our assets in a way that was fair to both of us. It took about a year for us to settle our affairs and then I was able to return to Canada. In financial as well as other matters, our parting was reasonably amicable and we parted on good terms - remaining so to this day.

CHAPTER 15

A New Beginning, Finding Kathleen and Opening Drew House

Needless to say, Olivier was deeply affected by his parents' separation but made it clear that he loved us both and scrupulously avoided taking sides. And while his schooling was certainly not helped by the break up of the family, in the end he did very well on his final examinations. He went on from the Friends' School to study Hotel Management in Sydney for the next year and a half. Judith found a place for the two of them to live so that she could look after him while he completed his studies. The first half of his training, a year and a half in length, all took place in Sydney. After that, he was free to find a position in any four or five star hotel in the world. By this time I was living in Canada, in the home that I had purchased years before in Elora and Olivier called to ask me if I could find him work in Whistler, B.C. I was fortunate enough to know Anita Stewart, a local food activist and author of many cookbooks. Anita is particularly well-known for her championing of all things Canadian in matters of cuisine - from the rich variety of its cultures to its fabulous produce and talented chefs. Her work meant that she was on friendly terms with restaurant managers, chefs, and owners associated with the cream of Canadian hotels. She kindly offered to make a call to the manager of the Fairmont Chateau Whistler Hotel on my behalf. Soon after the introduction I contacted Olivier in Sydney and put him in touch with the department in charge of staffing, but after that he had to win a position on his own merits and I am pleased to say that he did so. He thrived in Whistler, quickly receiving a series of promotions, and he remains happily and very successfully employed there to this day. From the point-of view of both his father and mother (who now lives in the United Kingdom) distance is an obstacle to either of us seeing him as much as we might wish, but he has a wonderful girl friend whose family live in Ontario, so not all the travel is one-way.

I, too, quickly settled into Canadian life. My nephew Eric, who had been in Elora for some time running a small restaurant called Café Patisserie, came to live with me - which was pleasant for both of us. The village of Elora is a place of stunning natural beauty and postcard-ready old stone buildings so it was a great place to be, and it was also a joy to have old friends as part of my life again. It almost seemed as though no time had passed at all. But of course I still had to make a living, and as I had already been refused permission (twenty years before) to open a small hotel with a licensed restaurant I knew that I had to take a different tack this time around. My plan was to create a bed and breakfast using the main house, which dated from the nineteenth century, for both guest accommodations and a personal apartment which I would build on the top floor. The old stone stables I planned to renovate with a dining room on the ground floor and further guest rooms on the upper floor. I saw the dining room as potentially multi-purpose as it could also be used for hosting seminars. I received a great deal of advice from friends but I had always succeeded in the past by sticking to my central vision and that's what I did here as well. Now of course where legal or financial matters were concerned I paid close attention, but in the end I would be the one paying for it all so I stuck to the instincts that had always served me so well. But there was to be a long struggle before the first hammer could be raised.

One of the things that had been in my mind since my remarkable experience during the retreat was to make my place in Elora one that was not just a business, but a venue where spiritual seminars and other similar activities could take place as well. So when obstacles began to appear I had both the time and the inclination to take on all comers to make sure that my dream became a reality. To start the process, with the help of an architect I prepared an overview of the project for village officials[7] in which I sought permission to build a bed and breakfast with eleven rooms. It was rejected on the basis of size, but I wasn't disheartened as I was fully aware that I was up against a formidable coalition of municipal employees with tunnel vision, competing bed and breakfasts, and neighbours afraid of possible inconvenience. But the sword that the opposition was wielding against me was one made up of municipal regulations so I hired a Toronto lawyer who was an expert in

---

[7] These events took place before municipal amalgamation and the creation of Centre Wellington Township.

the area. She carefully studied all the local laws and by-laws and then asked me to make an appointment with the village clerk. She told me that her plan was to "shell-shock" the village and then ask them what they thought was in their best interests. The heart of her plan of attack lay in the fact that my building, despite its age, had never been classed as a designated historical property. As a result I could tear everything down and as the site comprised two acres in the centre of the village I would be free to erect up to six houses and offer three rooms in each one as bed and breakfast rooms. In short she was formulating a new proposal for a bed and breakfast with eighteen rooms rather than the previous eleven. I would be increasing my total of available rooms from eleven to eighteen – and all of it completely legal. Of course I had no intention of actually destroying my beautiful historic buildings; it was just a tactic to win concessions and although I let myself be persuaded to consent to this charade, I had serious misgivings.

Well when we finally met with the clerk, Mr. Wilson, a usually helpful man that I dealt with on a number of occasions, everything went terribly wrong. She began to present her ideas and as she did so I could see Mr. Wilson's face start to turn red. I was becoming more and more uncomfortable as she continued to present her absurd proposal.

After a few minutes of listening to her Mr. Wilson suddenly exploded and asked, "Are you mocking me? But far from being intimidated she continued to press him, although she did so in the voice of sweet reason. And as far as the law was concerned she definitely had the upper hand. But I was feeling terrible at putting the poor man in this situation and realized that I had made a serious mistake in bringing in a high-powered lawyer from Toronto to bully the clerk of a little village. I suddenly realized how insulting it all was, so I interrupted her and tried my best to repair the bridge that she was in the process of blowing up. I made clear to Mr. Wilson that I had no wish whatsoever to destroy one of the treasures of the village; quite the contrary I wanted to make it even more beautiful and was willing to make the considerable investment necessary to transform the property. I told him that I wished to make a contribution to the local economy and asked if he would at least carefully consider my proposal with the other councillors before delivering an automatic refusal. After he had time to calm down a bit, the conciliatory approach worked where confrontation was only making things worse. I was reminded once again that business dealings are always most successful when everyone is treated with respect. Now mind you nothing was decided that day, and wouldn't be for quite some time after, but a real process had begun.

The rest of the meeting was very productive and we managed to address his concerns one by one. Later on I was invited to meet with other village officials to try to resolve areas of conflict before the matter was referred to the village council. Through these regular contacts we began to build relationships and after a few months a real spirit of cooperation developed. In due course the first phase of my project was approved. But now the objections of every single person in the village who might have a concern had to be addressed and I set out to meet with each and every one of them. My friend Anita Stewart again came to my aid as she had in finding a position for Oliver. Anita too met with all the objectors, both the rational and the irrational, some publicly, some privately but she was a tireless advocate for what became Drew House. Perhaps the ones with the greatest concerns were those who had existing bed and breakfasts in Elora. Understandably they feared the competition but over a series of meetings I pointed out that if we acted together, setting common standards and advertising as a group we could bring in increased business that would benefit everyone. I also told them that I wouldn't have the capacity to accommodate everyone who came to my planned seminars and that they would benefit in that way too. They also came to understand that my reputation as a successful restaurateur in Toronto would bring visitors to Elora who might otherwise never come. In time we came to an agreement and formed what turned out to be a really great B&B association. We continue to advertise together and assist each other and the results have benefited all.

So after the happy resolution of the problems with getting my bed and breakfast under way I was once more able to resume normal life. After all the stresses of first the divorce and then my permit problems in Elora it was a relief to have only myself to worry about. I felt a lightness that I had not known for a long time. That lightness was nicely echoed by my living circumstances. When I returned to Elora I planned to live in the main house and a friend was good enough to provide me not only with a bed, but also a table, chairs and assorted cookware for the kitchen. It was enough to make the place liveable until my possessions arrived from Tasmania, and I took a strange pleasure in the simplicity of it all. In fact when my container finally did show up I felt that the house had become too cluttered and it made me a bit nostalgic for the bare bones furnishings I had enjoyed before. But additional furniture was about to become extremely insignificant when compared with another event in my life.

The old house had front and back sections. I was living in the front part and the back was leased to a lovely and extremely pleasant woman named Kathleen whom I had met only once in passing on one of my visits to Elora from Tasmania. She was working for a French company that had interests in the area and was very pleased to be living in my beautiful old home. So as the beginning of construction was fast approaching, and with it the need for her to move out, I took her to a good local restaurant to break the news that I would be unable to renew her lease. But as it turned out she wasn't at all concerned since her company managers were transferring her to the U.S., where she had worked for them previously. So she would be moving out in any case. Her new assignment was to be in Washington, D.C. and she had arranged a place to live in Alexandria, Virginia, a suburb. However she would still be in Elora for few more months and that little delay was to change my life.

Over the months that we shared the house we discovered that we enjoyed each other's company and as time went by we began to help each other in little ways. Kathleen travelled a lot for her work which meant that someone had to look after her affectionate but odd Scottish Fold cat-with-the-unnerving-stare. I was happy to do this for her – and there was also (you knew this was coming) the matter of food, or rather the lack of it. The two sections of the house were not walled off from each other and because of the layout I would often have to walk through her kitchen. On one occasion, being a chef I couldn't resist peeking into her refrigerator. I was astonished by how little food was in it, and that was true for the freezer as well. I decided then and there that I would have to invite her for a meal now and again so she didn't starve to death. The prospect of a shared meal and a good chat was very appealing and it turned out that we had lots to talk about. She even became very interested in my plans for a B&B and conference centre. But despite the socializing, at this stage we were still just good friends.

When the time came for her to move back to the U.S. she promised to visit Elora once in a while as she had friends in the area. She assured me that she would drop by to say hello and see how things were progressing with the B&B. I was sad to see her go but I didn't have much time to dwell on it as my life was getting quite busy again. I was involved in planning the construction of my upstairs apartment and added to that I would shortly be taking on the much larger task of renovating the stables. I was also helping Eric with his restaurant from time to time.

And so the time passed, but I still keenly missed Kathleen and began to wonder if she'd forgotten about me. But then unexpectedly one day there she was, happy to be back, and staying nearby with friends. I immediately invited her to have lunch with me at my nephew's restaurant the next day. Of course Eric made sure that everything was top notch and we had a delightful time, again finding lots to talk about. As the meal was ending she mentioned her coming drive back to Alexandria and how it would be more pleasant since her company had given her a nice new green Jeep to use. She went on to describe the considerable attractions of this historic city with its famous colonial architecture. It sounded wonderful to me and I said that I'd love to visit her there sometime. To my surprise she suggested that I go with her. She had an extra room and I was welcome to stay at her place. When I expressed concern about interfering with her work she said that she had a few more days off and could show me around. Luckily at that particular time I had few pressing responsibilities to keep me in Elora so she had given me all the encouragement I needed. We agreed to start out early the next morning. I would share the driving so the trip would be less tiring.

The day had dawned beautiful and clear when Kathleen arrived right on time to pick me up. I had my coffee mug in hand as well as nice sandwiches, fruit, water and juices. I told Kathleen that I didn't like the highway stops with their restaurant chains serving awful food – something that I had learned first-hand on earlier trips. And despite the length of the journey, with so many interests in common, not to mention the sheer joy of being in each other's company, we reached Alexandria in what seemed like no time at all. There I was charmed by her lovely eighteenth century home with its low door frames and miniature rooms. Like other houses in the area it had benefited from careful and expensive restoration. Outside, the uncanny illusion had been created that nothing had changed in two-and-a-half centuries. And American Revolution notwithstanding the streets still bore names like "King", "Queen" and the like.

We spent a few wonderful days together while Kathleen showed me around her lovely city, but inevitably our last evening together arrived. I was to fly back to Canada in the morning and feeling very unhappy at the prospect. She sensed my melancholy and asked if something was wrong. I said that I wished that I could be much closer to her but our busy lives and the distance separating us would make that very difficult. I asked her if she felt the same way. That question led in turn to a very long and frank talk about our "situation" and we decided to give our budding romance room to blossom. We had to settle for a long distance relationship for quite a while, but we worked hard at it with frequent visits and our love continued to grow. Then, near the end of the year 2000, we married - I for the third time, and she for the second. Finally, after fulfilling the requirements of Canadian Immigration, Kathleen came back to Elora to stay.

And what a difference having Kathleen in my life has made! At that time I had reached the point in my B&B project where I had to get down to brass tacks with contractors for the biggest part of the renovation. It was a difficult and stressful time, but having Kathleen with her keen intelligence as an ally in the struggle made it all that much easier to bear. Renovation projects are usually difficult but I had to deal with three major local contractors who refused to even give me answers to my inquiries. So I turned to the young contractor who had done excellent work changing the attic in the old house into an apartment for me. I asked him to go over the costs of the job with me in a completely honest way as his estimate seemed much too low. As I suspected, he discovered that he had lost four thousand dollars, but as the estimate was in writing he had no recourse. He was understandably very upset when he saw the trouble that his poor accounting skills had gotten him into, realizing that he should have quoted me a price at least ten thousand dollars higher. I asked him if he'd be happy to get that amount now and he answered that recouping even half to cover his loss would be enough. I hated the thought of his losing money through inexperience so I decided to ignore our contract and give him the full ten thousand dollars. Needless to say he was overjoyed and I took the opportunity to caution him to be more careful with his estimates in future. We now had a relationship of trust and I asked him to consider taking on the huge job of renovating the former stables. I offered to pay him monthly as I knew he didn't have the capital to finance such a large project and after thinking about it for a while he agreed. We settled the deal, not with a contract but with an old-fashioned hand-shake. And within ten months my renovation had not only been completed without any disagreements between us, but had been done with superb workmanship in every detail. I was of course delighted and the reputation that Scott gained from the project has over time made him one of the most sought-after contractors in the area.

It was now early July of 1999 and with the construction finished we began our efforts to prepare the new dining room in time for the opening day party. Kathleen's parents had come for the occasion and her father, Bryant, seemed puzzled by my certainty that everything would be done in time. Understandably so as the general state of things was a chaotic mess with many of the finishing touches yet to be completed. Smiling at me in the way that you do when speaking to someone who may well be deranged he asked me how I thought that such a huge amount of work could possibly be completed in three days. I told him that I didn't know but it would all be done in time. The seemingly impossible quickly began to seem less so when my dear friend Yves (a colleague from my days at Gaston's in the sixties) unexpectedly showed up and offered his help. This extraordinary event was followed only two hours later by yet another when Hugo, my old Maitre D from Maison Basque, suddenly appeared offering his assistance as well. What he achieved was nothing short of incredible as in the brief remaining time available he not only made curtains for the windows but also decorated the entire room. And if all those additional helping hands were not gift enough an Australian friend visiting me at the time offered to take over all the cooking, freeing me up for other things. So once again in my life the impossible turned out to be possible after all.

It was a great party. Kathleen proved to be a natural hostess, mixing effortlessly and putting everyone at ease. My future in-laws were clearly delighted to see their daughter so happy. Some of the village officials came and were pleased to see that their concerns had been groundless and that Elora had gained a valuable asset to its economy. The construction team received many compliments from these same officials. So the new enterprise having been properly celebrated I looked forward to being open for paying customers in two weeks' time. I was hoping to making a bit of money in what remained of the summer as my financial resources had become somewhat depleted; the winter, as in any tourist town, was bound to be a lean time. But income aside, the other part of my vision, the dream of Drew House becoming a spiritual centre, was about to become reality.

Rudy, my friend from the 1995 retreat in Australia, came to visit me from Sydney and with him brought the book that would help to change my life. It was entitled *Conversations with God, Book 1*. The author was of course Neale Donald Walsch whom I have referenced throughout, but this was the first that I had heard of him. Rudy was very excited, telling me that this guy had written a book that he claimed was an actual conversation with God. He wanted me to read it right away and tell him what I thought. Well I was fascinated by the book as well; it felt totally natural and somehow seemed true. Further, it made a lot of sense - echoing some of the things I had learned from my friend Doreen and other psychics. Parts of it even reminded me of the Edgar Cayce material. But what was very different about *Conversations* was the casual tone and lively humour – not characteristics I had experienced with spiritual communications in the past.

Doreen Bennett and me in Elora. (2000)

However what was beyond unusual, what was in fact absolutely astonishing was Neale's *impertinence* in the questions that he asked of God – almost as though he were arguing with another human, not the creator of the universe. And miraculously every question was answered patiently and in a manner that didn't just challenge conventional religious beliefs, but introduced whole new worlds of knowledge and understanding. It seemed impossible to me that anybody could just make this stuff up. Once I got started I couldn't put the book down. Of course I had to share this discovery with Doreen and she was as keen as I was. Rudy was a little taken aback by my response, agreeing with the core messages but not sharing my wild enthusiasm. And then Doreen made a suggestion that left me utterly speechless: "Why don't you ask Neale Donald Walsch to come to Elora?"

It sounded like a good idea in theory but I didn't have a clue about how to hold a gathering for the very large number of people who might attend and there was an additional element of risk as Neale was not well-known in spiritual seminar circles at the time. But first I had to see if he would come, so I contacted Rita, Neale's personal manager in charge of scheduling all his seminars world-wide. It turned out that he was free in June of 2000. I further learned that Neale's fee would have to be paid in U.S. dollars – a bit of bad luck as the Canadian dollar was at one of its lowest points. I had no desire to profiteer where this event was concerned but I hoped to break even – or at worst suffer a loss that my savings could cover. In any case I decided to go ahead.

Now I just had logistics to deal with. One of my first challenges would be finding a place to host Walsch as Drew House would be far too small. I decided on the local arena as a venue since it was the only place with enough seating. That alone was a pricey business (I would need it for three days) and then I had to factor in Neale's fee, any materials and equipment that he might require, and in addition, the cost of providing high quality food for all the participants for the two days of the weekend seminars. So I had to charge quite a bit, but no one complained and in fact many thanked me for giving them the opportunity to hear Walsch in person. In the end the turnout surprised even Neale: nine hundred for his lecture on the first night and one hundred and thirty-five for the remaining two days - which consisted of intensive studies of *Conversations with God* materials, including opportunities to ask personal questions and receive answers. When all was said and done I actually made a small profit of five thousand dollars - half of which I donated to a school that Neale runs. An added bonus was the fact that Elora was buzzing with people for the whole three days – many of whom would return in the future. The event served to put both Elora and Drew House on the map.

Connecting with Neale was a great opportunity, both personally and in terms of seeing first-hand the hunger for change in the world. All these people had come together for one reason: the message of *Conversations with God* had connected in powerful ways with their minds and hearts and they were excited by the possibility of changed consciousness. They were to hear emphasized yet again, the message of the books that only from a place of clarity and loving choices can life truly be worth living. The three days in Elora were a breath of fresh air in a world of false beliefs where the assumptions of an ego-centric and materialistic world somehow manage to go unchallenged. How ironic that we see our world-view as somehow underpinned by reason and science when the whole basis of the way politics and economics operate in the world is nothing but blind faith. Neale Donald Walsch's visit to little Elora gave all of us that most precious of gifts – hope.

With the success of Neale's seminar I was encouraged to follow up with similar offerings and we brought a number of prominent speakers to Elora. Some were very well received, others less so. I even offered a few seminars of my own, hesitantly at first, but when they went well and generated a tremendous amount of healing, loving energy I was elated and ready to do more. There was just one problem; while it was deeply rewarding to bring together people who were interested in mystical subjects it was not a way to generate much income.

"The Boys" at Drew House. Pictured left to right: Hugo Quattrochi, Eric (my nephew), Olivier, Jacques Labadie and Hugo Vasquez. (2000)

When I first opened Drew House things were pretty slow so I had lots of time to spare for organizing these get-togethers. But as time went on I let myself get sidetracked and gradually slid back into doing what I had done so well for so long, namely preparing food.

And by sliding back I mean that I began to do far more than was necessary to make a living. When old friends and customers heard that I was available again and suggested things like offering a Sunday brunch to go along with the B&B I found myself unable to remain with my intention to focus mainly on spirituality. So over time, especially as B&B room bookings began to increase, I found myself once again immersed in the food culture that I had thought I was leaving behind when I left Australia. Someone like my friend Doreen would say that by letting my mind depart from my original intention I once again began attracting food-related activities into my life. And once I let that happen, food quickly began to take up most of my time. I even started to accept requests to do private functions in the evenings, functions that typically required a whole day of preparation in advance. Kathleen was a huge help and I was also lucky to find some dedicated locals who were willing to work part-time. All that helped of course, but the fact is that I was now in the position of having to steal bits of time from my business to continue learning about gifted psychics whom I might want to bring to Elora. But even when I found a spiritual teacher who looked promising, weekends, the normal time for holding a spiritual seminar, were pretty much spoken for. In other words my priorities had become reversed.

Now at first, none of this change meant that anything terrible was happening - in fact quite the opposite and we have had many happy patrons over the years to testify to that fact.. But with those happy patrons our reputation continued to grow and with it the work load until the point was reached where my body forced me to stop and question what I was doing. As I mentioned at the beginning of the book an attack of shingles in 2008 forced me to stop and take stock, and I certainly realized that my failure to begin work on this book was at the root of my illness. But once I recovered my health, over the coming days and weeks I gradually rationalized my experience away and put the book on the back burner again. Then, almost exactly a year later, in the fall of 2009, I once again fell ill.

This time I began to suffer weakness and a lot of joint pain. The symptoms seemed to suggest some form of recurrence of the rheumatic fever I had in my youth, but the medical tests were inconclusive. Whatever the exact reason, I was reduced to a shadow of my former self. The pain was especially bad at night, perhaps because of the absence of movement and lack of daily activities to distract from the physical discomfort. In any case sleep was very difficult to obtain and I was left with a lot of time to think. I was convinced as I had been the previous year that the normal harmony of body, mind and spirit, was somehow missing. When our health is good, the preoccupations of everyday life can be enough, but when poor health or advancing age insists on a reckoning, the deeper questions usually have to be addressed. In my case the disability, which thankfully was gradually brought under control by my doctors, forced me to consider not only the fact that I had been ignoring this book but also the reality that with advancing age I could no longer keep up the tremendous pace that my natural stamina had previously made possible. And where this book was concerned I knew that I had to put aside my doubts and trust that any obstacles would be overcome. And that I have done, and as for the rest, I am resolved once again to make Drew House a centre for spiritual exploration.

For when you come right down to it, the issues that were raised for me by my illness apply to every one of us. Each of us, as a microcosm of divinity shares in the act of creation, namely the inventing of ourselves and our lives. I was shown that fact most dramatically during my experience of absolute isolation in space during the retreat in Australia, but the insights of that moment were and always will be true. We create what we are by what we think, what we intend. My life, both on the esoteric and everyday levels has been testament to that fact. When I have trusted, I have been trusted in turn. When I have loved, I have been loved in turn. And when I had faith in God's love, in His desire for the best for each and every one of us I have not only flourished in every area of my life, but even, as I have related, been saved from certain death – and more than once. I have come to believe that a life that is purely about material acquisition is no life at all, that fulfillment can come only when we acknowledge the presence of the divine in our lives and strive to give back to God - in the form of all life around us - the love and care that we ourselves receive in every moment. No matter what the religious tradition, or the name of the spiritual master, unless we are taught the centrality of love we have been taught nothing; unless we accept that separation from God and from each other, is nothing but illusion, we will always stumble in the dark.

So for whatever time remains to me I will strive to remain awake and not succumb again to the distractions of busyness. I am happy here in my adopted country. I have been graced with a wife who is infinitely dear to me, whose very presence fills my days with light and as if that were not enough, we have the good fortune to live in a place of astounding beauty. Every place that I have lived has been good to me in its own way and the blessings of this picturesque little village of Elora, from the grandeur of its river gorges to the warmth and generosity of its people, are great indeed. Do I belong here? That's a more difficult question as I have felt at home wherever I have lived. So maybe the answer is here and everywhere. I do know that when I look at that famous NASA picture of the planet, as viewed from space, my heart tells me without any doubt that this luminous blue orb is indeed my home. And it is that certain knowledge that will lead me to continue working to ensure that the wonders of our dear earth are cherished and protected for all time.

It is my fondest hope that the day will come when all of humanity will live to serve.

In the kitchen at Drew House with Kathleen. (2010)

PART II

Must take stock of myself

CHAPTER 1

Challenging Our Beliefs, Changing Our Ideas

Is spirituality truly real? Or, maybe, is it a hold-over from the pagan beliefs that were picked up at a later date and transformed by religious institutions? Each one of us has an opinion when it comes to living a spiritual life. Mostly, I've found that confusion exists and deep-rooted cultural beliefs take over. Thought is the root source of spirit. People believe what they have been told.

Our intelligence, critical mind and creative thinking with the added bonus of intuition, are left behind. Anything new or different to challenge established mindsets is viewed as suspicious. It is better to stick to the old stories from our various cultures, no matter how unreal or historically flawed they may be, rather than to question if they have been working or not for the good of humanity.

It would be beneficial to observe if the cultural beliefs work or not and then move forward, but history shows us, so far, it hasn't been so. In fact, our cultural beliefs continue to be highly divisive, violent and, at times, leading to horrors.

Whatever the origin of spirituality, it has always existed. Wherever our spirituality comes from, it defines our existence. I can only relate to my personal perspective, which is based largely on my own experience.

I marvel at the diversity of creation. It allows each of us to experience our personal "consciousness" in regards to the various perceptions of how we relate to life. Our endless acts of creating our life are made possible by the gift of free will and the unconditional love from a higher source – or the "all there is" – who many of us would call God.

We have been – and still are – confounded by beliefs of separation from each other. We do not accept a creator who asked nothing from us, but continues to love us unconditionally no matter our deeds. We have been told endless tales of a demanding God who favors one over another. The result is fear of one another rather than unity. We are becoming more and more "enlightened." This simply means becoming aware of our natural divine origin and this realization, when it truly sinks in, changes everything. We are faced with a new awareness of consciousness, accepting our oneness and love as the ultimate reality.

I believe in a genuine search, or an attempt, at a spiritual awareness. When it comes down to life choices that matter, our world can only benefit from good will. Who we are in each moment of our life is expressed by our behaviors. Is it coming from thoughts of fears, mistrust, or from accepting and attuning to the spirit of love?

I believe that the meaning of spirituality is life being in harmony with itself in all aspects of creation. It flows from the spirit of what we term "God". In turn, it is perfectly connected to the energies of love and universal consciousness. It is therefore natural to attune ourselves with our source.

The gift of our free will may or may not be in harmony with the God spirit. It is important to accept our beingness as spirit, body and mind, the spirit being the first cause, the body our physical appearance in this world, and our mind the conscious builder of our reality. The three are one unit in the larger expression of God. My hope is that more and more human beings are willing to serve as co-creators with God or life.

There are already plenty of individuals doing much good work with the intent to improve the quality of life. I strongly believe this is the meaning of a spiritual life of co-creating as partners with the Divine in being of service. Sadly, there is also much confusion about the spiritual purpose of our own existence. So many of us believe that our purpose is to simply enjoy life and profit all we can. To do so is, of course, natural, but not mindlessly. Many problems surface because we neglect, and even at times refuse, to face up to the true meaning of what it is to be spiritual in order to work in harmony with life.

To me, to be of service and genuine about it starts with being aware of how our human activities affect us personally and all we touch in our daily lives. Spirituality is as real to me as the air I breathe, not just a belief in a particular religion to give it value. We can argue about believing or not in a divine origin. At the end of it all, after endless arguments, only your own personal experience is the one that matters. I have come to view spirituality as the guiding compass to find harmony within yourself first, then with others. Most importantly, we search for meaning in our existence in order to participate harmoniously with all of life. Each one of us is confronted with a choice of ideals to give our lives purpose.

I see this new millennium not just like another passing momentum of "time" in the history of the earth or humanity, but as the beginning of a shift (a new cycle) that will transform all of our human perceptions and, as such, transform human history. The many world events happening all over the planet are already changing much of the traditional beliefs that have been so powerful and seemingly culturally strong and secure. No one can predict accurately what we are going to face to get us to a stage of evolution that will transform the way we live. Years, decades and centuries are but a passing moment in God's higher perspective. For us humans, those moments can be excruciatingly painful days, months and years of numbness of spirit and miseries to go through . . . Still, I believe you have to be blind not to see that the process of change has been picking up momentum. For me, life or God is ever changing, transforming and evolving. We cannot avoid it. Some of us are seeing many old prophecies from various sources about to become reality or already past history. Do we fear or accept the inevitable changes life has in store for us? We prefer to refuse to face up with intelligence and grace the impermanent nature of our own existence or all of life, which refuses to be "still".

Permanence being impossible, it is wise to observe that every moment is new and is created by us. We call it "the present" and it continually moves to another present moment. It can be said to be the perpetual moment of "now" with all the life changes, big or small, to make life evolve. We are all entitled to our beliefs and the rightful legacy of our cultural backgrounds. With the advent of immediate communications, we are often challenged to absorb and process the constant flow of information. I believe it is changing many beliefs. The time has come to find common values that are recognized as universal, regardless of the cultural or religious legacy; the spirit of love excludes no one. It is wise to pay attention to the ones that work for the benefit of the whole or our Oneness, and the ones that do not work, but create endless miseries because they are not rooted in love. That goes for the believers or non-believers. We cannot run away from the inevitability of transcending some existing beliefs to move forward.

It has now, more then ever, in response to tragic world events, become necessary to pay attention to groups of individuals with extreme views or beliefs, who under the cover of either religion or a political umbrella, have no tolerance, respect for life or love for other human beings, and even less tolerance for divinity. They refuse to consider the oneness of all creation.

The only tolerance they have is for people who believe the same as they do. Any fundamentalist extreme view is dangerous and offensive to humanity at large; their understanding and vision are far away from benefiting the "oneness" and turn into a mockery the gift of free will, because love is missing. As such, those small or larger groups cannot keep holding hostage others under the pretext of freedom of expression of religion or political rights. More often than not, they will deny their own people their personal free will, claiming to be God-inspired by serving a "just" cause. Their true colors exposed by their acts, reveal soon enough discrimination, then hateful thinking, which I see as a disease of the mind leading much too often to violent or murderous acts.

We all have free will by the grace of God and consequently are free to think and act accordingly, each one creating our own distinctive reality. Some of us believe they have authority above others, more worthiness, more power, and are not afraid to demonstrate it, even if violence is needed, no matter where it leads. Powerful persons in charge of decision making are not afraid to coerce old beliefs that have become absolute to start with, to entire populations, regardless of the catastrophic results.

The world has never been so open with so much knowledge available to improve and better ourselves. The old saying, "If there is a will, there is a way," has never been more true. Cultural beliefs motivate some to feel entitled to possess endless riches, refusing to even consider sharing the bare necessities with others who are struggling to survive. A decent and elementary education is not even accessible to a huge number of people in this world. We are witnessing a growing worldwide population with gaps in simple human needs that are far from any fairness or even basic spirituality. Heaven and earth involve the whole oneness. No one need be denied riches or opportunities. The natural abundance of the earth has enough riches for all of the world population. It is our free will motivated by many beliefs rooted in fear and selfish needs that has been the cause of the many abuses we see around us. They are strictly unspiritual human deeds. No matter how cozy and comforting our own personal arguments or beliefs, we do nothing or very little to correct them.

The hope of the world for a safe and decent standard of living is getting more attainable. I have been listening to many "psychic readings" from various sources where such information has been mentioned many times and is repeatedly similar. Neale Donald Walsch, who has authored many books, including the best-selling *Conversations with God* series, is by far the most complete at explaining so much of the new cosmology. Other authors and psychics have plenty to tell about this subject. Everyone, regardless of their place of origin, has access to information about psychic phenomenon. With the constant evolution of the "mind" and personal conscious awareness, we come to understand that we are divine human beings. It is our responsibly to act accordingly.

I realize the idea of being "one microcosm" in the immense oneness scares people more than it comforts them. The fear of being diluted in this "cosmic soup" is genuine and understandable from our limited human perspective. I believe we have an amazing loving God who has certainly much more in store for all of us, if only we allow ourselves to have true faith to realize and live it. Life is eternal and in many forms. Whatever "wave" of life we choose, endless opportunities abound. The cosmos has more forms of life than we can imagine. The choices are endless.

Absolution

CHAPTER 2

Social Systems

The last century has seen the fall of communism. It would be wise not to repeat the utopian communist ideas, which glorified communal sharing with a social brotherhood, altruistic in essence, to work for the benefit of one another. As beautiful in theory as it was, in reality, communism – as we know it – turned out to be the single biggest human cause of desperation, injustice and gloom, turning to devolution in so many of its practices. It has also held half the population of the world in fear of nuclear extinction for quite a while due to an ideology which claimed to convert the whole planet. The intent was to have people join the party of their own free will and, if that didn't work, they were forced to convert.

The biggest flaw of the communist system was the total lack of any spiritual freedom. Spirituality is first and foremost about love, and it can only be sustained and nurtured through holistic values leading to positives actions. Love without free will is like a plant without water to keep it alive. It is doomed to fade away; nothing survives very long when love is missing. The key to love is freedom and responsibility. When it is replaced by coercion, and the opposite of love, it just accelerates the failure and decline of the entire system.

There were some positives aspects of communism, as well, to give credit where it is due. It was good for education and health care, in general, as well as for the military, which benefited the most by their belief in fear tactics, holding their own people hostage, and then depleting immense resources that could have served a much better cause to benefit their own people.

The most popular thinking today, and being accepted by so many, is the "free enterprise system", which advocates that if a society accepts such concepts it has the biggest opportunity to evolve and give people the best standard of living. Our "pursuit of happiness" mostly emphasizes the production and consumption of goods to help us find that elusive state of well being.

It is true, indeed, that many nations have attained great status and a high degree of social comfort and cultural evolution with systems that are relatively free, and in direct competition with one another, to produce goods reaching great levels of excellence, availability, and which are affordable for all to enjoy.

However, today's world is now facing up to the excesses of something, if well intended to start with, and being grossly abused in too many areas with differences of income distribution and personal wealth reaching the sky for the lucky few and poverty for the many. Where is the spiritual wisdom of accounting for each and every one of us? Where is the will to redress what sooner or later will become totally unsustainable on a world scale? We cannot avoid going through obvious changes. I believe some wisdom may surface before a total lack of sustainability reaches the level where human beings become desperate for lack of basic needs. That can surely lead to disastrous situations happening as a consequence of spiritual inaction. I am referring to the simple need for food and adequate water supplies, decent work practices and lodging, with social systems that promote fairness.

Our human priorities are in dire need of spiritual reassessment or, as Neale Donald Walsch points out in the *Conversation with God* books, "Politics is spirituality applied in daily life." Taken together, politics and spirituality cannot be dismissed as irrelevant or unworkable. The true meaning of spirituality takes into account each aspect of life without discounting or depriving anyone.

Our many religious institutions are equally on the spot, for they do not practice what they preach (their core values are highly spiritual). They are going to become irrelevant. They need to evolve if they are to be truer to their teachings. The single most important aspect is that they open up to other religions to share and live their values. Religions should not exclude but rather include each other in the spirit of love. There shall be no more fights over dogma that is increasingly irrelevant and useless in our daily lives.

So, equally on the spot are the many tyrants, political dictators and corrupt leaders of many parts of our world. Their life span will be shortened, and a slow or rapid, but inevitable, transformation will take place. I do not believe in superiority of any human being over another, but sadly too many of us choose to give our divine power away. If you want to give your power away, that's your privilege.

Unfortunately, giving away your power never gives you the opportunity to truly participate in life with the greater purpose and meaning to become co-creators with God in the measure of your willingness to serve. Obviously, this service is dependent on each one's abilities.

Fear is keeping many in line to the delight of their oppressors. Today, another subtle form of control takes hold through the use of media coverage and twisted information, covering only the aspects of the news which are deemed to be directed for specific results and beliefs.

Let me give you a small example. Let's choose the field of commerce for now. If I want to sell you a product using a fancy advertising campaign, I will magnify the quality of the product and then try to convince you that you need it. It is best to start with the youngest and easily impressionable minds eager to be part of the day's trend. So far, it seems natural and the obvious manner in which to conduct business.

However, if my product happens to be flawed or has shortcomings, or even unhealthy side effects or is dangerous to you, I can minimize the negatives. It could be endlessly argued as the right of free business enterprise, freedom of choices, even when science is involved to point out the negatives. There is no rule of law to even mention it at all, unless it is classified as toxic after long debates. So much of what we consume daily is truly toxic, but unclassified as such because it is unchallenged, for not many individuals wish to question and confront enormous powerful companies producing the "goods." As a result, these products are allowed to be sold. Let's assume I choose today's business rules, instead of a spiritual state of being, and I can sell you all I possibly can and get away with it. A genuine sense of spirituality would challenge the pro commercial benefits not with the intent to dismiss any product, per se, but to responsibly ask: Is it needed to feed us? Is it safe? Can it be sold at a fair price? Does it truly benefit the individual and society at large? And, most importantly, is it produced ethically and is it sustainable with no harm to the planet?

Ethics, the higher truth, the health effects, or the slowly poisoning of masses of humans or animals by the consumption of many products, are not intended to be exposed or debated in public. There is, of course, plenty of questioning and debating going on behind the "curtain" before it reaches the marketplace. At least now, in our western society, we are more and more informed. As a result, we are aware of many doubtful practices. We are not as willing as we were before to buy with the old trusting attitude of believing that if it's for sale, it must be safe.

The slow or rapid consuming of precious resources depleting the planet to satisfy our fancies is picking up momentum. We have passed the seven billion population mark. It's becoming more and more the subject of genuine concern for us and future generations for a safe production of what we consume and the evident reasons for sustainability. We are going to inevitably reach a critical time when we will have to choose between true "needs" and obvious non-essential "needs" to benefit society, and not just the rich and super rich. It is obvious to me that it cannot be spiritual to be promoting anything going against life itself. There can be many points of view about what is healthy and needed, or unhealthy and non-essential. That is a book in itself. I personally think our choices, as consumers, need to become more pertinent in light of what is truly beneficial to us all.

Today's thinking is prone to lean toward a self-gratifying use of what we believe to be our lawful rights. But what makes us believe we can use our free will or freedom for the good of "economics and business" with minimum ethics for the long-term good of our society? We believe a healthy competitive free market economy is what has served us well and it has become a western role model world-wide as the main contributor to reach the "goodness" of life. That we abuse personal freedom to justify our appetite for more power in getting above the competition has dangerously depleted the whole planet in just a century. To achieve our goals as super consumers and pay lip service to honest environmental concerns, and that we refuse to honor the very life that sustains us, is simply "abysmally mindless". It seems to me that regardless of your religious, political or philosophical beliefs, some urgency is drastically needed to wake up a sleepy world, or worse, a world stuck in contempt of intelligence and undeniable scientific facts about the prospect of what tomorrow may bring. It will happen slowly or even rapidly, but surely it will affect all of us negatively with more serious concerns in the near future.

My aim is not to deny any business their existence, but to point out the need for a newly enlarged awareness of ethics with any commercial dealings. If we understand the benefits to each and all of us, then it is only a matter of time until it becomes a conscious reality. That you think of me as an innocent or a crazy naïve person, thinking the world is going to transform itself because of my wishful spiritual ideas does not bother me at all. I will keep my wish and resolve to honor life or God as long as I live.

This translates into living simply and modestly. If you dare to pay attention and truly start to observe for yourself, the time will come when the many who truly wish to wake up a world in denial will not look so crazy or naïve. You, too, will wish for effective changes, not just endless arguments and cozy denials that are pushing away needed changes. Regardless of where we come from, we owe it to our children and future generations. Honest thoughts, hopes for meaningful spiritual or ethical changes, will benefit life itself and all of us in the process.

I am one of many in this pursuit. I believe lots of motivated people all over the world (some with high credentials and proven science) are searching for ways to bring sanity, decency, fairness, sustainability and transparent honesty back to our daily activities. With such a growing momentum, we are going to get to a tipping point where it will become obvious to more and more people that we need to get on with it. It will become acceptable to embrace real changes, however drastic they may need to be, even if painful or expensive for a while, by changing the whole nature of how we view "economics" and social priorities. The native people all over the world never took ownership seriously, believing instead in being the stewards of the earth and their community for a short time. We may again, at some point in time, take another serious look at what we have always thought of as being a primitive philosophy, dismissing the native wisdom.

There is no recipe for what may work for all of humanity. It is a complex world with endless diversity. Still, it is up to all of us to search and try any vision that is closer and more natural to benefit the whole. It is part of our divine nature.

Free will has to be equated with responsibility. The two concepts complement each other. It is part of our divine nature. We need to involve and account for love as the only guiding compass.

My friend, Neale Donald Walsch, often calls this "walking your talk". It is about being genuine and true to yourself and to the world. To do this, he suggests asking the constant question, "What would love do now?"

It is obviously easier to talk about anything, magnifying the drama and doing nothing, than truly participating fully or modestly. Your daily choices and how you "walk your talk", shows the world who you truly are.

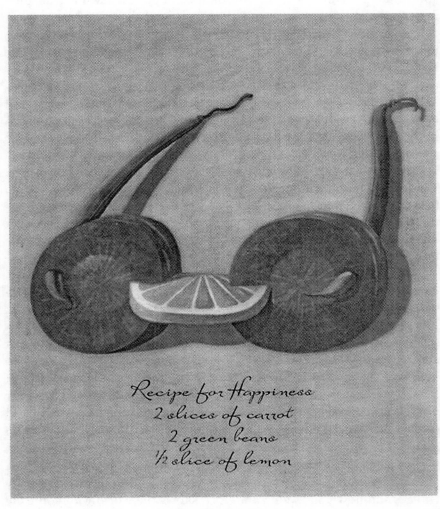

Recipe for Happiness

CHAPTER 3

Who Decides What You Eat?

The culture into which I was born has an old saying, "You dig your grave with your fork." There is a lot of truth in that statement, but the main element is missing. It all starts with the thinking process, which is the prime energy, the first cause of all that we choose to follow later. This is the reason I believe we need to bring back to our daily lives a genuine spirituality to guide us in all we touch, and the only effective way is to agree on core values or spiritual truths.

Eating has been the number one human priority for a long, long time, simply because of the need to survive. We obviously need sustenance to keep life going. There is a lot of interesting historical research of different cultures, some with advanced techniques in the art of food preparation, and others going a long way back in time. I am not a historian or scientist, or even a nutritionist, but a human being with what I believe is a good sense of observation.

I will tell you what I believe is decent and good, and expose what I perceive to be dangerous, maybe toxic, and certainly poor or unhealthy for humanity. There are many scientific findings and constant research initiatives that support what I have believed for a long time. It has become a duty to expose what made me feel so odd, uneasy, even repulsed. I hope a lot more people who are just like me will come to realize how important it is to be aware of what is really going on with the various aspects of production and processing of all the food that we consume. Many young people already choose to be vegetarians because they are appalled by what they see around them.

It is important to mention a bit of my personal history and the way I have been living since the 1950s. It focuses on the food culture, witnessing the many trends, then various ideas about diets and all that motivates our lifestyle, as well the many cultural beliefs that back all our choices. Historical events have had an enormous influence in setting those trends. It is impossible not to mention the major causes that have influenced our lives and, consequently, our choices. At times they are purely political before becoming motivated by economics or circumstances, like how to cope with periods of short local supplies due to extreme weather conditions. Another cause may be the many side effects of conflicts between nations or economic domination through abuse of power, with little or no competition, and our endless appetite for more of everything.

Wars, as they go, are pretty dumb. They do not reflect much evolution on the level of human spirituality. The one that deserved a particular mention for being "dumb" is World War I. It was senseless and insane by the sheer stupidity of what motivated the war to start with (the assassination of a duke in former Yugoslavia), and it dredged up old issues from previous times.

Past negative feelings that were never resolved lead again to misconceptions and result in a nation that feels "rightfully" eager to start a new war to show the other retribution for others' misdeeds. It was fought and endured forever and ever more between two sides that refused to engage in a dialogue of peace until one side finally blinked and gave up the fight. The result of any war is endless destruction and death by the thousands or millions. A bad armistice treaty created a repeat of war not long after, but this time it was strategically well planned, so the loser of old became the victor for a while.

It soon involved the world's major powers and they managed, after a long destructive fight, to stop the madness. My grandfather on my father's side was part of World War I and told my brother and myself endless stories about the horrors of that war. Then, my own father and mother were involved in World War II. I am the one to have broken the generational cycle of going to war by refusing to go to Algeria in 1962 when my time came to be drafted, choosing and managing instead to come to Canada.

The reason I mention that sad part of history is that I believe it had an enormous effect in the mindsets of our fathers to shape the world after World War II.

We felt endlessly deprived, not only of food and countless other necessities, but there were miseries inflicted on entire populations, the feeling of having missed living properly by not sharing the abundance of a normal life. An enormous sense of lost time gave a new vision of hope to build and create life anew.

The western countries with their powerful influences were involved in changing our lifestyles and mindsets. What followed were years of economic growth, prosperity due to so many inventions, and innovative business opportunities that no one could ever imagined possible before! A new world of cooperative spirit had emerged to elevate winners and losers by sharing a new vision regarding trade and commerce. The losers even ended up ahead of the "game," since they concentrated their energies in the business trade. Their military costs were forced by treaties to be minimized to the lowest use of their budget. Their political priorities could concentrate on rebuilding economic wealth and social benefits for their people.

The ones who were educated and smart enough to attain the greatest achievements, lifted up in the process all other levels of social categories, all benefiting in what we term a better standard of living. I do not believe our fathers had in mind such enormous development of endless proportions. They were happy to create prosperity and did not think in term of sustainability, using more and more chemical products and many techniques of extracting resources with little or no ecological concerns for the earth. The goals were to reach a scale of development to feed huge numbers of people and supply them with material goods. It was labeled later "society with foundations based on consumerism" as a way to create abundance.

All of this has been happening with very little interference, to debate who owns the resources or to question the huge inequalities of income distribution. The natives were not even involved in any decision-making for a long time. Their wisdom was scorned as "primitive". Since that time, more and scientists have dared to question the long-term effects of using chemicals to help methods of production reach such a feast of productivity. Today's priorities are very much about questioning all of our human activities. It has become inevitable; the challenges are real. There is an urgency to act. There are still plenty of individuals claiming that we are too concerned with protecting the environment and even have the audacity to claim there is not enough science to justify all the paranoia. As it will hurt economics, such bad faith is sadly the result of absolute delusion, for facts and truth about the real science has been available for a long time now and urgency is paramount to avoid the worst.

Are we going to find a healthy and intelligent balance between what we truly need and what is genuinely good because it is sustainable?

Are we willing to do away with anything harmful, toxic and unhealthy? The obvious objections are going to come from the many companies manufacturing and processing those products, with claims of no harm and freedom of choice being denied and more. Many will hire the smartest lawyers and advisors that money can buy so that issues can be stalled or even killed for years to come.

A good example is the ongoing fight by the tobacco companies, which continue to claim their right of survival. They simply moved their business to greener pastures and bigger markets and, indeed, survived and got stronger than ever. It can be viewed as a very smart business move, but cowardly as spiritual beings, avoiding any debate on health issues to keep economic benefits untouched. We are going to witness some lively debates in the near future about many hot issues involving mega companies. Their true *raison d'etre* to simply exist will soon become apparent, showing their true colors according to what they choose to defend. Some may even happily surprise us by adapting positively to society's wishes, and with the momentum of being politically correct, benefit financially as well.

We are talking about business entities and human beings facing great changes and at times total transformation. My wish is for much good will, of course; first, from all the different sides to come to agree to the slow but inevitable bettering of any activities judged unacceptable to the well-being of us, the people. The future of our society depends on such good will to move this millennium forward safely.

A few years ago, my friend Laird, who has the gift and ability to channel, and his wife, Patti, gave me a little booklet called *When Love Has Won, a Prophesy of Joy*. It explains their vision of what life is all about with much insight on the history of humanity past, present and future. The inevitable love dimension is placed above and included in all activities.

What has impressed me a lot is the premise to start thinking in terms of evolution over a thousand-year period. You may find a parallel with the "Thousand Years of Peace", which is prophesized in the Bible. It requires a total change of consciousness from us before we can start the necessary shift, but I believe it is happening more rapidly than it is obvious to notice, and over the next few years and decades it will accelerate exponentially. At some point, it will be impossible not to be aware. It is important to keep paying attention to events happening all over the planet that are shaking our traditional way of thinking.

I am using my friend Laird's words now:

> "This way of thinking admittedly requires a
> leap of imagination, but the current assumptions
> operate in such a narrow time frame that the long

term effects of human actions remain, to use the journalistic phrase, "below the radar." In every sphere of social activity then, human beings must operate on the basis of the same principle that guides the universe as a whole.

"These principles are as follows. Stated simply, they are those of THOUGHT, APPLICATION, INNOVATION and LOVE. In the context of the universe as a whole these four principles ensure that there is constant creativity being manifested amongst the great galaxies, amongst black holes, amongst the very, very powerful forces that as yet remain undiscovered. Each time a star collapses into a black hole, it means it has exhausted all its possibilities and is able to be concentrated in a very, very dense form that will constitute the seed of new creativity in the future. Everything remains in balance because all creativity grows out of LOVE.

"Love is the most potent force in the universe. It is more powerful than the greatest nuclear weapon. Love is the most basic building block of all matter and energy that exists. To take these principles into the human sphere, they could be described in the following manner: someone has an idea, large or small, and works towards making that idea have an impact, either in the physical or intellectual sphere. That idea can be taken by others and altered in various ways until all of its possibilities have been exhausted. At that point it becomes part of the intellectual soil that will give rise to new ideas in the future.

"But if the whole process is not governed by love, the inevitable result is anarchy. If the idea itself cannot meet the criterion of benefiting not only human beings but also all other creatures, visible and invisible for the next one thousand years, it is not based on love.

"One may have a wonderful idea, but if the applications of the idea are not based on love then chaos will result. If the innovations derived from those applications are not themselves based on love, the result will be the same.

"Take the industrial revolution; the idea was that of producing a greater amount of product while using less labor, a principle that continues to be the subject of innovation even today. However, because the idea was applied neither with love for humanity nor love for the physical world, for the environment, it became a closed system, where the criteria for success were based entirely on unit cost and successful marketing. In some cases, markets even had to be created through military conquest.

"If every idea, every application every innovation were to meet the criterion of benefiting all of humanity and the planet itself with a thousand year goal, nothing would remain the same. Cities would cease to be engines of economic activities; instead they would become laboratories of love. When love is the ultimate guiding principle, how does that change policies regarding use of mutually shared resources, distribution of income, housing, health matters and so forth?

"When the principle of love governs each stage, then all human progress will also be the progress of the planet, the restoration of health, beauty, optimal functioning, to all the great ecosystems. We personally think that would be quite a wonderful life to live for. It is surely better than the extinction of species after species until the turn of human species itself," they conclude.

Neale Donald Walsch, with his series of *Conversation with God* books, is more or less pointing to the same ideas and conclusions.

Everything starts with the thinking process, the very "first energy" with the question: Is it rooted in love or fear?

He goes on to talk about the principles of functionality, adaptability and sustainability. He promotes these concepts throughout his books. The values of love, joy and truth are the keys to living life fully and in harmony with God.

The various religions have the love aspect right, even to recognizing God or Divinity, and Origin as love itself. Where they fail is in the poorness of living and being examples of their very own teachings. Political institutions, kingdoms, or other systems with the goal of making life functional, are much too often at odds between themselves in their struggle for the most material possessions, which they believe will give them personal power. To make "loving for all" as their golden rule is far away or inconceivable to be even thought of as something that is spiritually natural. When you accept and enlarge what is loving as the very essence of what makes life possible, respect and gratitude show up in your thinking process.

The many events that the world is now confronting are undeniable facts of the lack of "love of life for the greater good", missing grossly in the way life is organized and structured in so many places and countries.

At a young age, I thought of committing suicide because I couldn't feel much love anymore in my daily life. I thought of taking my own life and thankfully realized that love was worth living, and even fighting for, no matter the obstacles. Wisely, after a surprise appearance by Maïté (her Basque first name, I learned later, means "love"), I chose love and life. From that moment on, I have tried to "walk my talk" in life, honoring love. I will do so for the rest of my life in what I sense and feel as loving awareness. I am far from being "all together", but is such a thing attainable as a human being?

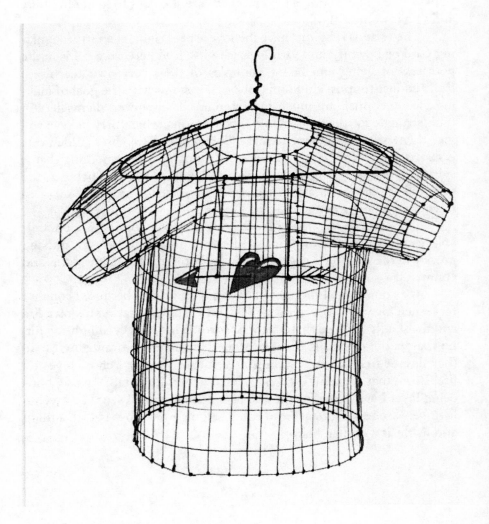

CHAPTER 4

Science, Technology and Religion

It would be wise for politicians and world leaders to truly look at life by being more inclusive of the whole and the real reason for existing. Maybe it is to move as fast as possible away from beliefs of exclusivity, power for the few, with control and possessions of resources grossly exaggerated, because of fear of lacking and mistrust of sharing with others fairly.

The world is rapidly changing and will not stand for the continuing gap between the super rich and super poor. The technology of communication, as Marshall McLuhan envisioned it in the mid-sixties, is changing faster than anyone could have thought. He talked about the boundaries of what is viewed as fair or unfair, possible or impossible, and challenging old concepts without fear.

These are the new facts of life in today's world, with superb electronic devices expanding ever more the networks of information; I believe to have only touched the surface of the endless possibilities ahead of us to transform this world. It is simply impossible to avoid major changes due to total transformation of perspective in the way we think of this new emerging world. The time factor is the only unknown question mark.

Let's start by giving ourselves the credit of incredible achievements in the last 50 years. Such a successful period of development is evidently regarded as creative and rewarding. In countless ways, there is so much to report; it would take a kind of "Super Guinness Book of Creative Achievements" to list them all!

Many human beings are very concerned with climate change, the state of the planet and health issues accentuated by the sale of toxic products. Add poor or stressful lifestyles and, on top, a mindless consumerism contributing to depleting resources at alarming rates. All these negative effects on our personal health or the life of the planet are challenging many scientists and engineers to find solutions. Some have no roots in spirituality; they simply believe all is permitted for the sake of science and the thrill of new discoveries benefiting them materially. Some scientists and engineers add a spiritual or even a religious dimension to their research. Often it is confusing in the understanding of what are the real life consequences to justify motivations to proceed. Confusion can lead to paralysis. Others, with intelligence and the added bonus of inspired spirituality as their yardstick, are challenging suicidal practices, like genetically modified crops, for the long term, not science or know how. Life has its own source of balance and self awareness.

To accept spirit as the all in all behind every single atom or molecule that create life forms makes sense to me. According to the *Conversations with God* books, every particle in the universe has indeed a certain amount of "intelligent awareness" or spirit backing. If every particle has an intelligence of its own, why would we want to tamper with our crops and plants, fruits and vegetables? It may not be such a smart move, for who is really so clever and knowledgeable on the bigger picture of life, to genetically manipulate without full know-how what nature has taken millions of years of slow evolution to balance itself.

No one can guarantee the future effects that genetically modified new life forms have on the long term of natural life as it used to be.

An enormous amount of data is available to measure complex life codes, even though much of it was believed impossible to tamper with before. Advances in technologies are far from safe if they are not balanced with a counter evolution of our spirituality. The monarch butterfly and bee populations are dying by the millions for no apparent reason. Don't you think genetic modification has something to do with it? I do not mean to pretend here to get into a debate about religious institutions that debate the morality of the use of stem cells or cloning. If it works for the benefit of mankind by curing disease, regenerating or rejuvenating and, in short, helping life, then it is obviously positive. If it is for particular gain to gratify or benefit the few, or worse claim dominance or advantages through such research over others, it is not spiritual.

Science can be used for helping to create something great or destructive. A good knife can be used like a great tool in any kitchen or it can be used to kill someone. We cannot run away from the purpose, then the ideal, that motivates our choices.

This new millennium is creating a new order that has to challenge each and every one of us to truly decide our truth. The approach to make anyone responsible regarding anything negative in a society is education. What are the ideals and values you wish to represent? What place do you have in a healthy society? Naturally, how on earth, if you take these aspects of yourself seriously, could you ever consider or wish to harm yourself and the people close to you.

Any issue with beliefs can become the sort of debate that is scary to any intelligent scientist or true humanist. There are sadly many examples of religious leaders or politicians totally lost by the advance of technologies and the new challenges they create, who are not able to rise to the proper level of spirituality to decide what action to take. Still, the golden yardstick has to refer to love with the very powerful question, "What would love do now?"

A lot of the world chooses to be in denial of love of anything, cleverly arguing to delay or cancel the intelligent steps to stop the spoils. The mass media can change and form perceptions by creating doubts when it suits them. This leaves the confused average consumer sticking to his basic immediate benefits of looking for price advantages and convenience of supplies. No such pain of being confronted; it's easier to leave the pertinent questions for others to worry about.

Those with more concerns at heart recognize easily the lack of spiritual awareness in so many of our daily transactions and wish for genuine changes. No one is looking for retribution or, worse, hateful revenge when love is at the core of any beneficial change for the higher good of the whole. It is sad to observe that, regardless of any growing common sense or scientific data pushing for changes, there is so much bad faith when it comes to anything viewed as a threat to the healthy survival of what is believed to be the law of the fittest and best for business.

We have certain inalienable rights, such as the right to vote and the freedom to spend our money the way we chose. These actions are done according to one's ideas of truth and spiritual integrity. I profoundly believe these choices show how much you truly care about applying your life's ideals.

Your family, your friends, life around you and the planet are also a priority. You cannot afford anymore to be a bystander and not be part of life's decision-making process. My suggestion is to be authentic in your ideas of spirituality in order to act. It is paramount to participate. Not to do so is to deny our divinity and our human responsibility as co-creators with the Divine.

Looking back at what has been thought of as okay and good for the world, we are indeed very functional and extremely adaptable.

However, we all need to seriously focus on what is sustainable, using love as the yardstick of creation. We cannot blame our parents for their lack of wisdom, given the state of the world that they left us. They were well meaning and didn't know any better. Certainly, we are left to face questions and ponder, "Could it be that our fathers, in the pursuit of happiness and with their spectacular achievements, built their castles on sand?"

Is it a success story that is wreaking havoc on our little planet? A *success* story? Who then is responsible for passing to our children a legacy of having to solve enormous challenges? It certainly has a shadowing effect that could negate so much of our ancestor's merit at being so hard working and successful. After years of humiliation and lack of basic needs and freedom, they made a decision to move forward. They went grossly super abundant. They just traded as they wished and did not bother about international rules for trading. They did not feel the need to abide by an ethical vision before competing freely between themselves and nations. It is obvious that the love aspect is almost reduced to the bare rules of courteous civilities and efficient accountings for both sides to profit. Nothing more was expected of them; the language of protecting the planet didn't exist. The next generation has been following the same pattern with even more daring pursuit of economic prowess and huge salaries or profits to outdo their fathers.

Those governing the market forces and who wielded power of money made no effort to study or even contemplate any sustainability for our earth. They contemplated even less the effects of vast social imbalances, our health issues due to a stressful lifestyle, or endless commercial additives. Just look at the chemical components, fertilizers, methods of raising animals, and now fish. An enormous number of animals are being raised under extreme conditions that were never ever contemplated in the history of mankind.

To reach these goals of mass production and all the new challenges it created, many new techniques and various factors came to the rescue. For example, antibiotics are used to avoid diseases brought on by cramped conditions. Hormones are mixed with food to speed up growth. That, in itself, is now being questioned as counter productive, since it affects us negatively over time. All of this is done to constantly maximize the number of animals being brought to market with an emphasis on a fast sale. The brand new world of genetic engineering with rapidly developing "wizardry" will achieve the biggest incentive – PRICE ADVANTAGE. Market forces are constantly coming up with innovations in production and solutions that are not concerned about long-term sustainability or love of anything natural.

Everybody competes and wants to be ahead of the other guy. Bigger is better. It seems that no wisdom can stop the madness until big problems or calamities occur. Why are the factory farms shrouded in secrecy? If pushed, the owners will debate and submit diverse scientific studies to prove that their practices are totally safe. To consider even thinking in terms of a hundred years planning would be already a great step forward, since a thousand years (as my friend Laird suggests) seems so far out of reach of our present belief system. Long-term benefits are meant to be immaterial in today's commercial thinking. Sooner than later, it would be wise to start thinking more long-term and include the love aspect to make it sustainable. There are many concerned individuals searching for ways to introduce a more wholesome approach to the larger effects of some manufacturing and the existing trade practices.

We are taking for granted our abilities to modify and alter the nature and origins of life. The attitude of so many scientists is pure manipulation without any spiritual input, let alone love.

Who will be responsible if calamities surface? Is it going to force us to face up and re-evaluate our life ethics or the highest spirituality for the good of all? I believe our fathers or most of the previous generations had little sense of preservation or ethics for the earth's sustainability, and even less for a spirituality that is all inclusive of the whole humanity. Once the focus is on competition through prices, productivity goes naturally with this goal. Add in the shortcuts that lead to the reduced cost of production, regardless of the genuine effect – short or long term – this competition may have on the workers.

The wheels of the "market force machine" take over with incredible efficiency, armed with trade agreements that are far from fair, creating excesses of gigantic proportions in sharing the riches of the earth and all the various deals favoring the few. Meanwhile, employees are subject to poor working conditions and low salaries, and are fearful of being outsourced.

This is far away from any concerns about anything spiritual, of course. It is considered the way to act and compete. We label it *business* and, as such, see and perceive it as being acceptable in our world. The priority of our human oneness is out of the question, as true spiritual evolution cannot fit into today's notion of business. It will indeed take much change in consciousness to switch the ideas of "getting" for the opposite – or giving – and sharing fairly what is truly the riches of all mankind.

The various legal systems of the planet are obviously catering to support old and rigid practices until human beings all over the world will start to seriously question:

Is it serving me, us, and the larger picture of humanity? It has already started, of course, but certainly not in the measure that will put some big business and their questionable methods in peril overnight.

I am not against business. I have had quite a few businesses myself. It is the conduct and the highest ethic behind each business that we seriously need to explore here and, more to the point, act on to correct the abuses. All that exists and is practiced has value and is of service. It is the exaggeration of profits for profits sake. It can be seen in the loss of a trained workforce to satisfy unfair competition, the hiding of unpleasant facts, the looting of too many precious resources, and anything done with malice or deceit to win advantage in the market. All activities serving the world are in need of reassessment with a spiritual motivation to truly be of service to all of us.

For example, do you consume with your family your own produce or what you sell? Does it give you joy and pride? It seems strange to many of us, but like many merchants who sell cigarettes to anyone, but will never smoke or have their family participate in smoking, they are able to separate what they call business from their true beliefs about themselves.

In the same manner, you can sell drinks or food products to others that you will not dare to consume yourself or give to your family. Now, if we are to be serious about ethics or any decency, it is obvious that choices that support your true beliefs have to be practiced by you first. Or, as stated before, walk your talk in the spirit of love, joy and truth.

If something is flawed and you know it, no matter what it may be – food, a bad product, a corrupt deal or something dangerous to your health – there is a contradiction in your make up to even consider making a living or a profit out of it, by convincing yourself that it's only "business" and therefore okay to do so.

The belief that we are separate (when in fact we are one human race) leads to nasty practices and poor behaviors. We need to find ways to re-invent ourselves for the benefit of the whole. We have to re-evaluate honestly what serves all of mankind. We, the people of the world, need to claim and demand total transparency in all affairs. This would change many of our present perspectives about each other and the way we act.

Another tragic fact is the ownership by a few mega companies of almost 80 percent of all food supplies to cater to all the North American market, and food production of specific items to secure those supplies. Included are enormous agro farms and vast factories to process our meat, grains and vegetables. There are the distribution systems, and vast supermarket outlets that work together to bring goods to consumers. Now, we even have countries like China or Saudi Arabia that are buying huge plots of land in Africa. Who are they out to benefit? The whole food cycle is at stake of being soon controlled and closed up in North America, unless we sponsor whatever is left free from the control of the mega producers. That system is not very old, still in the seventies almost 80 percent of our farms were small operations run by modest families making a fair and happy living. No one was starving or complained of paying too much for their food, and certainly animals and crops didn't require all the chemicals or additives in ways of hormonal substances they do today. A complete reversal of ownership and control has taken over. Now the big agro companies have enormous influence on the media, advertising and politics, and what do you believe is left for the remaining 20 percent to accomplish? Is fairness or any democratic ideal left free to balance itself?

Let's question the true benefits from such giants of industry to the average human being. Does it serve us well? Is it good and beneficial to our well being? How happy or sustainable does it make your life?

The first obvious benefit is that it is highly functional, and for that if you come from an ex-communist country or a poor developing one, you are in awe by the sheer display of so much abundance and efficiency.

The second benefit is the amazing creativity at adapting to market and reinventing itself in new ways to constantly profit or simply keep alive, since the competition is fierce.

Thirdly, we see the not-so-positive effect of these mega-operations. It has to do with sustainability. Their ideas of food are grossly flawed, not to mention the effect their foods have on human beings and the environment.

The dimension of love has never been part of any process, or even thought of or mentioned. As such, these processes are not sustainable for the long term. (I may not be alive to see the causes that will at some point destroy many of the food-generating giants.)

I can speculate that diseases, new germs and social rebellions will create upheavals that may become the very sources of destruction. Now, if we dare to bypass the silly clichés or false connections that we attribute to love in our daily life and truly give it the attention it deserves, what would be the outcome? What would happen when businesses put love in their dealings, starting with their own workforce? When love is part of any business transaction, it impacts first on the workforce where people are treated fairly. The productivity, the quality of any product, the fair price that is charged, and the rapport between the company and consumer are all improved. This is based on trust.

I am against world trade agreements that discredit any worthy local workforce for the sake of trading goods at rock bottom prices. On top, these goods are much too often of poor quality with no lasting life. Taxes or penalties could become a way of limiting outsourcing production to foreign countries. New taxes can be levied on firms for depleting the planet of precious essential resources, for polluting, or for producing poor quality wares that are wastefully unsatisfactory. Much good will need to be established with total honesty regarding prices, as sound work practices need to be international and ethical first. Otherwise, trading is going to be simply another way to perpetuate human misery and create an even more abusive gap between rich and poor. The world is in dire need to see itself as ONE, and assess the world's riches in terms of the ownership of the whole. I do not know how long it will take to have a human race that will envision such a future, but if we continue to operate as we do now, our species will not be able to sustain itself for even a few decades.

That will not be the end of the world, or end the situation which exists between the poor and the rich. It will simply end the huge gap between the "haves" and "have-nots." The differences will be reduced to levels which the new race of human beings perceive as fair, honest and acceptable. A new spiritual perspective can be established for rewarding the different levels of abilities working for the common good with excellence being the guiding yardstick. I believe that today's notion of rewarding work is closer to insanity than true authentic values. Just look at the new law passed in France that is aimed at fairness in compensation.

In May, 2012, the new president of France decided that the CEOs of major companies should not make more than 20 times that of the lowest paid worker. It reminds me of the example of Mondragon in the Spanish Basque country. In 1936, after the Spanish Civil War, the company decided to set new trade practices and established a salary structure whereby the highest paid executive would make no more than seven times the lowest paid worker.

Many books are exposing these various new ideas and progressive philosophies. They seriously question through research, and the help of science backing their facts, to expose what is often not thought of or hidden by those giants of industries. (See list of books at index.)

Do we need giant institutions to cater to the welfare of our world?

Why have we broken up the multitude of smaller institutions and encourage bigness? Is it truly "serving" us or the larger reality of our oneness? Right now, monopolies dictate the course of our lives by choosing a vision solely rooted in their perception of market forces. When a small company fails, it doesn't affect the larger picture of life. Perhaps it serves as an example of functionality not working or a lack of creative adaptability from which to learn, or sustainability never properly accounted for? Sadly, small companies can be sold out by trade agreements done behind their backs and leaving the big ones to become even more competitive by slashing costs. I don't believe they have our best interests at heart.

When it comes to bigness gone sour it affects us all. Financial calamities have created havoc in the U.S. due to the gross irresponsibility of giant banks acting in the competitive mode. They try to make money by offering unsecured mortgages and creative derivatives to sell to others financial institutions, regardless of the sound and honest practices of old. In the 2008 collapse, the whole world was affected. It has been hard to understand how a few unethical people and companies could nearly destroy the trust in the financial systems.

European countries have their own share of mistrust between themselves. Some have grossly overspent, and the hard-working thrifty countries are forced to bail them out. Where is the mindset of not spending what you do not possess or haven't yet earned? The new thinkers of economics have promoted credit and credit cards galore to the point that if we all had to pay our debts today, where would the money come from? Governments are doing their utmost to keep the status quo. There is absolutely no VISION; the goal is just to keep alive now by keeping the economic machine running.

Imagining a future where functionality, adaptability and, most importantly, sustainability are valued, is far away from most political dialogues. We are lacking the courageous political leaders who, while fully aware of the many problems facing our world, can be part of the solution. It is political suicide to go against economic powers not willing to change their ways. Many elected officials are not concerned with putting secure and sound policies in place which ensure that the lives of their people will be safe and worth living. They look for the short-term benefits that protect a very small elite who claim to protect the stock market! Strangely, they seem to forget that the stock market only existed for a century. The world had been going around for a long time before the market was created and will keep going around should the stock market not exist one day.

Food-wise, you can also make a parallel. The competitive madness created by the giant food chains is poisoning us by methods of food production working against what I term a decent spirituality. Add infamous agricultural subsidies at the expense of the regular taxpayer and the world prices are being corrupted by unfair trading.

The traditional little farmer has no chance of making even a small living in poorer countries. How can you compete with false prices and enormous economies of scale, making any of your production irrelevant, if you happen to be born outside of those protected zones?

But the world needs food, even at higher prices, and to grow it locally will always be the natural option. We have corrupted the livelihood of too many little people and I strongly believe we are endangering the future security of our food supply in the process should anything go wrong. Weather changes and natural disasters can affect production. Genetically modified crops are used in abundance right now at the expense of many heritage varieties of plants that survive the test of time, but, unfortunately, are not so productive. Soon, old seeds will be kept in crop banks instead of being used to feed us.

We are depleting nature's endless varieties for the sake of short-sighted economics with no one able to guarantee any lasting security of productivity for the long term. I believe our wise schools of economics, with savvy techniques and know-how, consider themselves ahead of the game and refuse to consider the love aspect or ethics. Who will have the courage to stand up for what they believe? If you dare mention the word LOVE as a motivation in any business school, the teacher will probably send you to the nearest psychological institution for a check-up! To me, spirituality is a full-time state of "being" and is constantly demonstrated by the choices we make in life. Again, what does love mean and why does it matter?

Simply, it is to serve the preciousness of life. Remember that, in truth, all of life in the grander aspect is God physicalized. Since God is life, anything proven negative is unsustainable, devoid of love or dysfunctional. Anything in life is using God's energies, positive or negative. The single difference is that negativity can only be permitted to last a short time to demonstrate that life in the bigger picture doesn't work against itself for long.

It doesn't require a belief in God to realize the wisdom of such observation. Love is the universal binding glue and nothing can hold for long without it.

But, like any attempt at wisdom, it is muddled in the concepts put forward by politicians, academicians or businessmen and women who are far apart in their vision and beliefs. Those who selfishly fool themselves with gratifying acts while shortchanging others are taking gross advantage. To manipulate the food chain as nature (life or God) intended is wrong and indecent, and does not serve humanity. They only see the short-term affect of their actions, but the damage done is often permanent, leaving others with mistrust and unable to survive.

The perpetual misconception of believing that all of life is separated is tragically working against all of humanity. We conveniently think in terms of total separation How else could it become even conceivable, for example, to loot the biggest shares of the pie, then be self serving between the few earning hundreds of times in salary what their own workers would be paid? This is a tiny example of the much larger aberrations taking place all over the planet. They are insults to any kind of true ethics or spirituality that lead to serious evolution. No one is truly worth a hundred of times more than another. God hasn't given anyone special DNA, making him or her king, queen or emperor over anyone. The sooner we realize they are human constructions, the faster we can come to understand our true nature. Our common sanity resides in elevating all of us. No one will be left out.

The world cannot go on for very much longer without a serious reassessment of the many distorted beliefs about the way we treat each other or the lack of true and meaningful spirituality regarding all aspects of human affairs. Many are conscious of what it means to be spiritual or living the highest ethics.

Most are confusing it with beliefs set in religion. It is true that at times some religious people are living examples of a very high spirituality demonstrated in their daily interactions.

Sadly, from my many observations, most human beings – religious or not – believe in the power of politics and money. This has become fully accepted internationally. Money, and the power it gives you, will be the motivating factor behind much of the mindset to act one way rather than another. This is what we have chosen to value, promote and believe. It serves us because of our economic success and, at times, our personal power gives us a better standard of living.

Obviously, we cannot discount the fact that some act out of goodness. The minus is the horrendous lack of fairness in the distribution of our riches, plus the added excesses that are working against securing a sustainable planet.

We are facing challenges of major proportions internationally. How on earth are we going to seriously tackle our endless fears of never getting enough of everything and the lack of trust between us to truly act for giving to the common good? For many years, my dear friend, Neale Donald Walsch, has been on the world scene conveying his messages of *Conversations with God.* To believe in God is not a prerequisite. The stakes are too high to believe that one or a few people alone can change our world without divine assistance. Everyone needs to contribute to saving the planet. This requires a massive worldwide spiritual evolution.

I believe this evolution—or revolution—is our doorway to sanity and it will be essential for the survival of humanity. How else can we secure a bright future for our kids? How can we evolve in peace and find harmony as a human race? Do we have the will to start a revolution that spares no one? There is much to ponder; much to learn and observe. There is much to discuss and much to decide. Every human being has internal challenges, but no evolution is possible without a conscious awareness. Clearly, we need to overcome what stops us from moving forward.

I have a friend, Rudy Eckhart, who specializes in helping people correct dysfunctional beliefs. After you realize how powerful issues can be and how they can affect your life, it becomes possible to move on and explore your life and your place of belonging. The interconnectedness between all of us and, to a larger extent, all of life, is to be seriously considered to gain a perspective that creates real and lasting changes. What is fashionable may change with time, but not your new sense of consciousness which allows you to finally grasp from where you came and who you are. The answer is a divine part of God. Once you understand who you are and it becomes true to your consciousness, you can clear yourself at last from the millennia of distorted beliefs. You can start fresh and choose a path forward that you trust and on which you feel secure. It will inevitably lead you to spiritual awakening. Ethics become paramount. Looting, shortchanging, showing disrespect, lying, and selfishly profiteering at the expense of many has no chance of impressing your heart and mind.

The golden rule of Jesus: "Do unto others as you wish them to do unto you," makes all the sense in the world once you start to grasp the meaning of "oneness" and realize that life is all about giving, not getting, this is the way to learn how to truly love.

Think about the many aspects of loving and how to apply them in your own life. It is not necessary to become a boring automaton, but by exploring the endless and creative ways of love, being loving comes naturally. Freedom and truth liberate you to joyfully express yourself. The amazing surprise is that in giving from the many aspects of your personal gifts or talents without expecting a reward of some kind in return, it does, in fact, come back to you multiplied in the most unexpected and wonderful ways.

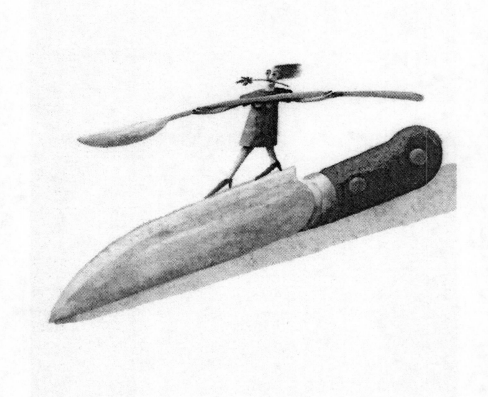

Balanced diet

CHAPTER 5

The Importance of Healthy Eating

The growing success of what is termed "organics" is a welcome trend. The love aspect is definitely alive in this movement. It is balancing the mindless and too often strictly commercial abuses practiced by the major food producing companies. Some are already paying attention, because most are feeding the world so far with good success, and that is indeed an enormous plus. They probably see themselves as saviors for the future. Companies are aware of the growing trend for more healthy products and they are already "cashing in" by utilizing the wording of organics and natural foods. Rather than just sticking a label on a package to get your attention, they need to abide by stringent rules in order for their products to qualify for the true organic label.

Let's talk of food being manipulated genetically. No organic label would ever reach such products. That, in itself, is not a clear issue that has a proven record of being safe in the long term. It goes against the natural selection process that took millions of years to evolve. Which scientist can honestly guarantee a total seal of safety with those genetically modified products compared with the order intended by nature? When you mix genes from totally foreign species in order to mimic an idea of a product, it is done with motivations of "convenience", meaning longer shelf life, a consistent look and better appearance. More production means more profits, which sadly benefits a few smart companies that aim to monopolize farming. True and serious studies need to be done to study the long-term affects of genetic modification. Does all this tinkering serve humanity?

The butterfly population was the first casualty of such practices with their pollination being compromised. Now, we are learning that bees may be the next species to be affected. Those who promote genetically-modified crops vigorously deny responsibility. The endless number of plants once available to us has been reduced to a few species of genetically-modified crops. Growers claim they don't mind sacrificing variety for the sake of convenience and economics. So, where we used to have more than 200 types of corn in the world, we will have only a handful if this trend continues.

The very powerful companies that supply the genetically-modified seeds are convincing the farming world of the benefit of using their seeds. It is at the expense of the little farmers who have traditionally used their own seeds and naturally selected their crops, even though much more labor is involved.

The increased production created by the mega-companies is jeopardizing the livelihoods of traditional farmers. Who knows if those genetically-modified seeds can withstand new pests and new pathogens tomorrow with catastrophic outcomes if nothing exists to fight them? Then, when the natural variety that has served us for ages to fight diseases is gone, what are we going to plant if those modified seed fail?

Why not create a culture of real natural food backed up by an ethical science at least as genuine as possible in promoting what nature took so long to create? We need to seriously question the true function of the fast food franchises that control so much of what we eat. Serving food that is poor in nutritional value, these companies have achieved mega success. They capitalize on yesterday's vision of giving people not "real" food, but an illusion of gratification in their eating habits.

These companies are no longer growing in the North American market. Are they questioning their *raison d'etre*? Some come up with brand new looks and some moderate menu changes, and it seems to be working. To revolutionize their business and serve real food is a huge risk. They are not going to do it out of the goodness of their hearts; their survival instincts and anchored beliefs about business are not going to wash away overnight. Their aim is to gratify consumers and make sure they stay hooked by constantly reminding people with clever advertising about their wonderful products. Those very products are addictive and loaded with sweets, too much salt, and plenty of flavor enhancers from chemical origins that mock or mimic real food. The movie *Super Size Me* is a "must see" for anyone who cares about what happens to you and your body after a steady diet of fast food. Pure facts; pure science! The giants of business usually crush anyone who they perceive as attacking their business by threatening lawsuits. However, since the movie carefully documents what happens day after day of eating only McDonald's products, it is difficult for the company to fight back.

To McDonald's credit, they chose to improve their menu and have cut down a bit on the gratifying "Super Size". Now, years later, we see public awareness increasing. Look at what Mayor Michael Bloomberg is doing in New York City. He is out to eliminate super sizes of all soft drinks. Bravo!

I personally believe these giant fast-food chains have a future ahead of them if they are courageous enough to start recreating themselves with genuine products fresh and alive with natural nutritional content, and with new healthy and authentic flavors to engage a food loyalty from their base of young customers. I give credit to McDonald's for providing clean and even visually-pleasing places with a side area reserved for kids. They have started to serve good coffee and are competing in a crowded market, offering bottom basement prices. This move to provide quality at fair prices is a positive sign. I hope this trend will continue and that much will be done to improve the nutritional value of their menu.

They can become good caretakers, not just serving humanity as a business, but for the purpose of providing true service. Then their advertising will not only be smart, but authentic as well. Maybe even their shareholders will see in this new rationale another incentive to contribute to service human beings instead of just a way to profit regardless of health dangers. Who can tell if they may benefit even more in the long-term with love in the picture?

One uplifting example of a company doing things right is the Chipotle restaurant chain. The fast food ethicist and chef Steve Ells serves pasture-raised pork burritos and free-range chicken tacos. In an interview with *Time (July 23, 2012, by Joel Stein)* Ells said his goal is to "destroy fast food" as it is now. "No more frozen patties, no microwaves, no more factory farms." As a trained chef, Ells is serving good quality food and his approach is working. His management style is to have responsible and happy staff. His views of the world and about food integrity to satisfy his customers are indeed "high end". I think they are highly spiritual, as well.

If you have a spirit of discovery, the movie *Fast Food Nation* is another eye-opener. The movie is a bit more serious and awakens us from our present torpor, state of apathy or mindlessness. However, these immense fast-food chains which provide food for so many people are ultimately responsible for the negative impact that their products have on the health of consumers. Another aspect is what the agro giants of the food industry, by their methods and practices, are creating what I believe is TOXIC food. It is left unchallenged and largely ignored by a sleeping world unwilling to wake up. Food poisoning is real, nasty and responsible for thousands of deaths every year. However, the food giants have managed to dilute the source and specificity of their products to the point where it is impossible to find them liable or to sue them. Let me explain. A hamburger is only a tiny part of a larger body of minced meat, as *Fast Food Nation* suggests, from a pool of mixed cattle (in that case, four hundred are slaughtered), so which farmer is responsible? How do you trace the origins of a diseased cow that contaminates the whole? Do you naively believe that there are enough government food inspectors to monitor the quality of beef? With so few of them left, it becomes impossible to do so.

Lobbyists have done wonders in making sure business goes on, regardless of causalities. The only time a big food chain is responsible is when there is a specific label on their produce, and poisoning happens repeatedly and from the same source. Then it is too obvious to deny.

The U.S. border was closed to Canadian meats overnight when a Canadian cow, dead six months previously, was reported to have tested positive for Mad Cow Disease. In Canada, any cattle that is found to be ill is required by law to be tested, so when cattlemen observed that the cow was sick, the animal was separated from the others and destroyed. That instant decision to ban Canadian meat created absolute havoc for the many people involved in making their livelihood from cattle farming. From ranchers to abattoirs, processing plants to markets, everyone was affected. Talk about having one rule for foreign meat and a different standard for U.S. beef. The U.S. system is such that it does not permit a true and honest check-up like their Canadian counterparts.

It took over two years and much effort by the Canadian prime minister to please President Bush over many unrelated issues to reopen the border to Canadian meat. If the U.S. is truly serious about food safety, there is much they can learn from Canada. Much needs to be worked up to have a true and genuine safety net where food poisoning can be eradicated.

Lately, Canada is setting up a bio-security program, the latest initiative by the Ministry of Agriculture, Food and Rural Affairs, to trace the origin of the food we consume. The idea is to quickly find the source of food-related poisoning or an outbreak of strong contamination. That could be from the field to the supermarket, and anywhere in between, until it reaches your fork.

The program also promotes the freshness of produce and the advantages of local farming, as it can only work if you are part of the system and agree to totally cooperate.

Eventually, it will cover the entire country. Will other countries wish to participate?

This is a step in the right direction. With good will and intelligent motivation, much can be redressed and the future can be promising again. Executives of large and powerful companies need to reassess their true *raison d'etre*. Will love get into the picture? Safety and caring for the health of the public is indeed part of being loving.

The last thirty years have seen the creation of monopolies and food giants at a pace that no one could have predicted. The question comes to mind, "Is it good for us, the consumers?"

I personally believe those giants have been too successful, and in the process have neglected to question or even consider the long-term effects of their actions. They created poor products under strenuous labor conditions and minimum concern for the environment. Animals suffer and new strains of viruses are created.

Another minus is that most major western powers subsidize their mega-agro farmers, undermining the traditional farmers all over the world who cannot compete with false prices of production, high mechanization or plain dumping by the same giant of food supplies in their own backyard.

I have seen it in Australia, which at the time tried to play by the international agreements that obviously were misleading or crooked. Those who attempted to sue or correct some trade imbalance were met with bad faith or plain denial of truth in the international courts, plus lasted forever at a huge cost before a decision was made.

The sad reality of unfair international trade practices are still very much alive today, not only with agriculture, but with fishing quotas, endangered species, copyrights, inventions, false subsidies or manipulating the rate of exchange, blocking foreign competition by administrative means. The world is mired in old practices of raw survival methods, waiting desperately for genuine people willing to stand up to such aberrations. I believe it's not that far away. It may be coming slowly, but the courageous, altruistic and dedicated ones are going to make their print. It doesn't mean that all is going to drastically change in the way life is going. Only the spirit that motivates anything has to be corrected where it is missing, not what is positive and already works well for the greater good.

Let's start with sale prices to minimize costs. The gurus and wise men of economics have promoted economies of scale, the law of bigness with the buying power and ability of marketing anything judged sellable in the market place. It is what is believed we need daily, even if some huge waste is going into the garbage for excess of supplies. In *Conversations with God*, it is suggested that half the poor of the world could be fed by the waste of the rich.

The supermarkets have made their remarkable success by putting together as many goods as possible in one big surface to attract customers. The idea is to save shopping time by having everything under one roof. The progression of such new and effective ideas of marketing have led to even bigger and bigger super stores.

To attract customers, most big box stores sell their products at the lowest prices, making it even more appealing to move masses of buyers from one place to another. To follow the logistics of such philosophies or mindsets, the next natural step was to expect and demand from any suppliers the same commitments, even dictate prices and pay back as late as possible to benefit from not using their own money, in the turnover of supplies. We are once again far away from fairness. The lion's share is twisted to serve one side first. The amazing thing is that there are plenty of new suppliers eager to work with them. The need to compete and survive overtakes ethical concerns.

I'd like to mention Costco as a huge supplier that practices fairness using the advantages of bigness. The idea is to belong for a yearly fee of $50 or $100. It is disposed like a huge warehouse with no frills. The products are first local, if possible, then further apart, as fresh as possible and then international, to satisfy the local demand. For food products, the mark up is only 14 percent, or 15 percent maximum, over the wholesale price.

At Costco, the consumer benefits by getting the maximum buying power with the most quality product available. It works extremely well. The workers are happy and there is a constant increase in the numbers of customers. Love is indeed in the picture and customers know it!

Farmers are also being squashed to lower prices by super producing, regardless of many adverse consequences. You can take many sectors of food producing farmers and often wonder how long it can be sustainable. How much can the very soil of the earth take with constant fertilizing each year to give them the crops they expect?

Is there a possibility of creating a dead soil, burned by overdose at some point?

At the moment, it is simply amazing to observe the quantity of food they are able to produce. I would be so happy to stop writing right now and congratulate them for their prowess and abilities at managing so much. They all are decent and hard-working men and women, so what else is there to say? To follow what I have endlessly referred to as spiritual or ethical approaches, it has to account for what we now call fair trade practices in all activities of life. It cannot be otherwise and, if the larger part of humanity will see and understand the new wisdom, I am sure that negotiations between groups involved and the working out of all the necessary transactions can be done in the spirit of good will and truth for all to benefit. It is a new belief in "trust", leaving no one shortchanged, cheated or dismissed as irrelevant in their old ways. Again, why not reintegrate instead of eliminating slowly and ruthlessly decent and useful human beings?

To pay more (reasonably so, the sky is obviously not the limit) and know that it is serving the higher good is not exactly a penance, but rejoice that it serves you and all of us as well. To avoid the immense amount of wasted food in North America generated by an excessive competition will be a challenge, but cannot be ignored. It is an insult to starving and deprived human beings, wherever they are in our world. In many cases, some just barely survive. Some action is required with minimizing or eliminating such aberrations. Food is precious and does not deserve to be thrown out for reason of convenience or not lowering prices, or ending up for meat-based products in rendering plants. We must challenge ourselves to find ways to channel our energies and serve others who are in need. The situation has to be reversed and we must find a decent solution.

To be obsessed with pure economics by ignoring what could be serving others is of no comfort to the ethical or spiritually-minded individual. One of the goals of this century is to slowly but inevitably evolve out of our most insensitive or abusive manners of doing business.

If we are willing to pay more for changes that are intended to improve all of life, I believe we are on the way to a bettering of our health and lifestyles while building more pride in our work. We can find trust, which leads to harmony and peace between ourselves. Whatever you are in need of, if it is of better origin, quality and workmanship then no one is at a loss. Love is part of the picture.

To protect and value good workmanship and restore pride with the use of life saving techniques in food production going with the laws of nature can only promote a healthier way of life. That it may again cost more in the short term, but save a bundle in the long term due to the costly treatment of health related issues, is a NO BRAINER to me as the obvious and only spiritual choice.

The present system is not harmonious and conducive to long-term health. I am not a scientist trained in agro farming or economics; I simply try to understand how it is possible to supply the ever bigger and bigger demands. It requires methods that confuse, scare and concern me.

When I see chickens by the thousands in small confinement, I feel sad for their treatment and wonder if it is really necessary to give them so little space. Even worse, some live in cages with their beaks cut off and amputated so as not to pick on the one next to them.

To avoid diseases by such proximities all sorts of antibiotics are part of their food. Then the antibiotics are passed on to us, even in small amounts, when we eat them. At times, their feed is even dubious. Some farmers are more genuine than others with what they choose as proper feed meant only for poultry. I am referring here to animal-based "flour" or bone that is mixed with grains or other feed. Make sure you see a label that mentions only "grain fed" or vegetarian-based products, and if the meat has no hormones, even better.

The pig farms are a success story of managing to produce so much at such low cost they are almost their own worst enemies. The market can barely absorb their endless production. Again, the confinement of so many animals is a question not many wish to elaborate on or even talk about; it is so much easier to avoid a confronting truth. Can we ignore a minimum of loving care and accept again to pay more for the comfort of those animals during their short life?

Very seriously, it reminds me again of my own father who was overly successful fishing and what sadly followed up only ten years later. With agro farming the concern is not availability, but the risk of any particular virus or plague of some kind able to decimate thousands and thousands so fast. It may happen some day; the concept of nasty new lakes created by the feces and urine of those giant farming factories, accumulating year after year, is pretty close to the shed hosting them. (See Toxic Food by Raymond Devos under "Recommended Reading" at the back of this book.)

Can anyone affirm it has no effect on the environment or the long-term health of those animals?

It is also disposed of in the spraying of the earth, sometimes way more than the earth could absorb, so the rest in toxic residue may end up in water shed deep in the earth.

Europeans have laws that force a recycling of feces and urine, but the same giants of industry from North America have convinced their government of getting away with such regulations. Some of those unethical giants are now setting up new divisions of their own existing plants in ex-communist countries with no regard for the environment avoiding stringent regulations, arguing it will scare "business investments". Those new emerging places are blinded by the success stories of production, as it is a well-known fact that when their own regime was all powerful one thing they never managed was to produce anything in sufficient numbers to benefit their own people! One aspect you cannot even mention yet in ex-communist countries is the "LAW OF LOVE", as they may laugh at you.

To add insult to the whole process, their goal is to export to other countries that are protecting their environment by fair methods. Again, like my example for Australia, you can be a decent player to protect what you value, but the other one can use chemicals, different feeds of dubious origin forbidden in your own place or country, but then allowed to export them and compete with you.

A world madness of trade rules over-protectively at times or completely open to unfair levels of competition by the ones involved. The "masters of business" of old have moved to new pastures in this world of competing for the lion's share, producing and selling with new vigor what is judged unhealthy in their own countries. For example, the cigarette companies and some chemical companies are not allowed to produce many of what used to be legal and is now illegal and, of course, all the giants of the fast-food industries are flooding their new world with western-style fast food or soft drinks that are far from healthy.

Add the very primitive labors laws of those countries, safety reduced to the bare minimum, inexistent fairness in salaries except for the ones on top, and it becomes a human tragedy that has to be minimized or best hidden from the consciousness and eyes of the world.

It is not much more growth in their own countries, but an endless new one for a quarter of century or more in the developing ones. All you need is to make sure what you promote is being perceived as the best thing from the West to make you a worthy and equal human being with the rich ones. It is amazing how twisted and false ideas can impact your psyche to believe in superiority as a very effective comforting thought.

The advent of mass media and advertising has created the decisive powerful effect on the younger generations. It has worked miracles for those big giants of industry. I often wonder if one day advertising will be challenged by true ethics, not just commerce.

If anyone would have told me, when I opened my first restaurant in Toronto that McDonald's would become one of the biggest companies in the world, passing General Motors long ago, I would have laughed and never given credit to it. But today, I truly wonder about their intentions and what they have in store for the next decades?

A fact of life is that they are powerful, aggressive for expansion, and cannot be dismissed. My hopes are with those giants to move forward and maybe lose temporally on their income by changing for the bettering of their menus toward a healthy oriented trend. They need to explain to their shareholders that money is not the sole priority, but a means of income that needs to be ethical. Their own personal sanity as worthy human beings, plus the safe feeding of masses of people, can turn into a true love affair; it will make their own offspring part of the picture to be proud of their dads or moms.

What is the sense in accumulating riches at the expense of the well being of others? If they believe even a little on the other side of our world, the world of the absolute, when the time comes to call it quits, they would see the bigger picture and be proud of their earthly choice. And if they don't believe in the afterlife, just to be decent and responsible human beings will do. Either way the result is beneficial and serves love.

Our long-term survival with our present food lifestyle is being questioned more and more, then proven by any worthy nutritionist as being mostly unhealthy. It seems too efficient to my perception and overly motivated by that vicious circle of cheaper and cheaper at the expense of genuine goodness, all in the name of competing madness. How far can it be pushed up and guaranty our food supply is truly safe to consume? When will a proper and beneficial human organization devoid of political influence, but backed up by the most ethical and qualified scientists, emerge to slow down at first what is toxic for human consumption, and then have the power to forbid any such concoctions to ever reach a marketplace? Most of today's institutions in charge of our safety are a joke, simply able to forbid the most obvious when trouble surfaces. If they were effective, thousands of people dying every year of food-related poisoning would be quite rare to witness. This is not to question the abilities of men and woman themselves in charge of our safety. The structure of the system needs total reassessment starting from growth to your mouth.

There are great books on the market right now with proper research and interviews with the relevant scientists or persons involved in the vast areas of the food chain.

The very first scientists with the backing of their own government (Quebec in this case and assorted institutions) are Richard Beliveau and Denis Gingras, both PhD researchers in molecular medicine. They came up with their first book, "Foods That Fight Cancer" with much scientific work to prove how important diet is in preventing cancer and many health related issues. Much is recommended in the way of freshness with emphasis on fruits and vegetables.

Not a surprise at all for my own understanding, since for a long time now it has been very comforting to know that my old vegetarian know-how was making a lot of sense. What could be added are animal proteins (it is your choice, of course) and a sense of ethics by accepting those foods.

For me, the bonus of their research is science that has value, something that has been dear and true to me for a long time.

There is much more I learned from those gifted and courageous scientists going against the flow of our abysmal neglect, ignorance or plain stupidity when it comes to a beneficial daily diet. Not a single fast-food chain is promoted as "good" for you or the giants of the soft drink industry, or to justify the many processed concoctions flooding our supermarkets.

There is not much joy in my heart to point this out. I often think in terms of time and space. When I visualize our actions and the way a future student of history is doing his homework on our present civilization, let's say a hundred years from now, what will he think and report? Do you believe sweet and complimentary notes, or wonder how we could have been so smart as to reach the moon, but fail to care to promote our most basics true needs for a healthy lifestyle. Do you believe they will be impressed by our intelligence in many aspects or lament at reporting our self-destructive habits?

I strongly suggest you do your own research. Again, I have a list of what I believe is the most relevant publication on those subjects. You will soon realize the neglect or mindlessness we are prone to let happen, simply because we have naively believed in our institutions or publics servants, or the giants of industry have as goals and a purpose to serve us well. I truly invite you to have a closer look.

This is the very argument most of the organic movements are claiming as dangerous to our health. Their beliefs are in total contrast to the mega agro industries. Their popularity is growing every year. Prices are obviously much higher now, but with the adoption of economies of scale in much more modest ways, their giant counterparts will improve prices and reach an affordable level if we are willing to support them in larger and larger numbers.

So far, it is proven over and over that their food nutrients are more potent in all elements of their nutritional value. Their flavors are superior and the appearance attracts people stopping to purchase them. The idea of the perfect look has had an amazing impact on the younger generation, as they generally don't pick fruit from granny or grandfather's garden and realize the vast differences the natural order represents.

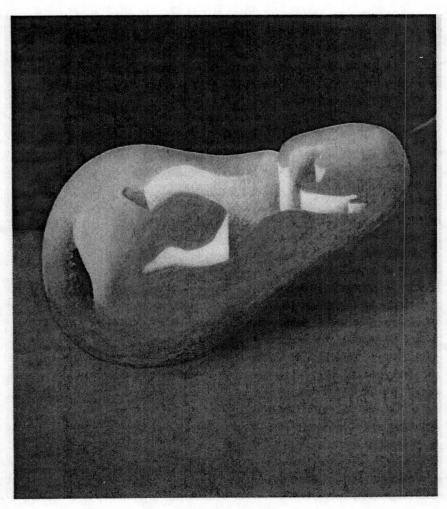

I fell in despair

CHAPTER 6

Are Our Foods Killing Us?

The health of millions of people is at stake every day. It is not difficult to observe that much of the North American food culture is part of the "cause and effect" it has on its own people.

According to the World Health Organization, the U.S. is leading the world in obesity, followed by Kuwait. In part, this is because of the American food culture that Kuwait adopted since the first Iraq war. Lack of exercise (the extreme heat makes it nearly impossible to walk outside during the day), combined with the consumption of fast foods and traditional dishes loaded with fat, has created an epidemic.

Many of the soft drink and fast food industry giants are hard at work convincing countries like China, India, Russia, Indonesia, and those in Africa that life is so much better once you adopt their products. In this way, the companies can become a powerful influence and reach billions of people. From a business point of view, this is simply a natural expansion of opportunities.

I choose to live up to my life choices, not to see them as simply business as usual. Long ago, I made a spiritual and ethical decision not to feed — or sell to — anyone something which I would not eat myself. This is especially true when a food has been proven to be bad for your health if you consume too much of it on a regular basis.

I'd like to tell you about something that happened to me when I was very young, just after World War II, when the spirit of American expansion was on the rise. It was my first exposure to a very powerful U.S. company and the way in which its products were marketed.

I was a young boy not old enough to stay with my Basque grandmother yet, but able to spend a few hours of organized time at the beach under the guard of a local beach club. It allowed for our parents to mind their own business free of our presence.

I remember a particular week of being entertained with wonderful games at the beach under the umbrella of a U.S. soft drink sponsor which shall not be named. We had plenty of fun with the various plays and toys all marked with the company logo. Even the local flags were looking small compared to the company ones. It was a full week of promotion to make us aware of this new drink, and on the weekend we could try one bottle for free. When the moment we all had been waiting for arrived, our sense of excitement and joy was hard to contain. After the various jumping up and down, and cheers for our sponsor, the time of celebrating by trying that famous drink was at hand. We were each one of us holding our beautifully shaped and distinctive bottle!

We still had to wait for the final approval before the climax time of drinking at last what we so eagerly had been waiting for during the whole week. I have to point out here that it wasn't available anywhere to be found. We were the ones to open the market of this new American drink!

However, when we all finally had our mouths ready to gobble up our precious drink, it wasn't the reaction expected from the ones in charge of the promotion. The vast majority ended up spitting it out on our first try with a noise of "harrh" and "yuck"! We looked at each other in dismay. Our expectations were so high and what we believed to be so special ended up as a huge disappointment. The bottles ended up being collected almost full.

The taste was totally foreign to our taste buds. In those days, soft drinks were made from some real natural base products. The chemical, even medicinal flavor and the dark color to add to it, was hard for our sense of taste.

For many years I forgot this experience, but not for long after a new and successful advertising campaign.

This time no one was making you try it first; the whole marketing campaign was emphasizing happy people, trendy and smart, adventurous in life. It seems that with this soft drink as part of your life, you were about to become that person. It took some time to sink in, but amazingly it ended up working!

The brilliance of marketing genius was about to transform old perceptions to new ones to suit any company willing to pay for and take the challenge of "Make Believe".

Today nothing has changed in the core message; it has simply become worldwide exposure with a few specifics or minor adjustments to suit the local market.

I have nothing against anyone in particular, as I am well aware that those human beings working for any company are first workers, and I do not wish to judge anyone. However, it is, I believe, more pernicious than just working and doing business, as the choices become far from ethical. For a long time real sugar cane was part of the soft drink industry, then corn syrup was used instead. In science it's called HFCS (high fructose corn syrup).

Was it cheaper? Better? I do not have the exact answers about prices, but I believe it was cheaper to make economic sense. However, it seems obvious why corn syrup was chosen with an extra-added bonus.

Here's a little story to point out the way. Every Sunday during my youth, my mother would send my brother and me to buy some pastries at one particular excellent pastry shop for desert after a beautiful lunch. We were allowed two each; no more. Our family did not eat much dessert the rest of the week.

I remember my brother complaining, and sometimes my father as well, that they could eat many more! Personally, I did not have too much of a "sweet tooth" and my brother or father were fighting for sharing the extra pastries left! So, one day my mother decided to feed my father and my brother just pastries for a Sunday lunch! My mother, my sister and I decided on a normal lunch, maybe with a pastry at the end if some were left. My brother was so happy when Sunday came and his excitement was hard for him to contain. My father was more subdued, but happy as well. The time came to eat and even though we usually bought a dozen pastries, that particular day we bought twenty-four for five people!

My mother was clever to put a dozen at the table to start with. After arguing a little bit about preferences of this one over that one, my brother put six pastries on his plate to the dislike of my mother, who suggested that he start with three first. It was an odd experience watching my brother gobble up the three or four first ones easily.

The fifth one went more slowly, however he managed to clear the sixth. My father took his time and finished his six pastries.

What happened after was not so funny. My mother got the other pastries out at the end of the meal and my brother and father decided on more! My father was joking and had enough, but my brother, I guess showing off, went through the other pastries, but never got the time to finish them!

Fortunately, the kitchen sink wasn't far away; he would not have been able to hold it until he got to the toilet!

Sick he was, and ashamed as well, because from that time on my brother's desire for sweets was very modest. My mother explained that anyone working in a pastry shop was offered the first day or so to eat all they wished, and four times out of five the new staff would lose their desire to gorge on sweets after their first excessive free binge. You may wonder what the relevance of this story is.

A lot, and again and again we are facing a world based on competition where what is honorable and good for the human beings eating or drinking those produces. I mean that being "ethical or spiritual" is related to a faraway consideration and probably is dismissed altogether as irrelevant for our time.

If those companies were using cane sugar or beet sugar, traditionally used for a long time, your body and natural reflexes of being repulsed by too much sugar will respond well. The smaller size of old bottles from previous generations reflect what I am saying here. Even if you had plenty of money to gratify yourself, you couldn't swallow more sugar than what your body could accept.

However, with corn syrup your body's natural response seems not noticeable. The part of the brain responsible to react to sugar saturation does not function, so you can gorge almost as much as you wish without that awful feeling of rejection, or worse, repulsion! It would not serve the market forces to warn the consumer about the health effects of consuming such drinks. The sacred right of doing business is simply perceived as freedom of choice along with the opportunity to buy or not, regardless of the obvious dangers to your health. No serious scientist would dare to object about the many negative effects. Compare this to the enormous size of today's bottles and imagine all the extra calories you are adding to your body to cope with.

Science has no understanding of why HFCS or corn syrup makes your brain not respond properly to sweet saturation or natural rejection, but you can be sure that all the executives of the many companies involved with sweets understand perfectly why they choose to use corn syrup!

It doesn't take a PhD in nutrition to deduce why so much obesity suddenly coincides with the enormous use of HFCS only in the last 30 years! To realize that if your brain does not react in the over-consuming of sweets because it doesn't recognized it as harmful, means you can load on extra calories and get away with it. To make matters worse, those sweet concoctions are going hand and hand with poor value food for the health of your body that are sold by powerful franchises. The constant hammering of all manners of smart advertising on masses of consumers is very effective. They seem quite happy and prone to indulge as their fancy wishes. Respect or concerns for the well being of their body is clouded by a convenient ignorance for their personal or kids' long-term health.

However, the whole body has to cope daily with extra, extra calories that it cannot eliminate anymore. To observe a sea of human beings grossly overweight is tragic and I agree that obesity is complex to explain at times, but those super-size calories do not help.

On top, it seems to go hand in hand with poor people who are also prone to consume deep-fried foods cooked in oils which are used over and over, the food itself being processed, meaning devoid of the fresh natural elements that your body requires. It is a culture prone to fall prey at the imagery of a smart advertising lifestyle accepted as convenient and pleasing to live with.

The truth is closer to ignorance and laziness of spirit to account for your personal well-being. There are so many products viewed as convenient, pleasing and falsely advertised as good for you!

Margarine is used by so many people who believe that it is good for them, but is it? Just browse any scientific data about the true nature of margarine and you will find out it is almost close to silicone in nature with one molecule missing! Even the bugs are not interested in eating it, but we are! The good news is that food manufacturers are offering newly-improved styles of margarine which are better for you.

The sad spectacle of major fast food chains being lined up with grossly overweight people gives you plenty of clues, especially when you observe what they choose to eat. The same observation can be from supermarket lines, when at times you have a close look at what many overweight people choose to eat. They are trapped in a vicious circle of poor nutritional food choices with the added plague of endless soft drinks to add even more calories to their diet. They have become addicted to JUNK FOOD. Sugars and salts are addictive, plus the pernicious effects of many "legalized" chemicals are added to hook you.

A mix of abysmal mindlessness on the part of any business involved in promoting such products may one day be recorded in history as "crimes to the healthy well-being of humanity."

Another recent movie that is a "must see" is called *Food, Inc.* It justly exposes the many aberrations our businesses are practicing as they feed masses of people.

This time it is even scarier to realize that telling the truth is okay, like in the case of *Super Size Me* or *Fast Food Nation*. The giants of industry are immensely powerful with government throughout their generous donations and lobbying powers. They have managed to have laws backing them up in case of lawsuit if someone is judged guilty of affecting their profits! Your personal health is irrelevant!

It means for me, for example, they can sue me not for what I am revealing true or not, but for the fact that it may reduce their sales and therefore their income. If you are impressed by what I am pointing out, it may have a negative effect on their business. Would you dare to mention any real sense of "justice"? It seems personal connections with the lawmakers to protect their business is what "justice "has become all about.

To affect or change their ways and demand more genuine and healthy products is long overdue. Where is the sanity of business and appropriate responsibility when the outcome is misery through disease for endless humans at some stage of their life? Then to add insult to the life itself, they are protected by the laws of big government against anyone daring to confront their practices. It sadly gave us the true colors of the political identity in charge and what is believed are life's priorities.

I have to repeat again that you are more powerful than you ever thought. It only takes YOU not to buy anymore whatever you are using and things will change very fast! This is part of a "unity" in conscious awareness to benefit all human beings.

The only way of being POWERLESS is to believe that nothing can be done by you, and let insanities of one sort or another stay alive and well, profiteering regardless of cause and effect. The addictive properties of the chemicals in their products make it very difficult for the users of such food and drinks to stand up and quit their habits. Your body deserves proper care and love. Young people of the world: Wake up to your true destiny and see your power at work.

Do you wish for true justice, a place in the workforce with decency and pride with a fair salary? Have you thought about how to eliminate unfair or corrupt competition of all kinds now on the world scale?

Unfair practices devoid of love will keep perpetuating injustice throughout generations.

Our present world is attuned to the influence of monetary supremacy, so to affect the very core of what is powerful and influential is to find out what will change it. It doesn't take a PhD in economics to realize that what is powerful is at the same time extremely vulnerable once deprived of its source of existence or to translate into plain language money, power and corruption of spirit which create enormous imbalances of income.

To choose a "status quo" that will affect your own well being and the one of your family, your precious health or our precious planet is definitely not commendable, all is interconnected.

Anything that you choose to boycott or refuse to be part of in relation of what you have clearly and authentically assessed as negative, toxic or unsustainable for anyone's well-being is a good motivation to act and respond with your POWER.

Be first the change you wish to see in the world (a quotation from Gandhi that he proved during all his life to be very powerful).

It becomes obvious not to participate in how far bad faith can be pushed or the survival instinct. We realize how insensitive, petty or ignorant our justice system can be in protecting toxic practices and institutions producing those products. Our actual leaders or persons in charge of most of our institutions may even be good respected members of our social life, including churches, synagogues, mosques, private socials clubs, and the good neighbors next to you.

The new millennium brings a series of relevant questions in all of our human affairs, from the daily bread and all food intakes we consume to all social relationships, activities and production of goods of all kind to useful effects. Much has to be worked up to eliminate with time the purely senselessly gratifying ones.

All actions need to be addressed from a new vision of justice with a more global meaning: "Is it good for me, others, or for humanity and our planet?"

Commerce alone with the enormous wealth it has created needs to be reassessed. The reasons are self-evident. Our planet, due to our insatiable needs, cannot sustain itself indefinitely unless we learn to prioritize what we truly need.

To make things worse, most emerging countries with their cheap labor costs and the competitive madness of the West are eager to give them the best technologies, but are not really helping them to make decent salaries to help themselves evolve faster.

The paradox is that we have limited resources, but are promoting cheap and useless wares (instead of long term) that come from those developing countries, even if in the process we sacrifice our own long-term manufacturing and all related jobs. To make some sense and save precious Earth resources we need to manufacture only for the very long term, saving jobs and the know how of good workmanship. Another case of competing against ethics, common sense or creative love, is giving the priority to "raw profits" and adding to the cause of so many destructives practices affecting the planet and us. I was suggesting earlier to tax wasteful unsatisfactory production. Something has to be work out, but hopefully not so extreme.

Another sad picture is our insecurity. Just think in terms of enormous military spending going constantly up for fear and lack of genuine trust between human beings. A good start to peace will be to exchange as much knowledge as possible between nations and have our kids staying with different families from both sides. That will diffuse issues of racism leading to hatred through the help and learning from each other, and establish friendships for life.

Some countries have done this as an "exchange student" relations program that has proven great for learning about others. So much is wasted on resources misplaced, misused and mismanaged. We are in urgent need of true reassessment of the enormous amounts of military budgets all over the world, all because of our suspicions of each other. The few bullies or dictators eager to stay in charge in this world, no mater how drastic and oppressive their ruling, cannot sustain their power for very long once peace truly becomes the spiritual goal and duty of the entire world to work for. It can be secured by the good will and power of the many countries participating in such a great achievement.

Imagine the immense resources going to education or to help in other areas, leaving a minimum military world until it may not even be needed anymore at some point in time. Who needs to fear the neighbor if we are reasonably happy, friendly and peaceful? Because we truly know and value each other, we can come to gradually understand our oneness.

Our medical system is being strained by even more enormous expenses. The super wealthy giants of business have contributed to accelerate a continuity of diseases to even younger and younger age groups.

Are we going to understand the necessity to involve the most brilliant minds, the most ethical thinkers, the most able and altruistic ones to get us out of a growing set of problems and assorted challenges? Much is starting to be seriously debated. At times we are witnessing true good will evolving. Even our political leaders are starting to believe in ethics. There are many politicians emerging on the scene, including President Obama, who, I believe, bring a fresh point-of-view to politics.

During the first election, the opposing party was constantly magnifying his lack of experience of government affairs, but his message was always clear about who he was and what to expect from him. I believe people all over, regardless of color, race or social background, have a hope for true changes meaningful to them, and the first one is TRUST, then DECENCY, then TRANSPARENCY, as well a belief in HOPE and a more just and equal opportunity in life choices.

Without promoting any particular political party, I think there are certainly values worth mentioning. The abilities, the conduct of daily affairs, and the solving of multitudes of enormous challenges is for us to witness and act our part in for the ones involved. Maybe a new approach has started, a new beginning in the conduct of human inter-actions. Will opposing parties see it as an opportunity to cooperate or will the old instinct of political adversity take over to sabotage oppor-tunities?

What the future has in store is uncertain. There are so many problems to solve that this president needs all the help he can get. It will be great to see a willingness to have both major parties cooperate in view of the magnitude of challenges to work up.

Will it be possible to lay aside olds attitudes of competing for "being the right one"?

Mr. Obama has been targeted by constant opposing forces. His modest attempt to give Americans what many countries of this world enjoy in medical benefits cost Mr. Obama the support of Congress. Not much power is left to move the country to a place of fairness and places value on the genuine sharing of wealth and spiritual wisdom.

So much is waiting for a fresh and new attitude at solving so much of the world's problems or unfair engrained habits, regardless of the politicial party.

Fear has been sadly a tool used intensively by religious leaders or politicians in charge of deciding what's good for you or not. Eccen-tricities and endless rules poison life for lack of true personal responsi-ble spiritual awareness. If we were simply more honestly spiritual or ethical in the daily conduct of our lives, all those harsh or primitive laws in time will become irrelevant. The ways and manners in which laws are written and applied gave us a good degree of knowing how civilized or evolved we truly are as citizens who are part of a national identity.

God has been used to validate endless human constructions with no shame, and worst, no intelligence to back them up. It is just plain fear with harsh stories of retributions in case of no compliance. Some will even go as far as pretending that God wants your beard that way! Again, Neale Donald Walsch has been the courageous one to write about this in his book, *What GOD Wants*. In it, he leaves 10 empty pages, then adds . . . NOTHING! The book is remarkable by all the concepts being clearly explained. If you happen to find some relevance in this book, all of Neale's books are a must. As mentioned before, much is suggested in the way of exploring at the end of this book.

Our presence on this earth at that very delicate time in the making of a new paradigm for humanity may not be for the faint hearted. I believe that the religious fundamentalists who refuse to evolve and open up to a true meaningful spirituality do not have much of a future. Much too often it is simply impossible to even engage in dialogue with them. Their mindset is rigid and self-righteous, and they are full of certainties. Nothing gets in, even less is given, and nothing has a chance of transcending anything. But I respect them; they are human beings following what they believe to be set in stone for eternity! Let's hope for them and to the greater common benefit, maybe they have the audacity to explore even a little, or they will end up as being irrelevant in time from their own offspring.

Sometimes I totally agree with diverse views like edicts or rules. Some rules make a lot of sense. From India, many faiths will emphasize vegetarian over heavy diets dependent on dead animals. No matter how great a chef you are, it still is more natural to pay attention to food that has the most life force in it!

Some serious thinkers and scientists are even recommending that at some point in time we will need to become almost fully vegetarian in order to save our planet. The simple truth is that a growing and richer population eating more and more meat cannot be sustained for very much longer in the future.

During my vegan years, it was explained to me that the elephants eat grass and find in it much life force. That very life force had many factors contributing to enhance or reduce our personal vibrancy. The sun has the most to contribute to life itself. Any growth will develop and mature well with the sunlight. Then the earth's magnetic field has a big effect; something not very well understood yet. All the many conditions for actual growth of life itself have to manifest under good care. That can be from the natural forces of nature or with the extra help of the know-how of human involvement, as both involve love.

To eat meat is to eat something dead and find your food elements to nourish you as second rated, since all life deprived of the life force that made it alive is diminishing rapidly. The point is to realize that all is vibrating. What is termed life forces are energies, electrical in nature, sensitive to magnetic resonances. The various rates of those energies or vibrations give us the vast diversity we are witnessing all over. To push a little further in a very simplistic way, all energies stem from one source or what we call God. To call love the universal glue that holds life together or the most powerful force is the true reality. Science may use others words for it, but the outcome is the same. If all of this makes some sense to you, as it does to me, you can understand what motivates my choices. It makes sense to take the most powerful vibrating foods which are easily assimilated by our digestive system. To achieve this goal, freshness and the natural authenticity of the produce is essetial. As well, the food needs to be grown under appropriate and ideal conditions with respectful care. To think that love has no bearing in the choices we make or the way we produce anything is sadly shortsighted; we will reach a time in our evolution when no one will dare to ignore it.

You may choose to keep your traditions of meat eating that have been going for a very long time mixed with a balance of vegetarian products. I personally like the Muslim, Jewish and Hindu traditions, and especially the Ayurvedic, which insist on basic rules to ensure a genuine food culture.

Some of those traditions take into their own ethics the way animals are fed, then being taking care of, then the way they are killed with minimum fear or unnecessary stress, even being blessed. That beats the gore of what the large agro scale industries are doing to our daily meat.

That religions, institutions or businesses manipulate beliefs is obvious. Does it serve us well or maybe we can use the yardstick "does it work or not" in life for the greater good? Whatever the story or label is added on by any institution, we have a duty to find out and assess how useful, valuable or not they are to us, and ultimately our oneness in the big picture.

I believe we are at a turning point in time where to be made aware of what's going on is going to become more and more the "order of the day". We are part of an age of information, or it can easily turn up to misinformation if we gave up our power of demanding scrutiny of facts, intelligence of discernment, and transparency at all times.

That will involve all essential life aspects that are relevant to our well-being and long-term evolution. The younger generations have a golden opportunity to start the process. Pretty soon they will be the grandest majority of people with the relevant intelligence and numbers to offset the "dinosaurs of the old order". All institutions that are inflexible and at times dangerously stuck have little life left. It is strange they refuse to see or accept that creation is constantly moving moment to moment. The last life is not is a fixed certainty.

Natural choices beneficial for the greater good with the backing of science and spirituality will at some point become a priority. Even without any belief in God, the very act of being decent and ethical in all of your human interconnections is totally self-rewarding, and the spirit still gives you much to be happy about! In fact, the whole universe conspires to help you once you choose true spirituality over fears. Remember, the choices are only fear or love. Which one is worth standing for?

I will keep promoting endlessly a personal vision at times, as well as many other spiritual influences that I believe are keys to help change our actual consciousness. I am part of the food culture and very happy to live in a little village now. I have lived in big cities and happen to have dedicated over 50 years of working in the food industry. Even without awareness at first, I have never divided the spiritual aspect of food that I believe starts with nature as the number one "miracle" of food suppliers. After that, the cultural expertise complements the endless creativities that resulted from the necessities of eating food for our sustenance.

As I have mentioned before, I was born in the part of France called the Basque Country in the beautiful city of St. Jean de Luz. My hometown was, for a long time when I was young, the first fishing port in France for tuna, sardines and anchovies. My father, being the engineer, began taking care of the many mechanical aspects a fishing boat required to stay at sea many days or when traveling for weeks. He was also part of the fishing team when the various mechanical systems of the boat were working at a minimum. All men were needed to fish those yellow fin tuna, some reaching a thousand pounds in the early season of May and June. Later, in July, August and September, it was albacore. I went fishing with him only twice a few days at a time when I was in my teens.. I have strong memories of those days at sea.

The Gulf of Biscay is not known for being flat like a small lake. I had the worst bout of seasickness and nothing was available at the time that was effective against it.

My fishing experiences had to wait until living in Tasmania to again reconnect with the love of the sea, and all the myriad of beautiful fish and sea life living below those vast impressive deep blue waters. This time I had a hard bottom, sea rescue, rubber boat called a Zodiac, a Japanese outboard motor to propel it and a trailer just made for the boat – easy to attach to a car – and my son, sometimes with his friends, delighted in going fishing or diving in so many of Tasmania's natural harbors, islands and coves. There was rarely a totally flat sea. The weather at this latitude of 40° can change rapidly and the sea will become very rough very fast.

This was the reason I bought a rescue rubber boat. We have been through many stormy adventures, but always made it back and with plenty of good catches.

The reason I am mentioning these passages of my life is that fishing has changed so much since I was young. In fact, the fish stocks are so low and the way of life of a fisherman no longer exists in the same way that it used to. Expecting some abundance somewhere by just searching particular spots in the vast sea becomes harder and harder in spite of all the electronic gadgetry available.

I remember very well discussions in my family in the mid-fifties about the many differences of opinion regarding a regulatory system that some wise or visionary fishermen already had in mind, and were trying to convince first their own people, then their Spanish and Portuguese counterparts. As I have already explained in the previous chapters, the concern for the future of the industry and sustainability of the fishing stocks were being questioned and assessed. It was again an attempt by some decent people to include some sense of responsibility and sustainability to what was good and loving, obviously beneficial to so many. It will start by agreeing on a fishing net with a size large enough to let small fishes go through. That simple demand was never to reach agreement! Larger issues of quotas to restrain over fishing and give life a chance to sustain fish stocks never materialized. NO TRUST!

I did explain the sad results of no intelligent ethical or spiritual agreements. History keeps on repeating itself and you are left wondering *can the human race ever learn anything from one another's mistakes?* Is wisdom ever going to be applied?

Nature can only take so much abuse or mindlessness; the failure to agree on some intelligent practices of loving sustainability have created what today's world is. It is a world where everyone is thinking of their immediate self interest, afraid of missing their share, and not trusting the others to be honorable in sharing or to agree for the common long-term good. The total mistrust of my own people, and close neighbors to agree 50 years ago in what makes intelligent sense, can be witnessed today in many of our global interactions. Some are more scavenger-based than ethical, but all competing for whatever is left with total mistrust in each other. To see them in world councils trying to agree on anything is a true show of denial, lack of trust and sadly devoid of true and common long-term interest with no ethics or spiritual commitment of any kind for intelligent preservation. There are no serious international rules of law to abide by which are truly effective and accepted with the personal honor to comply. Some people are displaying their worst behavior by refusing to face up to the facts.

That has proved to be evident in the Kyoto agreement, where on one side countries agreed to sign and commit to cut pollution, but in fact did not keep their agreements or are so far behind that you almost side by proxy with the ones that have bluntly refused to sign anything. In the short term it will cost them something financial, or alter their precious lifestyles. Even with the knowledge of losing the very lifestyle they enjoy so much, it makes sense to fight for the preservation of that precious lifestyle; instead, they are denying it, refusing to sign anything that will preserve it. Talk of madness made incomprehensible! Maybe there is a secret desire for "Hara Kari"?

In Copenhagen, the world seems more serious to commit and have some results. Even if nothing much was agreed upon, the heads of state of many countries have shown good will, there is a dynamic of hope, and we will see how it will turn up in practice soon. The host country, Denmark, is certainly a leader in showing the world what is possible. They are committed in many beneficial ways and even have managed to earn many economic benefits from their long-time practice and vision that started in the eighties to actively find solutions to greener energy and ways to preserve it or cut down pollution. They are serious about committing to what life needs to sustain itself.

What has been named the new vision to save our world in Rio (Brazil) twenty years ago is now, in 2012, after the last international meeting, not so comforting. What will it take to temper the mindless and suicidal tendencies of big business or shortsighted politicians to take responsibility for their actions? Sure they will be long gone or out of being prosecuted after leaving a legacy of destruction, maybe reaching a point of no return.

Some hopeful changes are soon coming. Our younger generations are getting very aware of the facts, and with intelligence and common resolve they will push away the old to restore some urgent sense of responsibility and appropriate action. Many companies understand the enormous potential of work and the benefits for all to find ways to minimize pollution, wastes to recycle into energy or new materials, and food to grow with new methods all year long.

I recently heard a broadcast by the BBC about a British scientist who was mentioning something called "thorium" cheaply available in the world. It has the same prospects of creating nuclear energy to produce electricity, but with the huge bonuses of being totally "burned", meaning no radioactive wastes!

The mind-blowing fact is that this was known since the early fifties, but all research and resources were focused on uranium. The sad and obvious reason is, you cannot make atomic "bombs" out of tho-rium! To give it a hopeful twist, serious studies are underway in various countries right now to find out how it can serve the world.

Another good prospect at work is some fish farms that minimize pollution and even use their waste to recycle it into other useful organ-isms. The list is growing and growing about human beings serious at changing our world for the better and moving forward. Animal farming hopefully may get a chance as well to find ways to be kinder and only use the proper feed devoid of animal-based flour, rendering plants that can transform themselves into fertilizer plants, and as such, free the world of "unethical feed" that has previously been the cause of Mad Cow Disease.

For what is economics? Wealth and prosperity? What is the good of social aggrandizement if our planet is in danger of not providing enough? The risk presented by new and old diseases contributing to malnutrition is real. On top, we often see workers who resent what they do and food safety is compromised. We are already witnessing many earth transformations, new strains of viruses and bacteria that leave no doubt about the future scenarios. My hometown had many boats in the harbor in the 50s and 60s. Now, it only has a few left. It is living no more out of what was once a number one fishing port with industrial canning factories. Expensive apartments have replaced the factories, and luxury sailboats and yachts have replaced the fishing boats. The reason is that there are almost no more fish left to support even a tiny fishing industry.

I was in Tasmania not long ago and the same pattern is occurring there. The only difference is that it's happening so much faster. It makes you feel very worried. I was enjoying, a few years before, a spe-cial bond with fishermen, so naturally I always had the best choices and quality reserved for our restaurant, "Panache", in those days.

Our menu changed daily. Our lunch and dinner menu was based on what I chose to buy at the market. I was the only old-style crazy chef operating in this manner, but our patrons loved every morsel of food we served, our prices were very fair, and the restaurant was always busy. And with time my young partners actively participated at locating beautiful new products.

The young cooks working with us were delighted to participate. At times we gave them free reign to come up with their own recipes, the whole staff being the first "judges" before it became part of the menu. That way, we ate the same dishes that the customers were eating, with a little wine or beer as well.

Supplies have changed now. Over fishing has been the same as in my home region of France, so prices are very high now for whatever is left and except for aqua culture of salmon, oysters, mussels and scallops, with reasonably good availability if you pay the price, the wild fish of plenty are gone.

I have reported previously of using only what I believe to be the best available products, often encouraging many locals to start their own businesses when they had something special to offer.

I profoundly believe in excellence, nature being the top in providing endless rewarding products. Loving and respectful care is part of the process of any culture or animals farming. To respect nature or life, or ultimately "God's creations", is to be a good caretaker or provider, steward or a good worker in any of life activities.

No more no less; just be what your personal abilities permit with grace and joy of participating at the making of life itself, even in the smallest activities. To wish for more is your natural heritage, if you so desire, then learning is the door to your evolution. I believe God will always give you the increase as you evolve. In that sense, the sky is the limit. Some of us are true demonstrations of such abilities, but nothing is required as necessary. It is only by our free will that we choose our personal meaning in the larger picture of life itself.

We have a beautiful and amazing earth, endless opportunities, and now with our technologies even grander and more daring possibilities of achieving greatness in so much of life's adventures ahead of us. Let's choose a pursuit of happiness that denies no one of their natural heritage, and come to see and understand that peace, prosperity and harmony between ourselves requires us to evolve in recognizing each other as precious spiritual beings.

No science, no higher knowledge, no political system, no religion or any human grouping can evolve in peace without adopting a system of values that is sound, secure, and always searching for a spiritual source that has a genuine source of love to back up any of its core foundations. With this new consciousness, our old and tenacious beliefs of being separated will fade away, opening up at last a genuine human fraternity ready to cooperate.

Each generation builds their own addition, their own creative print, their own glory.

Nature has an endless variety of species, each one adding to life harmonies. Our human differences are to be treasured for us to recognize and learn to appreciate them, not to be used with spreading and cultivating false fears to separate us and perpetuating our mistrust in one another.

It is with this vision in mind that I comprehend the thousand years of bliss in the making.

It is up to each and every one of us to actively participate in serving this new cycle of our earth.

My personal story has only relevance if I recognize how my life events and experiences have made sense or not. I mean, in view of a genuine spiritual awareness to serve as a modest contributor to life itself, all there is, what we call God.

I hope I succeeded in honoring my promise to the "heavenly figure of light" in my dream a few years ago now. It refuses to fade away until I act. By accepting to do so, I certainly feel I have found a constant flow of personal observations and have benefited from the assistance of others to make this book possible.

I hope I have triggered in you, the reader, something to think about; maybe a desire for soul searching, and most importantly a desire to act in any productive manner by using your "power of choice" where it matters. Soon, with more and more of us involved at making the necessary changes, we will all see some positive results.

Let each one of us be as authentic and as spiritual as we sense it in our hearts. We will soon accomplish so much for all to see and enjoy as we go along.

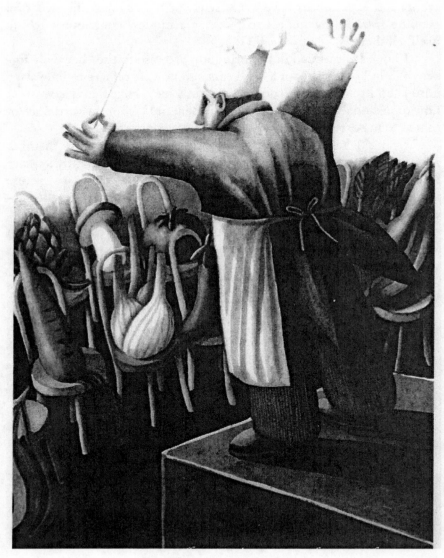

The Maestro In His Kitchen

CHAPTER 7

Food for the Body, Soul and Spirit

There is a questionable correlation between spirit, mind and body. It is essential that you grasp these three aspects of what we call you or me. Without the harmonization of these three in one, nothing serious will be possible in making your life a happy experience for the long term.

From the spiritual aspect and ideally first, the spirit leads by the goals you set, then the mind makes up a plan of execution in the manner and ways to accomplish the goals. The mind is always the builder and spirit the motivation. However, it takes some effort and practice to differentiate the mind's motivations, often clouded by the noise of our own ego self (full of fears and age-old survival instincts, and not always pretty) and the real self or the small voice of our true self or spirit (soul). The body will follow and respond to both according to our seriousness of beliefs, followed by the application of our choices.

If your life is great, your table abundant with great food, your health in good order, there is not too much in this part of the book for you! You are already ahead!

Before I suggest anything, I'd like to refer to my personal experience in the choice of foods from the markets around the world which I've had the privilege to visit or buy from. I would like to share my personal family associations with farmers and producers of specialty goods, and making the food for the many cafe-bakery-pastry shops and restaurants I have opened and managed in three continents.

France is a small country in size, but enormous when it comes to anything cultural, food being paramount, in view of endless other activities. The world has now opened up and we all benefit from multi-cultural exchanges. The easiest manner to learn how to relate to one another is greatly facilitated around a table by sharing some beautiful food with a loving joyful attitude. It creates bridges where conversations flow, and if you respect others' views and mindsets, much can be explored. You truly learn there are many ways to see a particular issue. As long as you don't insist on being right, we can manage to live and let live.

The *Conversations With God* saying, "My way is not necessary a better way, but another way" becomes a reality in the understanding of tolerance by not judging anyone. The world is an incredible display of human ingenuity. Cultural advances of nations are certainly expressed in the way food is grown, nurtured, processed and distributed, then cooked and served. Much is reflected with the many techniques and availability of choices. Traditions are equally magnifying the excellence of workmanship, or the lack of it!

Today's focus on the food scene is shared in TV shows where great chefs compete. There are endless cookbooks being printed every year, and revues by food critics more and more refined. Our food culture, local and international, is part of the way of life for everyone. The world has opened up to cater to our senses like never before!

Wherever you go, food glorious food is available for a price!

So, let's start by defining what our idea of food is and what motivates our choices. Our cultural background, for most of us, has probably the biggest effect in choosing our daily menus, although not necessarily on a regular basis. If you happen to benefit from a good source of cultural tradition, and your parents are still alive and healthy, enjoying meals surrounded by people they love is wonderful.

It is quite obvious that all is well and nothing needs to be improved, but hopefully they live as long as they wish. Sure there is always the opportunity to add some unknown recipes to the existing daily fare, and we should eat less as we age.

We have witnessed, in the last 50 years, people of my generation having absolute mindlessness, bordering on total comtempt for the well-being of what is good for them in the ways of nutrition and quality of life. The hectic pace of modern life has minimized a food tradition if not eliminated it, making convenience, speed of eating, and choices of food motivated by prices and fast gratification the new priority.

So, what has been pleasing, sugary, or salty, and practical to use regardless of true nutritional value, and perceived as not expensive, has been promoted endlessly throughout smart and efficient advertising. Our kids are flooded with images promoting a false culture of food. Real and good honest food is not the goal, but any concoctions pleasing to the taste buds or highly profitable for the ones selling those products are. My personal belief in food includes uncompromising seriousness in providing what is natural, genuine and consequently good for you, since this is what the earth has been giving us for a long time.

I am convinced that at some time in the future what is permitted to be consumed now will be banned forever as extremely dangerous to your health. Why is there so much inertia from our government, nutritionists, doctors and parents? True, there is more and more awareness, and we can see transformations and movements opposing poor food value products often referred to as "junk food".

Still, the bulk of our present general culture of food is flooded with products that are killing us slowly. Being healthy could be resumed as what ancient Greek philosophers coined as a healthy mind in a healthy body!

Easy to say, but not so easy to accomplish, especially since all of us are constantly brainwashed by advertising totally aloof to any ethics of what is beneficial for you as a human being. In this competing world, the game is to convince us that we can have constant gratification. If it was oriented for just adults, we could argue that we can make our own choices. Sadly, it is much more pernicious and tragic, as our kids are targeted very young through smart and creative advertising. The kids cannot make up their minds. They believed blindly the world of adults and, make no mistake, those same adults are very aware of what they are doing.

The U.S. Food and Drug Administration has been silent to explain the side effects of most of the chemicals, sugary products, or too salty items used in processed food manufacturing. They are fretting with recommending more sanitation, more antibiotics, more radiations, or cooking to death to kill bacteria. There are always new ways to dispose of evolving germs that are constantly more difficult to deal with. But avoid the true debate; review all foods one by one as healthy or toxic for consumption, or at least explain the risks.

What about truly being honest and start at the beginning of the food chain? Powerful groups are minimizing whatever truth or genuine good will is voiced so far by the few courageous ones willing to question and act.

We are fascinated by entertainment. You can watch on TV the cream of the crop in terms of the world's chefs. You may be indulging, sipping carbonated soft drinks, filling up on salty chips, or from an oversized bucket full of popcorn gobbling up sugary confectionery, all in the comfort of your couch or cinema, that even goes as far now as to sell you burgers and fries. And we don't see the contradictions. I have witnessed doctors, nurses, smart waiters or some cooks, very picky in their work, but aloof to themselves or what they give to their kids when food comes to be consumed. If you question them, they kindly reply that's what they want. Many of us have lost in the past two or three decades a social discipline of sitting at the table sharing genuine food prepared by a mother or father, giving in the process a sense of tradition of real food in a loving set up.

Today's environment is so filled by activities; the easy option of manufactured and processed food is part of many menus at the dinner table with maybe the weekend left to take the time to cook again.

With more interest in food in the way of being entertained, where is the reality of using what impressed you so much, but used so little in your own life?

Restaurants have never been so numerous; it has always been social and popular to eat out, especially on weekends. Some restaurants are excellent, some fairly priced, and some reaching the sky in audacity to value them. Still in the simple daily life of most of us, the cafeterias of hospitals, schools and institutions are serving mostly poor, convenient, food chain items!

A hospital bed will cost our government close to a thousand dollars a day or more, but the food cost allowed per patient is only a few dollars! It seems doctors can save you from disease at whatever cost, but the food you consume may be "dangerous to your health" or at best mildly acceptable.

The duty of anyone involved in manufacturing or processing food of any kind will obviously be questioned more and more. Simply by the facts of life we can already observe multiple negative results. We will then wonder how it is possible we went so far away in dysfunctional thinking. For the sake of convenience, budget choices are made. In hospitals, equipment that costs the world seems to be okay, but the food has to cost the minimum.

The degree of present massive obesity in the average population, including in our kids, or the increased risk of diabetes at an early age, or a surge of cardiac problems, liver and digestion, is related not only to a lack of physical activity, but mostly to the consumption of more and more dead and toxic food. Today our body is mostly "acidic" than having the proper ph balance. According to the Edgar Cayce readings, no virus can live with a proper ph balance. It is when we are mostly acidic that our body prepares the way for virus to develop. And guess what kind of food makes for more ph goodness than acidic?

Look at all the fresh greens, vegetables, nuts, grains and fruits that promote a positive ph balance. The acidic "imbalance" is created by all the death food which is deprived of natural goodness and freshness.

I will keep repeating that our business leaders need more ethics or genuine spirituality in their vision of today and tomorrow, including first the well-being of their clients, not just a fast and gratifying profit in competing or surviving, but to change priorities. Some of those leaders of the processed foods are using more chemicals to keep the "shelf life" of those foods from rotting, changing colors or bettering the appearance again. More is being asked from our digestive system to assimilate. Can any science truly confirm that these chemicals are really safe?

Who is going to stand up or even be allowed a grant to study in total freedom with no interference by the powerful food establishments? We also have preservation practices which make you wonder at times, is irradiation safe? Does storage for months still keep food as nutritious as nature intended? Sometimes frozen food seems a better option, as long as it is doesn't sit in the freezer for too long.

The focus is on anything that ends up saving money and is practical is magnified and easily adopted. In general, the food companies don't care about the manner in which animals are cared for and fed, before being processed for the burgers, sausages, deli food, chicken nuggets, and small goods of all kinds that flood the shelves of supermarkets. Do you really want to experience visiting a chicken farm, or a pig farm, or anything that is mass produced?

The natural order has been mocked for a long time now. Most animals in those production houses are never to see the true light of the day, much less be exposed to the sun, or rain or wind!

Imagine human beings living in such conditions? Diseases of all kinds would manifest pretty quickly due to the constant proximity and the stress of missing your freedom of movement. Maybe people would even fight one another to the death after a while by going insane.

Well, animals can do that, so the chickens have their beaks cut off. That way, they don't pick at each other's feathers or worse, their eyes. Pigs have their tails and some teeth missing, but they still can eat all the food they want. Some keep their tails and teeth, but live in a cage allowing them only two feet of movement back and forth. Sometimes even their feed is questionable.

Beware! Buy animals that are fed real food. There are a lot of questionable practices that from my personal point of view are dysfunctional. (Anyone curious about these practices need only inquire about the purpose of rendering plants.) I do not recommend going back to strictly old ways. There is a huge world to feed. I hope to see, at some point, a new and more decent and humane approach in the manner we treat the animals we consume as food, because we are fooling ourselves by expecting from our farmers and food producers lower and lower prices.

In turn, they have become way too smart at being efficient at delivering by finding new ways to produce more and lower the prices. That obsession is becoming the number one problem in the mindset of consuming, since most of us buy only according to price. The cheaper the better. Some big chains even claim that they will not be "beaten", as their prime advertising motto! Consciously or not, we, the consumers, are forcing most big chains to constantly be creative at finding ways to make a good profit and have satisfied customers. We also create gigantic conglomerates that are simply wiping away smaller and traditional family businesses or traditional farms of old. Bigness claims to benefit us by reaching an "economy of scale" in many aspects of any operating organization. If this is true to functionality and adaptability (although many ethical practices can be questioned), we are at a huge loss when it comes to sustainability. The methods and philosophies of cutting costs to compete with other giants is creating, more often than not, a total lack of ethics for the animals or the environment, or even the treatment of employees.

At least smallness has a heart and much variety, with a large display of products not found anymore. The exception is the specialized farmers who are betting on the niche market and who cater to the well off. With a rise in family farming, I believe that the trend will be reversed. Prices will become more affordable and choices will be plentiful.

We have espoused a philosophy of consumerism, motivated by the lure of low prices with the added belief of necessary endless gratification through our buying power.

We have accepted and equated the idea of happiness by constantly buying more and more, even if in the process we end up diseased and far from being happy, since we never have enough. We have lost the sense of measure and the wisdom to draw the line in our needs. Few of us are paying attention to what goes on at all the different levels of production. It is odd that television shows can delve into a pertinent subject, let's say about obesity, and at the same time bombard you with advertisements glorifying food habits that contribute to weight gain! Are we serious about life, or are we going insane by nurturing a culture of make-believe feeding on denial and absolute mindlessness?

Only when calamities are making the news for a short time do we dare to question a little, but then it is back to the routine of our daily life, for not many have the stomach to demand decency, honesty and real safe food, as it will end up costing more.

Science has proven, and any dietician will confirm, that to consume poor nutritional foods is harmful to your health. So why on earth do we still eat them? Even to go one step further, how can they be allowed to be sold? I don't want to put people out of business, but I want to challenge existing practices. They have the means and science to make products healthier for the larger population anywhere in this world. I support the expansion of these businesses worldwide, as long as they are ethical and loving. The way it goes now, when companies move into foreign countries, they keep the old ways of doing business, even making the people of those countries feel they are now part of the big, sophistocated world! The companies ignore the new science of knowing how their products affect people and do nothing to redress the causes, creating health issues for the whole world with impunity. Instead, it is turned around like they are doing them a favor to be there!

I do not have any personal grudges against anyone, but will certainly not be afraid to expose what I see as totally dysfunctional and dangerous to us human beings. When pushed to the next level, it means that we come under a general "spiritual amnesia" where we don't care enough to correct the problem.

Enormous amounts of money are being manipulated by those with poor or very little true sense of the highest ethics when it comes to dealing with the future of entire populations according to their actions and decisions. We are in dire need of trustworthy people with the gift of not only being able to do the work, but mostly have the qualities of spirit or highest ethics to make a meaningful print.

I do not believe that a new race of humans will be self-serving like the ones in charge of high positions today, paying themselves gross amounts of money, adding titles, shares or endless benefits at the expense of so many.

I truly believe many wish for a future where their kids not only can have their share of the goods of the planet, but mostly share them fairly, and by this process be at peace with one another.

Under the sun, or as God sees us, we are all equals. That certainly does not translate as sameness! A simple observation with each of us is obviously showing that we are not equals in human abilities, character, beliefs, socials identities and other multitudes of different aspects. However, we all deserve equal opportunities and our many differences will create our own share of life, we all end up creating the reality we choose. The key is first to make sure you can create that reality in fairness, because the earth's riches will not be boycotted by the few smart ones believing falsely in their entitlement of self service first.

Our new challenge in this millennium has to do with evolution of our spirit, or if you prefer for my many atheist friends, a new code of ethics for the world. Redefine the word love maybe, but use all the values it represents, for what we truly need as mentioned over and over is a dramatic change in consciousness. It means what and who are we going to choose TO BE during that new millennium?

That will involve many drastic reassessments of our human identity, our connection to higher forces and a new sense of belonging to our common source.

All previous masters were not kidding when they declared, and showed by example, their amazing abilities, their great wisdom, and their total indifference to accumulating material possessions.

They certainly were not indifferent to the daily activities and life events, their sense of where they came from and belonged. The key to their joy, love, total truthfulness and endless abilities was to share and make the pursuit of happiness a reality, and they showed us the way.

One of them, Jesus, even says: "Do not be surprised by what you see and witness. What I do shall you do and even more! Seek first the Kingdom of GOD and all the rest shall be added unto you!"

You certainly can ask for divine guidance, help and understanding. What are we afraid of, since it is our natural heritage? Will we have the courage to see things as they truly are and have the intelligence to move forward in beneficial choices for oneself first? I am not talking of material selfishness, but what benefits you spiritually, for if it's good for you, then it is good for the world!

Issues are part of all of us; they often hold us back from moving forward. On a spiritual level they are referred to as patterns of negative energies blocking or stopping our progression or evolution.

They are like an extra load to carry on the long journey of life, sometimes poisoning our good will and relationships.

Total honesty with oneself is very helpful in observing our actions and the motivations behind them, as well as the way we react, especially in unpleasant conditions. It tells a lot about our personal awareness in true consciousness when we choose easily healthy behaviors.

The big question has always been: who are we? Who can truly listen to one's heart without fear of being mocked or taken lightly?

When it comes to our personal health it is paramount that we pay attention. Let's take our body, for example. When you are told that our medical system in Ontario consumes more than 40 cents of every dollar collected by the Canadian tax system, everyone has an ethical obligation to smarten up, change behaviors that cause sickness, and demand that food supplies, or overly stressed lifestyles, are not massively contributing to creating diseases. This trend is totally unsustainable. Parents and educators have a duty to elevate young minds with the highest ethics and values. Only after the spiritual values have taken root can all the useful data be taught. Then comes the experience of whatever teaching is taken or chosen in view of what science has discovered. Science and spirituality are not far apart, but complement each other. Only when the two are working in harmony will the best opportunities to be of service for humanity materialize.

Even from the perspective of an atheist, with a minimum humanitarian approach, such a move seems natural. Our true evolution cannot ignore science that works in harmony with life or God.

There is plenty of scientific research focused on how to increase production through genetically-modifying our crops. In addition, farmers trusting science are tempted to take shortcuts when it comes to feeding their animals.

In 1998, I attended an interesting meeting at the University of Guelph. Anita Stewart, a dear friend of mine, is a food activist and food writer of many great cookbooks and is also involved with the promotion of Canadian chefs who promote local food. In 2012, Anita was awarded the Order of Canada for her contribution to Canadian food culture. She certainly deserves it. She has promoted food excellence from local producers and supports farmers who deal with originality and quality all over Canada.

Since she knows my background of food and we share many common beliefs, she recommended that I attend the meeting, which concentrated on three aspects of the food chain. One part dealt with the science of food and featured scientists from the university. A second dealt with producing and growing produce that involved the farmers, some of whom advocated the latest genetic wizardry. The third aspect focused on restaurateurs, caterers and cooks. We gathered around a big table before the meeting started. I sat next to a nice gentleman and we exchanged ideas and opinions. Keep in mind that just a year before, disease decimated England's cattle industry. I could not resist telling this gentleman what I observed when I was a young boy and spent every summer at my Basque grandmother's place where old-fashioned farming methods were still practiced.

The disease in question is what is called Mad Cow Disease or BSE (Bovine Spongiform Encephalopathy). I pointed out that I couldn't understand why science accepted the use of dead animals or other sub-products from animals as food proteins to feed vegetarian animals. That was transgressing the order of nature!

He explained to me that the process proved to be safe in the making of such proteins, but the British had an accident of production in one of their facilities they called "rendering plants", not getting a temperature sufficiently appropriate to kill all the bacteria in the making of that immense soup. He even added, "We will teach you food science if you wish, and you will teach us about good meals!"

To add a bit more on the making of that "soup", it is basically composed of all animal substances, such as carcasses, regardless of origin, unwanted offals, blood, and even past-dated meat from supermarkets. It is a very appetizing list of prime ingredients, as you can imagine.

In the old days you would find a use for such products and they usually ended up in fertilizers. I guess someone inventive and obviously prone to prove that animal proteins are valuable got his way! May I add that it is still very much alive today, so the relevant question is: Where is it going to, and which animals are being fed with such proteins?

No wonder you see more and more labels "grain fed only" or "no animal by- products" as part of the diet. If you wish to know more details, just do a little research into "rendering plants".

Back to the meeting at the university . . . The purpose was to talk about all the different stages and advances in creating and improving production, along with consumer expectations, trends and demands.

I have to point out here that the program never mentioned if all those products were of real good nutrition or healthy value for the consumer. I believe the focus was more on how a finished product finds its way to a market and satisfies the customer.

Everyone was welcome to comment, suggest or ask questions. When my turn came, I thanked all the scientists for their contributions at expanding knowledge and finding smart techniques to constantly improve and facilitate the farm life, increasing crop production to feed a world expanding so fast in numbers! I also thanked the farmers for the bounty of their production and the quality of their products.

I asked how safe it was to modify with genetic manipulation the various species of the food chain, even if the genetic imprint is totally unrelated.

They told me that pure science is complex. The genetic code and discoveries related to genetically-engineered food is reserved for scientists. Their answers did not satisfy my inquiring mind! So, I touched on ethics and spirituality, asking if the scientists were violating the laws of nature. It was the very same conversation that I had just had with the gentleman sitting next to me! There was a big silence and I felt quite uneasy thinking that I might have pushed my opinions too far and embarrassed my host. I did not get any answers, but when the gentleman next to me stood up, he was introduced as the president of the university – the boss of all the others!

I felt even odder for a while, and regretted my boldness. However, he mentioned that ethics is very much a part of the research process, but that pure science and any related discoveries cannot be questioned first as ethical or not. Otherwise, it may slow down the chances and the opportunity of being a first-class university open to all aspects of research. I understood that at the level of pure science all knowledge is good. What left me uneasy is what people choose to do with it.

I never got any answers to my questions about feeding meat proteins to vegetarian animals. I went back to my seat and apologized for not being "proper" to my famous host. We exchanged a few jokes, smiled a lot, and Anita and I went back to our little village. I got invited again, but it took many passing years.

I have been asked for years to cater various private functions organized by major universities in our area, with the University of Guelph being very special to us. I guess I didn't have much credibility representing "my ideas of science", but I am taken seriously when food is part of serving my patrons with flair. My philosophy has always been if it is not good for me it's not good for anyone!

I have never had a case of food poisoning so far with all of those years of feeding people. I certainly do not claim it is impossible, since so much of today's world is inter-dependent and little is known about how food has been treated or if it has been exposed to risky locations or stored under questionable conditions.

With all the antibiotics and other drugs that they give to animals these days, there continues to be a surge in food poisoning with viruses and bacteria that are much stronger than ever before. We have enjoyed a period of relatively "easy going control" of the many "bugs" that were efficiently wiped out with the many new wonder drugs of the 60s and up. We are facing new strains of super bugs that have managed to evolve with impunity. To add to the complexity, we are sharing now the "world bugs" by the mixing of food from distant foreign origins. Any

253

food from foreign origins needs reassessment when it comes to compete with the local ones. That is my personal view of a world more prone to sanity by keeping an existing domestic supply independent of foreign origins. To take only into account the fact that you cannot produce all year long makes you an importer, as is the case in Canada during the wintertime. Otherwise, you are harming your own people and depriving them of their source of living, and I dare to have any politician or business entity prove otherwise. Not even mentioning the negative carbon effect for the planet of transporting unnecessary food supplies that you have produced for generations locally to everyone's satisfaction.

Does it truly serve us and is it meaningful to open our borders and contend with an unfair world competition? Will our own immune system get stronger or weaker? Could it be that our new diet will be filled with even more dangerous chemical substances? (Most countries do not agree on banning dangerous pesticides or doubtful fertilizers at times, but are allowed to export their produce.)

Will our quality of life improve and contribute to make us go one way or the other; healthier or more prone to diseases? The competitive spirit again, not the spiritual one, is going to be the predominant factor in this new-age world competition and it may become ruthless, creating more human drama than good. Do you foresee a world at this stage interested in true ethics? What science has promoted is the constant use of antibiotics in large doses. There are common practices from the bad cold or flu to more serious conditions, and our dependence on chemicals drugs of all kinds has been the mark of modern medicine for quite a while now. And it has been mostly effective so far.

The part that I personally find appalling and sad is the way it has been transferred so fast to animal farming. The logistics of this kind of farming is to cram many animals in small areas, from chickens to pigs. Livestock, including cattle, is being fed wheat and corn, mixed with hay or other crops so that they grow faster and fatter. A lot of animals are deprived of their natural environment and of decent conditions of life. Can any serious scientist prove that the rays of our sun are unimportant to the welfare of animals? Right now most of the agro farming deprives them of natural light. Then they give the animals antibiotics and hormones. Drugs are given to survive their short, unnatural lives. Even their digestive systems are mocked. Cattle were never meant to eat cereals or corn or proteins from other animals. They were meant to eat grass. We can move the argument to many other species. Even fish from farms are being fed pellets which contain a certain amount of meat proteins. My viewpoint stems from the simple and respectful observations of what I saw when I was younger and from my experiences as a chef. I admire the many farmers who are trying to preserve the old traditions of farming. They will, of course, use all the latest know how. The farmers are not denying a genuine science, they simply refuse to transgress the order of nature. I totally agree with that stand, knowing only too well the differences of taste and the satisfaction of using products of natural origin. All my customers over the years have benefited from eating such products. I never personally regarded myself as a great chef. In fact, I have always kept the feeling of being a perpetual apprentice. But I will certainly argue and defend my roots and my abilities to spot the best produce in any market! That has been my gift (plenty of learning from my mother when buying for her shop over many years) and from the awareness I have incorporated into what I truly believe is best for my customers.

It is impossible to go backwards and expect everything natural and organic overnight with happy animals filling the warehouses or compounds, having glass roofs to see the sun, and access to big pastures to pick endless bits of food or grass to compliment their daily addition of grains.

Many in Europe are doing such farming and have no problem to sell all their products. North Americans are catching up with the Europeans in demanding quality goods from farmers who use humane practices.

Lately, I have been reading about the State of California banning the farming of geese and ducks for the production of liver, known as Foie Gras, which is a delicacy. As a chef, some of my friends have asked me what I think of it. Sure, I can understand that the animals experience temporary discomfort when force fed.

My own grandmother used to raise geese and ducks. I observed that you had to be forceful the first or second time you fed them, but after that the geese and ducks came of their own accord when it was feeding time. They had a life of freedom and looked happy to me.

This is a false issue. If you truly wish to be ethical, then, yes, ban force feeding. But, then, ban the cruel practices of many factory farms.

Strangely, Anglo Saxons are well known for protecting and caring for their animals. Why does their concern stay at the level of pets and not include all the other animals? You can be easily sued for neglecting your pet, or even, like the case in Toronto with ex-employees of a humane society (animal shelter), be taken to court for various offenses toward some sick animals. Much can be said about the pros and cons of this interesting case. It will magnify the offences from the prosecution and minimize the motivation or circumstances that made it possible to happen from a humane point of view. Big lawyers are involved, and there is lots of noise over practices that some see as humane and others the reverse.

Strangely, no one has the courage to question and expose in a courtroom the cruelty our mega agro farming is inflicting on millions of animals. The transgressions of the workers of the shelter pale in comparison!

Are not all species part of creation and from the same God? Who is going to argue for them? Doesn't life – in whatever form — deserve respect? All becomes a pursuit of efficiency and market fancies with the advantages that give the consumer a fair or cheaper price to pay. However, again and again we are facing a philosophy of bigness that has no long-term benefits to sustain itself because it mocks love.

The workers are low paid in those factory farms and working conditions are horrible. The workers must endure the stench of foul air while doing jobs that are demeaning and gross. On top, most of the factories are polluting the environment. Regulations are inadequate. Europeans have at least passed legislation to provide for the humane conditions for animal farming. The North Americans are in their traditional mindsets of procrastinating, lobbying politicians effectively for slowing or avoiding anything that might affect their ideas of pricing, and ultimately profits. But they have no shame in trying to flood the world with their poor products, spreading bad examples to emerging countries, some of whom have even more disdain for animals. Tomorrow you may buy their products believing everything is fine and safe. And, because it will be cheaper, you will contribute to eliminate more local farming. My vision of spirituality cannot ignore any part of what we call life and the love for life, or God as the source of it all. For me, even if my atheist friends ignore the God label, and it is their privilege, they certainly cannot deny all the facts I have been exposing over and over, or pretend to love their pets and conveniently ignore other species.

We will benefit immensely by being more responsibly aware and even by visiting animal farms. I do not want to bankrupt our farmers; I know enough of them to understand what they are doing. Their way of thinking is they work hard, feed all of us, don't make fortunes, and, by and large, they see those practices as necessary to the way the market works.

To add to their plight, fierce competition is threatening whatever has been their regular livelihood. The doors are more and more open on the world, more in the way of unfairness than the reverse. It seems that big business has more chance of surviving because of their enormous financial resources and lobbying power.

At some point in time we must confront the many issues that our mindless beliefs are creating whether we like it or not. We do not wish to learn anything by observing honestly what works and what doesn't work in terms of ethics. We are too fearful of what the neighbor may do or not do, and now we can add other countries to the picture to make it even more difficult to be decent. Cause and effect cannot be denied forever.

If nothing else, it makes concerned citizens ponder, "What are we really doing to ourselves?" We are the ones creating the reality we will be forced to face. I can take all the scorn in the world and still not take it personally, unless trusted and ethical science proves that I am way out of line and need to reassess my thinking.

The conditions exist for much saner, humane and ethical ways to farm. Many are already hard at work to prove it. It is true that we will have to pay more for those products, but not a lot more so that it will become unaffordable. As well, many of the techniques that exist can still contribute to minimize costs and be ethical. Most importantly is the fact that people need to understand how important our local farmers are to all of us. The difference in cost can be largely compensated by knowing that it is ethical or spiritual to be supporting our community, not just large corporate entities with little or no concern for ethics. The most added bonus will be the disappearance or the reduced dangers of those super bugs, for they will be contained and will only exist on a small scale.

Animals, humans, and the whole of life has is own proper immune system to cope with reasonable and natural conditions. Life has evolved throughout millions of years and millennia to give us the wonder of wonders that we call our world.

Why not use science to protect what life has given to us naturally? To help nature is of the highest ethic; to resort to practices of profiteering using science to mock and distort life is not elevating humanity. It is sadly an exercise in aggrandizement to flatter one's ego and pass it along for the benefit of large and mostly money-oriented individuals. In the long term, we are responsible to pass on to our children a life where respect and true highly ethical science is working for our benefit. For me, and I hope more and more people, the answer is to preserve the beauty and health of the earth. It is to respect the fragile balance between all species giving life to all our present scientific know-how to protect and glorify the human habitat where we have our precious existence. To me, the cause is worthy and urgently important. I am talking as a simple human with eyes to see and feelings to feel. My friend, Neale Donald Walsch, points out that feelings are the language of the soul. I can relate to that. The dream that I related in the introduction was purposeful; my wish is that I have lived up to the challenge.

I didn't realize I had a wealth of food information with the added bonus of coming from a strong cultural tradition of glorifying food (sometimes with much excess). I have lived in many different countries that have rich food cultures. I have had the benefit of making lots of dishes and the privilege to serve the public for many years. This could only have been possible by having real food of only the highest quality.

The biggest surprise was to discover an inner spirituality that has always been there, even when I was pretending to be an atheist.

Intelligence has to prevail at the end of the day and the courage to stand for what you believe is decent and true, respecting what I understand now to be our oneness.

May the source of all and perfect love gently help you to evolve with the willingness to serve life.

A Word About Food and Diets

I have never followed a single diet in my life. When I was vegan, then vegetarian, I accounted for those periods as a lifestyle choice. Diets are restrictive and unless sick or living in a place of little food choices, I always buy and choose from the perspective of my desire for fresh, seasonal food. As well, I buy things with the desire to please my family and their food preferences. Prices are not my first motivation for buying. However, like most of us, I think I have to keep an eye not to over buy or exceed my budget.

I am making some minimum comments about different options and places.

From the Mayo Clinic diet, which is renowned and inspiring, to the ever-popular Weight Watchers diet, which can be restrictive and not very fun to follow, I can see where these approaches to losing weight make sense.

Raw food diet, vegan, and vegetarian are all very particular choices and have great benefits. My personal observation and experience is that they become so restrictive that it is not wise to consider doing it by yourself. You definitely need a dietetic and regular check-up to make sure you are not depriving the normal functioning of your body.

Ayurvedic diets are in essence very good to follow, since they have a long tradition of ethics. They are concerned about assimilation, digestion and processing nutrients, which many diets don't address. Some extra effort and patience is warranted.

Deepak Chopra has excellent menus to suggest about many aspects of diets from the great traditions of India. Some are vegetarians, while some suggest to eat modest amounts of fish, poultry, lamb and dairy products. Beef is not a prime choice!

The big question is, "What is your idea that you have of you?" Most people will be serious with diets for a while, becoming suddenly almost like fanatics and going crazy over a missing part of the food intake or very strict on following the guidelines precisely.

Then one day the diet is over. They have lost some weight, feel better about themselves, and now is the time they feel they can indulge again in old habits. What took you so much effort and discipline, and maybe some degree of paranoia to be precise, is washed away pretty fast. You are almost back to square one in only a few days of no dieting. Your body has reclaimed its previous weight and you are depressed, wondering if you have to diet for the rest of your life, or let it go and enjoy your old lifestyle, even if you don't like your appearance in the process.

Some diets are prone to be more efficient by going along with a series of exercises to keep the body tuned up or burn the unwanted calories. You realize that you need to be accountable for any excess food consumption that you have to burn by sweating with more exercise. A whole industry is at work with some claiming more success than others. We are made to be active and all of us need a daily measure of exercise. Much will depend on your age and the many variations in our genes. Each of us truly has different needs. The perfect approach will be the formula that works for your mind, body and soul.

Most schools of thinking focus on diet and the many techniques of exercising. At times they recognize the importance of the power of the mind to help in the process, but only the very few will discuss spirituality as part of the key element to hold the three parts together as YOU, or who you truly are.

To convince you of their fees ranges from modest to the sky, there are indeed many valuable and excellent spas, exercise rooms, or entire institutions providing good facilities and proper care to make you lose those unwanted pounds.

What makes much more sense is not to fall prone to lifestyles and bad habits that get you to look for those drastic reassessments, then painful changes and long periods of hard disciplined work.

At times, the financial aspects may be stopping you from moving forward or the inconvenience of lifestyle, especially if your partner is against change. Your health is going to be challenged at some point if you let go by reasons of ignorance, laziness of mind, or plain gratification of going for all your wants, regardless of the unhealthy effects on your body.

So, when you have heard repeatedly and still wonder what I really mean by who YOU are, it will be the number one question to consider before moving into any serious changes for the long term of your life.

Your body will adjust with much more ease once your mind, the number one aspect to be properly assessed, is clear about the power of your divine self, or the life force (for an atheist) that is in charge. It will definitely be easier to move with resolve in tackling the issues that have kept you dysfunctional in your lifestyle. It is at the level of belief first that any serious change can effectively work for the long term.

Most of us are reluctant to accept that we have issues. Any diet will have little effect from the outside to what are the core problems from the inside with a very subtle set of issues undermining our true conscious sense of personal worth and divine identity.

If the mind is left unchanged in the core beliefs you have held, any dieting is doomed to have only temporary benefits. The very same thing can be said about a healthy lifestyle. I am trying to magnify again the root of our dysfunctional state of being and it has to do first with the false beliefs we hold about ourselves. In the case of dieting, you won't be able to last in restrictive choices unless secure in your decision. The personal ego that had its way for so long will find it too hard to deny yourself of many of your fancies.

This will lead you easily to the idea that you can, at some point, loosen up and choose what your fancy desires. Your ego has no interest in your truest benefit, meaning no regard to your divine self. It is dismissing it altogether by looking mostly for short-term gratification.

Again, a change of consciousness in your idea of YOU is the primary reason why anything that benefits you as a human being is the reason to improve or keep yourself fully alive and healthy. With time and effort it will lead you to realize at some point your power, your grace, and your worth as a divine being.

It will become easier and easier to go along the lines of positive behavior and even see yourself as a future servant of helping others to wake up and see for themselves the fullness and goodness of life. Wellness, usefulness and joyfulness is contagious, and you may wish to share it.

It is not for trying to please a fancy anymore, or even the idea of a new image of you, as those have no back up for being long lasting and sound. The simplest reason for any true change is when you decide at the level of the heart, because you wish to reclaim yourself and feel secure and honorable in all aspects of living. You do not know of any outcome yet, but you wish for a new image of yourself. Soon you will glimpse your divine worth and see it in others, regardless of the temporary masks or attitudes, pleasant or unpleasant, we all project to the world.

You did many things yourself and learned to forgive, so to speak, your own "trespasses" in order to move on. It becomes only natural to expand the forgiving to others, and maybe for the first time you see and understand the meaning of the Lord's Prayer at least for that passage, "Forgive us our trespasses, as we forgive those that trespass against us."

You are moving away from your previous unsecured, selfish and limited sense of YOU to a greater limitless new sense of belonging to a much larger reality. It slowly breaks down the false idea of separation that your previous self embraced.

To honor your new self is to find your own balance by your emerging spirit. No one has the right to tell you what to do or coerce you to do regardless of the arguments, even if they are positive ones.

Any teacher worth his "salt" can only promote, persuade, convince or suggest. You are the one to choose, for then it will become credible and justified to you as you grow in experiencing the knowledge and results. You become the observer of your reality that you create moment to moment.

The major reason for dieting, if you do not feel well as you are, is to help you function at your best level and feel the energy of life flowing in a new way, giving you the freedom to move and participate in what is suitable and good for you.

Spirit, mind and body all work with the natural harmony of life to maximize the meaning you choose to give to life itself. You are the secret recipe. No one can do it for you; the choices of your experiences are yours. We can talk about generalities and what has been observed, and the conclusions that have been recommended by health and food nutritionist experts.

If you choose to be an omnivore, meaning free to try all you wish, the only restrictions are what is sensible according to your size, gender, lifestyle activities, and geographical location with the cultural print and climate. All those are to be considered as vital and valuable with years of tradition to back up the particulars of any culture. One sensible piece of advice: any of your real authentic food traditions will beat the processed, toxic food.

To minimize excess calories is to cut down on carbohydrates, especially if more than one or two are involved. For example, rice mixed with potatoes or pasta, then bread to add to all those starchy products, ending up with sweets at the end of the meal, and many alcoholic beverages to top it all off.

Some diets suggest proteins do not mix well with carbohydrates, meaning it's either meat, fish or chicken involving vegetables or salads, but don't includes the potatoes, rice or pasta, any starch, and for the vegetarians not to mix more than one or two of those.

When meat wasn't as abundant as it is now, for reasons of not being able to afford it, mothers and grandmothers had the natural wisdom to use three quarters more carbohydrates, including vegetables of all kinds, and only a quarter of meat per person, sometimes even less, having meat only on special occasions.

Most of today's portions are almost the reverse, with lots of meat and some carbohydrates, and few vegetables. The easiest way to see for yourself if it works is to put it to the test!

Try not to eat any carbohydrates every day, but skip them a day or two at a time. I personally have difficulty trying not to involve some amount of carbohydrates in my meals, but my choice will be on one rather than two or three, as well as using moderation.

I think that most of us are excessive wheat eaters.

In my personal life, I have promoted the amazing feast of products you can make with wheat. A close friend of mine who is a psychic and medical intuitive, Lori Wilson, is able to read your body's needs and health issues. She suggested that to relieve my allergies to hay, ragweed, pollen, feathers and dust that I cut down on wheat and cleanse myself with water and sliced fresh lemon two or three times a day. She said that my sinuses would clear up.

Since I had to deal with those annoying miseries for many years, I gave it a try. I'd had enough of those over-the-counter drugs that were totally ineffective after a while.

To my surprise, after only a week of drinking water and lemon, first in the morning then mid-day and afternoon, and cutting all wheat-based intake in my meals, my sinuses cleared up, allowing me again to smell and breathe properly.

Imagine that I, a chef, baker and pastry cook, having enjoyed and served so many wheat-based products, had to keep the wheat out of my life or risk having a stuffy nose.

I found out that indeed we do abuse wheat products, especially with white flour deprived of good nutrients. Countless people are affected without knowing why. It seems natural that we react to excess of any kind. I will still have a dessert or enjoy a good piece of bread every so often, but not at every meal.

Many people are now Celiac or totally affected by wheat. This is another step altogether where no wheat is allowed. However, many cereals are compatible with me, such as whole-meal pure rye bread or whole meal rice pasta, corn pasta and other grains. There are plenty of choices.

To be conscious of your intake of food is necessary, but do not get paranoid about it. If you take away the joy of eating, you are on the losing end of "the baguette". The food of life is meant to make you sparkle. It is an essential and important spiritual experience, as well.

Fruits are the number one "sparky" food, but to be truly beneficial to you, they are better assimilated by themselves and not eaten at the end of any meal. Make a habit of eating fruit first thing in the morning or during the day between meals and see for yourself how you feel. You will also benefit by rarely being sick. I have personally experienced this and believe its from the fruits' multiple protective nutrients.

Try, for example, freshly squeezed juice in the morning with nothing else or eat raw fruits. Then, twenty minutes or so afterwards, eat your choice of breakfast with herbal tea, real tea or coffee.

After only ten days or so of that practice, your body will crave its "fix" of genuine vitamins every morning. It has nothing to do with the false orange juice sold as freshly squeezed. That is just super-pasteurized with chemical vitamins added! Those juices are indeed freshly squeezed at some point, but then processed by getting rid of the oxygen content in order to store them in crates for maybe a year or more. Then, they are reconstituted, pasteurized and ready for the market with a time limit of sale.

We all believe it is indeed just freshly squeezed for us. It's just another trick of the world of advertising cleverly used to fool our perception of any true meaning of freshness.

Most of us neglect vegetables in our diet. It is proven now that all of them have tremendous properties to not only help keep cancers away, but to feed us with life radiance. It is essential that you slowly but surely re-program yourself to eat your vegetables.

Salty concoctions and cured meats are not good for you, and neither are overly sweet foods and deep-fried food of any kind. If you really wish to treat yourself with fries every so often, make sure you cook them in your oven. It will take a little longer, but they will definitely be better for you. Today's kids are notorious for avoiding their quota of vegetables, so it is no wonder that their own parents and our general culture has been minimizing such consumption. To see kids flooding their stomachs with gaseous drinks, such as carbonated colas with plenty of ice, or icy water during their meal is a sad reflection on the parents' ability to discipline them and guide them to healthier habits. Ideally, you need very little to drink during meals. Imagine your stomach is made of a fine muscle membrane and can be compared to a big pocket. To massively flood this sensitive and hard-working "pocket" on top of the food intake is to abuse it and make it work much too hard.

Drink between meals. During a meal, a little wine is excellent, but no more than two mid-sized glasses; red wine preferably. To include fish in your diet is now popular, but some kinds of fish are more beneficial than others. To be ethical is to avoid consuming any fish that is endangered. If they are farmed, some have methods and feeds more healthy than others, so watch carefully where they come from and try to find out if it's safe before the influence of the price alone makes you choose over sanity. The human ingenuity has, over the years, managed to find balance of food supplies in most cultures.

With our latest science we can even improve what is lacking and keep what has worked, and it is essential to the well being of masses of people. Western countries eat way too much in general. We could do with more quality food and less quantity.

To see new immigrants from what are considered poor countries with perfect teeth, probably they have never seen a dentist in their lives, and looking fit not fat, is a wonderment. When you see those same people years later, a drastic change often is very obvious. The North American way of life has changed their looks and has affected their once-healthy lifestyle.

White processed flour is slowly but surely fading away; not fast enough for me, as it has contributed to many diseases by the total lack of essential nutrients that were intended to serve human beings. Instead, those precious ingredients are taken out of the many varieties of cereals and end up benefiting animals to supplement their feed.

Even if you add endless chemical substances to compensate for the goodness you took out in the first place, it is still a poor substitute. Nature is always first and best at everything. The idea of white bread, white rice, white sugar or white anything was a fad or fashion created to imitate royalty, since they had access to it to elaborate endless sweet concoctions. It is indeed working much better in pastries. I have used it myself many, many times with success. For a long time, I also have promoted whole meal bread, whole meal pasta, whole meal rice and many other wholesome grains.

Today, with increased public awareness about healthy eating, I am encouraged to see the momentum picking up for more and more of what is genuinely wholesome. To cut down on excessive carbohydrates consumption, less sugar and salt gives you a head start. With time, you learn to taste food with little salt or none even, and find that most food tastes pretty good and has its own particular salt.

However, if you live in a hot climate you do need salt in your diet to help you retain the water in the body and not dehydrate or dry up too fast. We have lost the good habits of vegetable and fruit consumption. Our kids are happy to have a few salad leaves or a tiny portion of greens and pretend they have their "fix" for the meal. Not many people are tending gardens anymore, adding to the lack of what has always been essential to any good diet. I love the example of Michelle Obama, who has required a garden section with vegetables be part of the White House grounds.

It is, as well, great to have in the First Lady, someone truly concerned with the problems of obesity and an active participant at finding solutions. She has secured the help of Jamie Oliver, a great young chef from England, who is always keen to promote real and fresh food.

Changes are on the way, and great ones at that, but the momentum has to be kept up. Some powerful forces not happy with those facts are trying hard to slow the process of evolution.

Milk is very popular in the North American diet, with choices of one or two percent, or whole milk (which is still deprived of a lot of natural cream). Strangely, your body is not recognizing your effort to save a few calories and acts harder to digest something that has become hard to assimilate. Your body prefers whole milk to start with as more digestible. Did you know that the Queen of England recognizes that and only drinks full raw milk?

That information was given to me by a scientist that came to our bed and breakfast. He was going to argue in court to defend Michael Schmidt, a local farmer who has suffered endless harassment and lost all he previously owned to fight for the right to provide raw milk. That gentleman has been sued a few times by the all-powerful milk marketing boards.

To avoid the law forbidding the sale of raw milk, he sells you a "share" of his cows! And since it is your property, you are allowed to drink your milk raw from your own cow. But it is not something the local government accepts and has relentlessly been after him for the last 16 years.

That case is going now to the Ontario Supreme Court. He has won two times previously, but again very sadly the big industries are threatened. There is a monopoly that does not accept any competition, even an insignificant challenger, since it costs them a fortune to buy their milk quota. I agree with them to counter U.S. or some European unfair practices by keeping them out of Canada, and the battle is far from being won. Free trade, or rather free for the giants, to be more specific, has become an enormous worry to the small and mid-sized local producers.

It is important to pay attention, since it is the very food (controversial or not) that is going to fill the shelves of your supermarket in the near future. In short, the zero, one, or two percent milk does not deserve the exaggerated attention it gets. It is a marketing invention with no spectacular, concrete or beneficial effect. The calorie reduction is too small to make a statement claiming good lifestyle results in your diet.

Pasteurization is part of our culture and will not be challenged. This makes the legal fight look petty by trying to impose on a few individuals their freedom of choice and their right to exercise it. The health dangers are almost non-existent. All it takes is good veterinary services to survey the cows on a regular basis. Many French and Quebecers have produced raw milk and have not killed anyone. Those giants of the milk-related industries are claiming it is to protect us? I wish I could truly believe such a statement.

I agree that the large producers can be credited for many achievements, the most obvious being the many services and choices at fair prices from which we benefit. Will the health aspect be truly part of their future priorities? I sincerely hope so, and believe it will serve them and us even better for the long term if they are bold enough to realize it.

Again, without any personal science, but by simply observing nature's intent, I believe pasteurization is making it more complicated to assimilate by your body. But the habit is so engrained now that it is a waste of time to argue for plain raw wholesome milk! With today's veterinary services, the risk of contaminated milk is extremely rare, but we are forcing on our digestive system something far from perfect, not to mention the cheese industry that could produce even better products with non-pasteurized milk. To me the choice needs to be working like Europe where there is room for a quota of raw milk and the principal bulk of the market is for pasteurized milk.

A welcome addition is milk from goats or sheep; cheeses made from those milks are not necessarily pasteurized. In Southern Ontario, we are fortunate to have producers like Monteforte, or Baa, Baa Cheese. They make and sell their products locally and there is a welcome selection of excellent yogurts, creams cheeses, and various creative cheese from soft to dryer consistency, all very well made and tasty. I know those pioneers personally, and love their daring new approach.

I know many small farmers and locals who are responding to mega-insanity. Those courageous and straightforward human beings are not only rebelling against toxic practices, but trying alternatives at feeding us genuine goodness and quality. They deserve, in my view, all our attention, even if the cost is more. We will benefit in the long term by avoiding all sorts of health problems with the daily bonus of treating ourselves well and enjoying their excellent fare. Spiritually speaking, it is giving them the opportunity to serve the higher good.

When we refer to calories from milk or cream, the calories involved are negligible. This mad culture of percentage is another human construction with insignificant benefits. There are many charts about what are the daily calorie counts according to our daily activities, gender, age and type of person with an active metabolism or a slower one.

I have witnessed so many times people who indulge in rich food and desserts and then become paranoid because I didn't have one or two percent milk or five percent cream for their coffee! Surely those excesses in food and calorie counts bypassed by a huge number the little or insignificant affect of their particular cream or milk, but strangely the twisted perception in priority is misplaced.

To end my musing, whatever you start with, do it with joy. Bettering yourself is not to be viewed like a chore or to be in penitence, but as a lifelong process with trial and errors. Remember these three life principles: Functionality to make it work with your lifestyle, adaptability to adjust to change, and sustainability to know that you do not cause yourself or your life to be negatively affected.

The last and final key to unlock the gift of life in all its forms: Be aware of love, truth and joy. Add these key values to anything you think of and act on to serve yourself and all you touch.

May you rejoice in many blessings along the journey of life!

LOVE

Love

Recipes

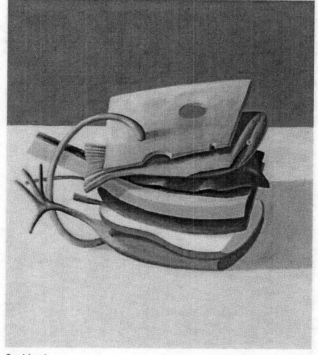

Cookbook

While I did not intend to write a cookbook,
I've included the following recipes for you to try.

— Roger

APPLE PIE OR AUSTRALIAN PIE MOLD

Flaky Pastry for "*vol au vent*"

Pastry will take 1 to 2 hours to defrost
Roll dough flat over some flour
Pierce with a fork to avoid lifting when cooking
Choose a mold of your preference
Cook in oven at 375 degrees f. or 190 degrees c. for 10 to 15 minutes
until light brown in color

For Apple Pie:

Sliced apples
Lay in a circular manner over flattened dough
Add sugar
Cook for 15 - 20 minutes
Add honey, cream, lemon juice – to your liking!

BEEF BOURGUIGNON (ABOUT 6 PORTIONS)

This recipe was the winner of the Toronto Star's Golden Whisk Award in 2008 for Canadian cuisine!

The strange part is that I rarely had it on my menus over my many years of cooking, favoring fish over meat dishes. (I also never have submitted anything to be judged in my whole life. This recipe was given, along with my family's "Gateau Basque" recipe to Anita Stewart for her book, *Anita Stewart's Canada*, during the same year)

Here it is:

You need some good quality beef. It also works well with bison or venison.

I prefer a mixture of good stewing beef morsels with some using the shank as part of the mix (half shank at least since it is more moist that other parts when cooked)

Quantity of Meat: 1½ lbs (750 gr)
The meat has to be marinated for two days before cooking.
You need to add to the marinade:
2 small carrots, peeled and diced
I celery stalk, diced
1 red onion diced
3 cloves of good fresh local garlic crushed (never to use the prepared crushed garlic preserved in jars)
1 tsp. of fresh or dry thyme
1 tsp. of fresh or dry tarragon
½ tsp. of black pepper or cayenne
Half a bottle of strong red wine (Californian or Argentinean)
1 ounce (or two tsp.) of olive oil

The cooking part:
Ingredients to have ready:
⅓ cup of oil (I prefer virgin olive oil)
½ cup all purpose flour
¼ cup chopped parsley mixed with some garlic (2 cloves)
½ tsp. of Tarragon (dried or fresh)
½ tsp. of salt, and a little more cayenne or pepper (up to you)
1 cup fresh diced tomatoes (or a small can of diced)

1 cup beef stock
2 ounces of cooking chocolate (or bittersweet)
The rest of the bottle of wine (half)
When beef is almost cooked, this becomes part three to pan fry separately with a little oil to add to the stew.
½ lb. of mushrooms, if small keep them whole (cremini or Portobello, sliced when big)
¼ lb. lean bacon diced or pancetta.

Part One: Cooking the beef

You need a good casserole dish (with a lead to cover and simmer later)

Heat at medium range add 1ounce of oil then garlic and parsley for a minute, add tomatoes, beef stock (if not available water instead)

Then chocolate, the juice of the marinade (not all the chopped bits)

The half bottle of wine (there is a motion to this part that is maybe too much for a beginner or even dangerous, if your hood is very low)

The wine has to be "burned," to remove the alcohol content, so just add the wine as is or, if adventurous, proceed as such:

In a small pot pour the wine and bring to a boil (if you have a gas range it will catch fire by itself until all the alcohol is burned)

The flames are going to go almost a foot high.

If you have an electric range, you need a match to start the burning.

When the flames are gone, just add to the rest of the sauce.

Part two: The beef morsels

In large cast iron or a good pan, heat oil over medium to high heat
Dredge meat in flour, shaking off the excess
Brown on all sides and add to the sauce
Cook gently for two hours with the cover
Check if cooked, or if seasoning is to your liking, add a little cold water and half spoon of corn starch if the mixture is too liquid (the flour over the meat should be enough for acting as a thickener, but it's up to you again)

You can add the bacon and mushrooms last on top when serving or mixed in the stew. Goes well with good whole meal rice, scallops potatoes (see my easy recipe) or pasta, or any mash.

If you are adventurous, use this recipe for a great meat pie (just add a few medium cooked vegetables to the mix, such as carrots hearts of celery, peas, sweet potatoes…)

DRESSING FOR CAESAR SALAD

<u>Ingredients</u>
1 tablespoon of Mustard (Dijon, if possible)
1 egg yolk
Juice of 1 lemon
2 ounces of olive oil
Garlic, parsley
Parmesan cheese
Croutons, crispy bacon
Anchovies, if desired

<u>Method</u>:
First mix mustard, egg yolk and lemon juice
Then add oil and the rest of the ingredients

GATEAU BASQUE DOUGH

Here is my family recipe for the dough used in the lemon tart. This will make three cakes. I suggest that you don't cut down the recipe, but freeze the left over dough that you don't use.

Mix together:

1 to 1 ⅓ cups unsalted butter, softened.
3 cups granulated sugar (raw sugar is best)
4 whole eggs
5 egg yolks (save whites for egg wash)
4 ¾ cups all purpose flour
1 tablespoon baking powder
Pinch of salt

Let sit four hours in the fridge before using. I suggest you use parchment paper to roll the dough. Roll it to ¼ of an inch thickness and lay it, with the parchment paper, in a pie plate. Cut the excess dough on the sides. Fill it with the lemon tart mixture. Bake 35-40 minutes at 325 degrees f. Make sure it is congealed (not liquidy) before taking it out of the oven. Let cool.

Lemon filling (you need to remember four ingredients: lemons, sugar, cream, eggs in equal measure)
For a 8-inch pie shell (about 6 to 8 portions)

Part one
4 lemons (nice firm skin preferable)
Grate the skin first, using the smallest grater
You need a bowl large enough to hold all parts
Juice the lemons (make sure there are pits) and measure what it makes
Add the grated lemon rind

Part two
Whatever is the measure of lemon juice and grated rind (about two thirds of a cup, probably)
Pour into bowl, add same measure of white sugar (use no other, as it will discolor the nice yellowy look, if, for example, you choose a dark sugar)

<u>Part three</u>

Add same measure of 35 percent cream in the bowl (not 10 percent or 18 percent or – the worst, of all — milk)

It will only work with 35 percent cream.

<u>Part four</u>

Add into bowl same measure of whole eggs

Beat the whole thing together gently pour over the prepared dough in the pie shell and bake at a low

Heat oven 325 F or 150 centigrade for about 40 minutes it has to be congealed like if you bake a quiche to be ready. Let cool at least one hour before you serve it.

LAMB CURRY OR CHICKEN

Ingredients:
A leg of lamb diced (No fat)
If you choose chicken, use a free range, preferably, or only grain fed, cut it in 8 pieces
1 red onion or echalottes (shallots)
6 cloves of garlic
Fruit (one apple, one banana, one mango)
Curry paste or powder (I prefer the paste)
1 can coconut milk
Same amount of white wine, two fresh tomatoes (or a small can of diced tomatoes)

Method:
Sauté lamb chunks (or chicken), until nicely browned. You may use a separate pan to fry the cubes of lamb, then, in the cooking casserole dish, pour sesame oil or coconut oil or vegetable oil

When hot enough, add chopped onion, or echalottes, do not burn, but cook until golden brown

Add crushed garlic

Cook one more minute add curry powder or paste

Sauté slightly for one minute

Add one can of coconut milk, then, using the empty can, add the same amount of white wine.

Season, cover and cook for 1 to 1¼ hours on gentle heat simmering (pick up a piece from the pot to check if it is cooked)

If you are cooking a chicken, it will only take 25 minutes.

Thicken with mixture of cornstarch (a soup spoon and an ounce of cold water, in the last few minutes, pour half first then the rest to correct the thickness, repeat the motion if it's too thin)

Add fruit during last 15 minutes of cooking. (You can choose to add the fruit after the wine and coconut. They will melt in the sauce and act like a thickener.) Serve with your choice of vegetables or whole meal rice.

ORANGE CAKE

Use only navel oranges.

Gently boil 3 to 4 oranges for 1½ hours (start with cold water to cover generously as it will take evaporation)
When cooked throw the water away.
Blend in a food processor the oranges with 2 cups of almond meal (ground almonds) add:

1½ cups white sugar
7 whole eggs (large)
1 cup flour (if celiac, add another cup of almond meal instead)
2 tsp. baking powder
3 ounces butter (soft and preferably unsalted)

If your food processor is too small, just blend oranges, sugar, and butter, then transfer to a bowl to mix the rest of ingredients

Fold into greased mold or, best, use parchment paper on bottom of the mold. Add the mixture over and cook for 40 to 50 minutes. Check to see if is cooked with a small knife blade. pinch the blade in and see if nothing sticks.
Serve with a toffee sugar sauce or orange sauce.

PAN FRIED FISH

Choose some fresh filet of fish like cod, sole, cat fish, tilapia, haddock, trout, salmon, artic char...

No thicker than ½ inch

You will need:
A good olive oil (virgin)
Salt, cayenne or pepper
Lemon or vinegar
Garlic
Flour (half a cup on a flat plate)
1 or 2 whole eggs (beaten in a bowl)

Method:

Season fish on both sides

Dip fish in flour both sides and then transfer to the bowl of egg and make sure to cover both sides again.

Put in hot frying pan with oil in it

Cook fish 2 minutes on each side medium heat, add crushed garlic from the beginning with the skin left on.

Add lemon juice or vinegar last when cooked.

You could also add chopped crushed garlic, parsley - white wine, a little butter to make a fast sauce ,it will only take one to two more minutes .Serve with salad or over a mash potatoes with cooked spinach blended unto it .Or by itself with half a lemon and chopped fresh herbs.

This goes well with a simple mayonnaise or mousseline or white butter.

PANFRIED SALMON

Ingredients:
Olive Oil
Salt
Cayenne Pepper
Garlic & herbs, ½ glass wine
Choice of salmon steak—deboned—with skin on (mostly fresh)

Method:
Reduce heat; add mussels, garlic and herbs.
Cover 2 minutes.
Ready to serve.

ROASTED CHICKEN LEG OR BREAST WITH FILLING

You will need:
Chicken legs or breast
Olive oil or other oil
Garlic
Herbs
Bread crumbs or almond meal
Dried fruits or cheese or both, one whole egg to bind the mix together add seasoning, a little meat like minced pork or minced chicken (use one leg no bones, for this if you have a food processor)

Method:
Remove the back bone of leg carving around the bone first or make an incision on breast on the long side just in the middle reaching the tail part.

You will need a piping bag to fill up the breast but a spoon for the leg is fine (try to keep as much skin as possible to envelop the mixture)

Baste with oil and dried herbs of your choice

You can also add a mixture at the last 10 minutes of cooking of crushed ginger, garlic, Kikkoman sauce and honey

Roast in hot oven 390 F. or 190C for 35 minutes (Cooking time depends on the size of the chicken.)

Deglaze after removing oil with ½ cup water or white wine (except for the one's using ginger mixture)

SAUSAGE ROLLS

This has been one of our many popular and much remembered items.

There are a few variations on the original one.

Here is the most popular one:

You need two good quality meats: half pork minced not too much fat and half minced veal (the fresher the mincing, the better)

It is illegal in Europe, at least in France, to sell minced meat, unless done just for you at the moment or purchased frozen.

Good fresh garlic, Italian type parsley or the regular curly one.

A good wine vinegar or best balsamic.

Some salt, some cayenne or hot sauce or black pepper.

Method:

Part one

For 1 lb. pork

1 lb. veal

In a bowl pour first the vinegar 1 -½ once, salt 1 tsp full of salt

Let the vinegar melt (this motion is the secret, so no messing around with trying to avoid the good vinegar!)

Add chopped garlic and parsley (add other fresh herbs if you wish)

About 4 cloves and ¼ cup of herbs, add hot sauce or cayenne or black pepper to your liking, about 1 tsp. for mild flavor.

Add meat and mix thoroughly, with your hands.

You can do this the day before to develop more strength or at the moment (keep refrigerated, if you choose to do it the day before)

Part two

You need a good puff pastry (also called flaky pastry)

They do come now in the frozen section all rolled up with parchment paper (non-sticky for baking)

Make sure you buy the ones made with butter (They are vastly superior to their mock "cousins" which are made with oils of different origins loaded with chemical stabilizers and emulsifiers.)

Roll up the dough over flour until quite thin (brush with egg wash, just a beaten up whole egg on the top side)

Lay the meat mixture folding it on one edge of the dough like if it was a sausage size, all along, it will stick because of the egg wash.

Roll it until it cover ½ inch more the dough, cut with a sharp knife, turn it over to have the double dough thickness on top. (The reason is simple. When cooking, it will develop nicely.)

Cut with a serrated knife preferably about one inch wide; add another little cut in the middle (acts as a chimney during cooking)

Lay on the parchment paper and brush each sausage with the egg wash on top. Make sure they are not too close together for cooking in the oven.

If you have a convection oven, it's better. Cook at 400 degrees Fahrenheit or 200 degrees Celsius for about 10 minutes or a little more, if they are too pale the puff pastry needs to be crunchy and the meat cooked slightly golden on the dark side.

Serve warm.

Variations:

You can use lamb minced by itself as long as it has a little fat in it (same recipe, but add a sliced banana and chopped mangoes. You can substitute the hot sauce for curry. I prefer the pasty one to the powder.)

You can mix minced turkey or chicken with pork instead of veal.

It doesn't work well with minced beef! They are too dry.

VEGETABLE SOUP
(COUNTRY STYLE)

Ingredients:
½ lb. Carrots (cubed)
½ lb. Pumpkin (cubed)
½ lb. Potatoes (cubed)
1 leek chopped
1 Celery stalk chopped
Savoy cabbage or another variety (shredded)
Rapini or Spinach or green beans (for the end last five minutes and only two for the spinach)
2 crushed garlic cloves
Parsley

Method:

Boil 3 litres of water (you can add some soup bones or a chicken carcass (bones); or use less water and add a tin of beef or chicken consommé.

When water is boiling add in order –Carrots, leeks, celery.

Add seasoning (sea salt preferably) black pepper or cayenne and let boil for ½ hour.

Add pumpkin and potatoes

If using Savoy cabbage, it has to be blanched before going into soup (separately boil it, rinse it)

On a small pan with a little oil add crushed garlic, parsley, or basil, or fresh tarragon. Just fry for a minute and add to the gently boiling soup. This motion will spark up and flavor the soup! Do it 15 minutes before the end.

Your last move is to add rapini (cook only 5 minutes or spinach two last minutes) it will green up your soup.

The whole mix of ingredients needs to boil gently with a lead on for at least one hour. You can serve it with a little cheese on top, a dollop of heavy cream or sour cream, or pan fried pancetta or bacon, or croutons, or chopped fresh herbs.

Makes about 10 portions.

GRATINEE (SCALLOPED) POTATOES

Yukon gold potatoes
This is a very easy recipe and always popular.

Use a nice looking, oven-to-table dish, so you can serve at the table when out of the oven.

You need some Yukon gold potatoes or the red skin variety will do.

For 6 to 8 persons about a good size potato for each person so 8 or 2 lb

About ½ pint or ⅓ of a liter of 35% cream (nothing else will replace it, don't try to reinvent the wheel!)

Peel wash and rinse the potatoes, then slice them and lay on a dish for baking.

Cover them up with exactly half water and half 35% cream, just to let them show up a little above the liquid. (You probably need a full pint being half the cream and water.)

Do not make them float reduce the liquid if this happen.

Season with salt and cayenne (I personably do not use black pepper, because I don't like to see all those black "spots," but white pepper will do or the black pepper if it's your preference.)

Bake in 375 degrees Fahrenheit or 170 degrees Celsius for about 35-40 minutes (You can add some cheese of your choice for a gratinee effect in the last ten minutes of cooking. Do not add before as it will dry up.)

ZUCCHINI CORN BREAD

You need for ingredients:

2 cups tepid water
2 zucchini chopped
1 cup of grated cheese (cheddar or other)
2 whole eggs
2 tsp. sugar
1 tsp. salt
2 tsp. granulated yeast (or 1-½ once fresh one)
Blend all together in a large bowl, add
2 cups plain flour
2 cups corn flour
½ cup corn oil

Work up gently with your hands until homogenous let rest with a humid cloth outside for an hour.

Work up again a few minutes to give it some strength.

Wait another half hour, lay in bread mold with parchment paper or roll into the shape you like. Let rest until it develops half size more in volume outside. You can also let it rest in fridge overnight and cook the next day. (If it does rise enough during refrigeration you can bake it, as well, without waiting.)

Add a little egg wash with a brush on top (One beaten up egg)

Bake at 375 degrees Fahrenheit or 175 degrees Celsius for 25 to 30 minutes.

This goes well with many dips or for dinner!

Recommended Readings

I've put together a list of books which have made a lasting impression on me and have influenced the way I think about life.

PRACTICAL SPIRITUALITY

These books are treasures of information and loving wisdom.

My first choices are from the people whom I personally know and trust. Firstly, I recommend all the books of Neale Donald Walsch, especially the *Conversations with God* series (Books 1, 2, and 3) published from 1995 to 2000. He has written many more books since then, the last one being *The Storm Before The Calm*, published in 2012. Visit www.nealedonaldwalsch.com.

My dear friend and spiritual peace troubadour, James Twyman, has written many wonderful books. I personally resonate strongly with *The Art Of Spiritual Peacemaking*. He has been kind and generous to involve my wife, Kathleen, and me in his most recent book, *Love, God and The Art of French Cooking*. Website: www.jamestwyman.com

Another dear and gifted friend Lori Wilson has written books that help to demystify the false concepts and beliefs about the nature of psychics and how wonderful they can be in helping us. Her book, *Medical Intuition*, has plenty in store to help you understand with factual and practical examples of what science needs to do in order to evolve to our next level of knowledge. Web www.inneraccess101.com

Michel Touzard surprised me a few years ago by pointing out Neale Donald Walsch's work as the key to opening up to his own personal conversations with God. He succeeded, calling it *The Dialogue with the Divine Within*. He also wrote a book called *GOD AND I, CLOwNING*, under the pen name Michael Inuit in 2006. Website: www.publishamerica.com

A very appropriate book to about the power of our thoughts is *The Law Of Attraction* by Esther and Jerry Hicks published in 2006 by Hay House. Website: www.hayhouse.com

When the Dalai Lama speaks it is wise to listen carefully. All of his books are simply treasures of wisdom, compassion, tolerance, vision and hope. I like one in particular, *Ethics For a New Millennium*, published by Penguin Putnam Inc. in 1999. ISBN 1-57322-025-6

Another primer to reinforce and prove the power of our thoughts is the groundbreaking work and books by Masaru Emoto, especially *The Miracle of Water* published in 2007 by Atria Paperback. ISBN 978-1-58270-162-2

Deepak Chopra has been a pioneer in waking up our world to a spirituality that is inclusive to all of us without offending major religions when the spirit of love prevails. All of his books are challenging us to move forward and truly evolve in the process of changing our consciousness.

I like *Grow Younger And Live Longer* by Deepak Chopra and David Simon, published in 2001 by Random House. ISBN 0-609-60079-6

Eckhart Tolle is another author who published a groundbreaking book in 1999. At first, it didn't catch on like wildfire, but a few years later it did. It is called *The Power Of Now*. He later wrote another excellent book, *A New World*, a remarkable attempt to help us recognize our true nature, and reorganize our beliefs.

The Nature of Good and Evil by Sylvia Brown and published in 2001 is an eye opener, as well as her other books. See www.hayhouse.com

Life after Death written by Tom Harpur, published in 1992, is a courageous and well-documented book to explore this delicate and important subject, since we all question if there is any reality beyond death. Tom has since written many valuable and challenging books on spirituality. McClelland and Stewart Inc. ISBN 0-7710-3941-7

The Lost Memoirs Of Edgar Cayce by A. Robert Smith, published in 1997 by the Association for Research and Enlightenment Inc. This is a remarkable association founded in 1931 and very much alive today to express with intelligence and integrity the facts of life in what we know "as seen and unseen." They have the most amazing library and collection of anything that relates to spirituality. Website: www.edgarcayce.com

Zero Limits by Joe Vitale is a fascinating little book about the power of prayer or transmutation in the name of love. John Wiley and Sons Publishers, 2007. ISBN 978 –2-89436-205-1

Gary Zukav is the author of many fascinating books I like, such as *The Heart Of The Soul*, written with Linda Francis. Published by Simon and Schuster, 2002, ISBN 0-7432-0567-7

Why Good People Do Bad Things by Debbie Ford gets at the root of the myriad of issues we all carry and often those that cause us to fail. It is an eye opener for the serious seeker who chooses love over fear. Harper and Collins, 2008, ISBN 978-0-06-089737-6

Every Day Grace by Marianne Williamson, a powerful communicator when it comes to expressing the longing and hopes of the heart and the true nature of anything spiritual. Riverhead Books, 2002, ISBN 1-57322-230-5

Take the Step, The Bridge will be There by Grace Sirocco was a book given to me by the author herself as a gift for Neale Donald Walsch following a seminar I sponsored in 2000. A few years later, it did reach Neale who was vastly impressed by the power of the book. It took me a while to read it and I regret the unfortunate waiting time, since it was a treasure sleeping on the shelf. Harper and Collins, ISBN 0–00-200071-7

Seth Speaks, published in 1972, the year Jane Roberts channeled Seth. It is a book that leaves you in a state of wonderment or absolute shock, asking, "Could it be real indeed?" The length and scope of this new awareness was simply too much to absorb for me at the time. It was in the mid-70s that I first was introduced to the book. I went back to explore slowly the information a year later and the second time it did make sense. Even today, it is not for everyone, however it has far reaching concepts and it does make more and more sense as time goes by and you truly evolve spiritually. Prentice –Hall, publishers.

Another fascinating book is called *Sai Baba, Man Of Miracles* by Howard Murphy, published in 1971 by Book and Information Centre, 290 Merton Street, Toronto, Ontario M4S 1A9.

Staying with old and extremely relevant books, I like the book, *As You Think*. This treasure of a work was first published in 1904 by James Allen and re-published by his son, Marc Allen, in 1998. I happened to read it only a month ago. Except for the timing, I would have loved to have quoted some passages with Marc's permission! New World library ISBN 1-57731-074-8

This one, too, is a primer and old, as well: *The Sermon on the Mount* by Emmet Fox, published in 1934 by Harper and Row.

Man's Search For Meaning by Victor E. Frankel, published first in 1959 and last reprinted in 2006. A true classic. Website: www.beacon.org

Victory before War — Maharishi Mahesh Yogi, by Robert Keith Wallace and Jay B. Marcus. The authors present a peaceful solution to world conflicts using the Vedic traditions (one of the oldest world religions). Published by Maharishi University of Management Press, Fairfield, Iowa 52557. ISBN 0-923569-38-3

Dream Healer by Adam. Adam is an amazing person! Published by Penguin Books, 2003. ISBN 0-14-3055376-0

The Scrolls From the Dead Sea by Edmund Wilson. Many books have emerged since, some with updated data. None of the three major world religions are keen to discuss these manuscripts in depth, as they would have to make drastic changes in some of their present theologies. Published in 1955 by Oxford University Press, Catalog # 55 –11322

The Gnostic Gospels by Elaine Pagels is very challenging to the same main religions. This book questions with much intelligent pertinence the various core beliefs that look more and more like the result of human constructions rather than true relevant spirituality. Published by Vintage Books, 1989.

Proof of Heaven, A Neurosurgeon's Journey into the Afterlife, by Eban Alexander, M.D. Published by Simon & Schuster Paperbacks, 2012. ISBN 978-1-4516-9519-9.

The Truth of Love and Fear by Rudolf Eckhardt, a dear friend and master at discovering your life's issues. He is a true pioneer, using spiritual teachings to restore your inner-self. Dog Ear Publishing, Anticipated publishing date 2013.

INSPIRATIONAL TO ETHICAL LIVING

The David Suzuki Reader by David Suzuki, 2003   Website: www.greystonebooks.com

The Ethical Imagination, Journey Of The Human Spirit by Margaret Somerville, 2006. Published by Harper and Collins Canada

A Basque History Of The World by Mark Kurlansky, 1999. Published by Alfred A. Knopf Canada

Stepping Lightly by Mark A. Burch, 2000, New Society Publishers

Becoming Human by Jean Vanier, 1998. Published by House Of Anansi Press Ltd.

$2 To Happiness by Vicki Stanley, 2011, Published by Dad Ink, 717 Main Street, North Canton, Ohio, 44720

Your Feminine Heart by Jessica Ashllie, 2005. Published by Heartfelt Press Calgary Canada

Voluntary Simplicity by Duane Elgin, 1993. Published by Harper and Collins

The Voice of Hope, Aung San Suu Kyi conversations with Alan Clements Seven Stories Press New York 1997

I Shall Not Hate, A Gaza Doctor's Journey by Dr Izzeldin Abuelaish, 2011. Published by Vintage Canada

BOOKS WITH A CRITICAL VIEW OF OUR FOOD

By far the most critical book, with the most research is *Toxic* by William Reymond, 2007. In French Published by Flammarion ISBN 978-2-0806-8763-3. Website: www.toxicfood.org

Food Politics by Marion Nestle, 2002. A scientific approach to nutrition and what politics is doing to our daily food. Published by University Of California Press ISBN 0-520-2406-7

Folks, This Ain't Normal, A Farmer's Advice for Happier Hens, Healthier People and a Better World by Joel Salatin. Published by Center Street, 2011. ISBN 978-0-89296-820-6

Fast Food Nation by Eric Schlosser, 2001. This book was made into a movie. Published by Harper and Collins. Together with the movies *Supersize Me* and *Food Inc.*, *Fast Food Nation* gives us an insight into the shocking practices and poor behaviors of our food chains.

The Omnivore's Dilemma by Michael Pollan, 2006. A more sub-dued, but, to the point, approach to what make sense and is good for us. Published by Penguin Press. Website: www.michaelpollan.com

Ma Cuisine by Alain Dutournier. Written in French by a wonderful chef with a flare for food. He focuses on the way our vegetables are nurtured and grown. For animals, he pays close attention to the way they are fed and raised. From the field to the fork and the sea to the table, he presents state-of-the-art cuisine. If you happen to be in Paris and want to treat yourself to a wonderful meal, stop by his restaurant, Carre des Feuillants, 14 Rue de Castiglione. Published by Editions Albin Michel, 2000. Website: www.albin-michel.fr

Nutrition Action by Michael Jacobson, Centre For Science In The Public Interest. This monthly magazine, independent of business influences, reports the relevant and accurate data about our food products from a scientific point of view. Website: circ@cspinet.org

Anti Cancer, A New Way of Life by David Servan Schreiber, MD. A look at life from all the different aspects. Published by Harper and Collins, 2008. ISBN 978-1-554468-221-8

Foods That Fight Cancer by Richard Beliveau and Denis Gingras, 2006. Two scientists in molecular medicine give their suggestions for preventing cancer through diet. Published by McClelland Stewart Ltd. ISBN 10-0-7710-1135-0

Allergies by Carole Bateson –Koch, 1994. She describes and explains how allergies are diseases in disguise and how to treat them as naturally as possible. Published by Alive Books ISBN 0-920470-42-4

Acknowledgments

Many authors have impressed my view of the world. Some have become close, personal friends. Neale Donald Walsch, James Twyman, Lori Wilson, Alain Dutournier and Rudy Eckhardt are wonderful, insightful individuals who have given their unique gifts to the world. I thank them with all my heart.

It takes the help and support of many people to write a book. I'd like to thank Tom Samek, a dear friend and artist "extraordinaire" with a pen, a brush, and with precious words, and, on top of it all, who happens to be an excellent chef, as well. His contributions are invaluable.

My special thanks go to my beloved friends Laird and Patti Orr, for their patience, inspiring conversation and long hours of hard work in editing the first part of this manuscript. In addition, I'd like to extend my gratitude to my devoted friend Doreen Bennett for her loving suggestions and support. Thanks also to Sandy Ditmanis for her constructive review and comments, as well as to my circle of close and loving friends in the Village of Elora, namely Maureen MacIntyre, Stu Oxley, Cheryl Ruddick, Anita Stewart, Brian Wark, and Molly and François Layton, without whom this book would not exist.

Finally, thanks to my sweet love and wife, Kathleen, for her unwavering support, advice and attention over the four years that this book has taken to complete.

EATING OUT

Maison Basque:
A welcome
addition
to our French
restaurant scene

Eureka! Lest anyone forget this auspicious occasion let it be inscribed that in 1973 a Torontonian (albeit of French origin) opened in this city a good, cheap, honest-to-goodness French restaurant.

Roger Dufau of Le Petit Gourmet takeout and catering was the guy who figured out that what the people don't want, in either food, decor or service, is another $60-a-couple restaurant or a pretentious imitation thereof. His newly opened Maison Basque is downright pretty to behold; each item on the limited menu is carefully prepared; and, most merciful of all, he's taken a cue from some of the finest French eateries of Paris and New York—a fixed price menu only, with full dinners priced at $6.00. It's about time.

Fixed price restaurants generally send you home less financially depleted than table d'hote ones, even if the entree prices on the regular menus look much cheaper than the fixed price. The extras on the bill, like salad, or that dessert that you couldn't resist as you mellowed towards the end of the evening, can send your bill soaring. The other boon of the fixed price is tranquility: You know what dinner will cost so there's none of that furtive adding up of the menu prices to keep the tab down.

We started dinner in the long narrow room with rough, tasty pate (that somehow vastly improved on its journey southward from Le Petit Gourmet) and a steaming, hearty tourtiere, the French-Canadian meat pie. Dufau also features different soups each night; if it's fish soup when you're there, don't miss the light tomato-flavored broth with chunks of fresh fish.

After the first course the waiter cheerfully explained the colorful murals. They depict Basque men playing their regional game called "le chistera." Rackets from the game adorn the walls and add to the

restaurant's individuality. The Basque region, in the south of France near the Spanish frontier, comes alive on Temperance St. with brown and cream embroidered tablecloths and napkins, tables lit by gas lamps and a dark, low ceiling.

Maison Basque isn't the only low-priced French eatery in Toronto, but somehow most of the others miss the boat even when they provide pleasant dining. Some of them go wrong by trying to serve complicated, overly sauced entrees that don't quite come off; others offer good tastes but cuisine too heavy to be called true French. Dufau has intelligently confined himself to entrees that he can produce consistently well within the financial and gastronomic scope of his operation.

At our dinner the fresh grilled grouper, a firm fleshed sea fish, stood quite well on its own without a sauce; Entrecote Bordelaise was a tender steak bathed in shallots and light red wine; Coquille St. Jacques come with fresh fish in a velvety cream sauce. The vegetables were all fresh and beautifully undercooked.

For dessert the restaurant usually offers Gateau Basque, a cross between cookie and cake pastry that comes in the shape of a cake with a heart of French custard. Obviously a specialty of the Basque region, it is beautifully reproduced here.

If the gods at the Liquor Licence Board so decree, La Maison Basque will be serving wine as of June 1, but until then it's temperance on Temperance St.

Whatever the Board decrees, don't miss Maison Basque. If you agree that restaurants, like people, come with various measures of integrity, you'll see a large dose of that all too rare commodity in this little restaurant.   — JOANNE KATES

Maison Basque: 15 Temperance St., 368-6146 Amex, Chz.

Eating Out – Joanne Kates, Toronto Star (1973) Maison Basque: A welcome addition to our French restaurant scene

Waterfront venue offers a relaxed approach to eating

Dining
By Michael Lester

PANACHE, Hobart's newest waterfront restaurant in Salamanca Place, offers a new style for Tasmanian diners. It's a cross between a café, a restaurant and a bistro with casual service, good-quality food and wine, but at pub prices.

The restaurant has been open since November and its mixture and style of dining has so far proved popular. It is owned by Canadian expatriates, Richard and Julie Perry, and their partner, Roger Dufau, who was the founder of the popular and successful La Cuisine restaurant and pastry shops.

Panache is at the southern end of Salamanca Place in part of an historic sandstone building. It used to be a trade union office, but has been renovated and converted into a modern restaurant while retaining some of the old ambience.

One of the features of the restaurant is a garden courtyard at the back which has been lighted for night dining.

Roger Dufau said that he has been pleasantly surprised by the continued popularity of the restaurant after nearly three months. "People naturally are curious about any new place and it is in a good location, with parking and within walking distance of the city centre," Mr Dufau said. "But we also think that we have touched the right chord with an upmarket café style that is more relaxed than many restaurants.

"The service is good but casual, nothing is overdone or too particular and our prices are pub prices, while the quality of the food is much better."

Panache caters for a range of clientele, from those walking in off the street for just a coffee or an ice-cream to those who want a full, three-course meal. Mr Dufau said that the average bill for a meal and drinks for two people was between $25 and $40.

If Panache has a fault, it is that space is limited which makes it a little noiser than the usual restaurant — yet that adds to its busy atmosphere. The lack of space also limits storage which is reflected in a relatively small menu and wine list.

However that is more than offset by the fact that all the food is fresh, delicious and well presented. Mr Dufau said the menu was changed regularly, depending on what fresh food was available at the market. For example, most of the salads served with the meals are grown hydroponically by a supplier in the Huon Valley and sold to the restaurant as a mixed package.

Panache also claims to be the only restaurant in the state serving Tasmanian wine as the house wine — the Pipers Brook Pinot Noir which is sold at a moderate $14.50 a litre.

My companion and I went to Panache on a Saturday night and it was busy until late. For an entrée, I chose the gravlax and oyster salad — thinly filleted ocean trout marinated in sugar and salt and spices and two fresh oysters served with salad. My companion had an interesting dish of baked

● Food with panache: restuarant owners Roger Dufau, Julie and Richard Perry.

mushroom caps with a ricotta cheese and vegetable farce. The mushroom caps were filled with a sauteed mix of zucchini, capsicum, onions and egg plant.

Although the menu changes regularly, two entrée dishes — the fish soup and caesar salad — have remained since the restaurant opened. On the night we were there the menu

Panache
89 Salamanca Place,
Hobart.
☎ (002) 242 929
Type of food: cosmopolitan.
Open: seven days a week, lunch to 10pm.
Prices: entrées $4.95 to $6.50; mains $10.50 to $12.50; desserts $3.75 to $4.95.
Wines: small range, but good quality and price range.

also offered chargrilled quail marinated in vinegar.

For the main course I chose the lamb shanks in cous cous — a North African wheat semolina made with flour and oil which makes a change from rice and adds another taste dimension to the meal. The lamb was tender and beautifully flavoured with orange, onion, capsicum, garlic and basil, tomato and basil.

My companion had grilled rib of veal served with a mushroom sauce made with white wine, cream and tarragon.

Both dishes were big serves and very good value for money both in terms of quality and quantity.

While the winelist is not extensive, it does offer a good range of reasonably priced wines and we chose a bottle of

Gramp's 1990 cabernet merlo to accompany our meal.

Panache's desserts chang daily, again depending on th availability of fresh fruits. A the moment, raspberries blueberries and loganberrie are used for the fruit flans. Th night we were there the res taurant also offered an apricc cheesecake. The restaura bakes its own fruit flans cheese and shortcakes dail and also offers a selection o homemade ice-creams and sor bets.

I opted for the fruit flan while my companion had the apricot cheesecake. Both wer well presented and delicious.

We finished the meal with Panache's special coffee. The bill for three courses and wine came to a reasonable $64.5C for two.

My last Tasmanian venture: Panache. Waterfront venue offers a relaxed approach to eating (1993)

TUESDAY | APRIL 21, 1998

UELPH MERCURY

The only paper on Earth dedicated to covering Guelph and Wellington County **75¢**

NEWS

Mercury, Tuesday, April 21, 1998

...Bloc Quebecois MP
...y leaves the Parliament
...s chair from the House
on Parliament Hill

...es his chair
ut of Parliament
... Bloc Quebecois MP

...laNews

ELORA | *Roger Dufau follows his Basque traditions*

Hanging out with an incredible chef

If you get a chance to hang out with Roger Dufau in his kitchen, go for it. Go for it in a huge way. Roger, who lives in a beautiful, grand home at the corner of Mill and Mary, in Elora, is an incredible chef.

You don't have to take my word for it. You could ask anyone whose dined at any of the 14 restaurants he's owned over the years in Toronto and Australia.

Those who love fine food may fondly remember some of his endeavours in the megacity – the Cafe Du Marche, behind The King Edward Hotel, the Maison Basque on Temperance, or Le Petit Gourmet.

Elora is so damned lucky to have Roger, in house, at long last. It's been a lot of years in the making.

In fact Roger told me, as he was making an incredible lunch for me the other day, that he first came to Elora 20 years ago, to visit a friend, and fell in love with the Drew House.

He snapped it up, dreaming of the country lifestyle, with a plan to create a fine country inn.

Instead, the changing courses of life's waters carried him to Australia. "We did a little chain of shops there, La Cuisine. It became a monster. It was so busy," Roger says, smiling.

Now we've got him back. And those of us who adore fine cuisine, and intri-

Bonnie Ewen Pyke
Rural Routes

esting company, can't wait until he gets approval for his plans to create a gorgeous bed and breakfast at his home, and we hope he follows through as well on plans to start a cooking school.

People like me could use one.

Meeting Roger actually gives me hope for my pitiful kitchen performance. It's inspiring to know that Roger didn't start out as a great chef. For years, Roger was actually an aeronautic engineer.

He left his Basque roots for Canada in the late 60s, hoping to work in Montreal, at Canadair.

"I came to Montreal, because it was French, only to find out I needed to

take three years of English because all the engineering plans were written in English. I had to go to school before I could work. So I asked them, how am I to eat? And they said, that's your problem!"

So Roger set to work as a handyman at Club Esterel in St. Marguerite, and gradually migrated into the kitchen. It was a natural migration.

Roger's Basque grandmother was a great chef. His mother owned a grocery mart, and his father was a fisher. He lived surrounded by food.

"Food was very important to the Basque. People were not very rich, but food was always very good and fresh. You know I find out now I was a gourmet (an environmentalist) without really knowing it. For years, I was doing what was natural, choosing what is good, what is best and fresh. It is the best to do."

After returning to France for a while, Roger recruited his mother, Madame Dufau, and his brother Michel, to join him in Toronto, in the restaurant business. The first attempt, Le Petit Gourmet, was disastrous.

"I was trying to do French take-out. It was a total flop. The Chinese food take-out was passing food out as quick as they could. They were lined up around the corner at the Kentucky

Fried Chicken. But we, we were dead!"

Not to be discouraged, the Dufaus tried catering, and started a smart little business among the well-to-do in Forest Hill and Rosedale.

Those cheeky Forest Hill ladies wanted to keep us for themselves, and did not tell anyone about us. But the Rosedale ladies, they would share, and so the word spread.

The second edition of Le Petit Gourmet was born, and business was fantastic.

The rest, as they say, is history. Great history.

The story is not done yet. I hope it continues in Elora. Everyone here should get the chance to meet Roger Dufau, a wonderful, and gregarious host.

He comes by it honestly.

"The Basque, we have a tradition of being hospitable, and liking to eat, to please. When you make people happy, it's a good feeling. People open up when they're happy, and have a good time."

You bet. Thanks for lunch, Roger. I had a great time.

Bonnie Ewen Pyke is news editor at The Mercury. She writes Rural Routes each Tuesday. You can reach her at 822-4310, ext. 272 or by email at ewen-pyke@guelphmercury.com

Bonnie Ewen Pyke, Guelph Mercury (1998) Roger Dufau follows his Basque traditions. Hanging out with an incredible chef

About the Author

A noted restaurateur and chef, Roger Dufau has owned and managed 16 restaurants and eateries on three continents, including *Maison Basque* in Toronto and *Panache* in Hobart, Tasmania. In 1968, he and his mother established the popular *Le Petit Gourmet* in Toronto.

Originally from the Basque region of France, Roger feels it is not only important to nourish the body, but also the spirit.

He is a regular contributor to the Faith page of the Guelph Mercury, a daily newspaper in Southern Ontario.

He lives with his wife, Kathleen, in Elora, Ontario. Together, they operate Drew House, a popular bed and breakfast known for hosting spiritual retreats, seminars, cooking classes and community events. He has one son, Olivier, who resides in British Columbia.

We are What We Think and What We Eat is his first book.

CPSIA information can be obtained at www.ICGtesting.com
Printed in the USA
LVOW08s2259180913

353058LV00002B/16/P